# VOYAGES
## ON BARINGO

# VOYAGES
## ON BARINGO

2003 – 2018

JULIA BILLINGHAM

# DEDICATION

This book is for my husband, our children Vanessa and Henry, our grandchildren, and all who sailed in the good ship Baringo.

# ACKNOWLEDGEMENTS

My thanks to my husband and skipper John Sanderson whose seamanship enabled the adventures described in this book. Also, to Glynis Green for help with editing and to her husband Malcolm Gibson for their company on the longest leg of the circumnavigation from Ecuador to Tahiti. I would like to thank my friend Catherine Pocock for her expert advice about the publication process and Laura Jones for her excellent technical editing and design.

# BARINGO VOYAGES

# 2010 – 2018

# CONTENTS

## PART ONE

Chapter One: Beginnings.................................................................1

Chapter Two: The First Voyage: *2002 – 2003*...............................7

Chapter Three: Thailand to Borneo: *Jan – May 2003* ................ 17

Chapter Four: Borneo to Hong Kong: *Sept – Oct 2004* ............. 23

Chapter Five: The Interlude .......................................................... 31

Chapter Six: Preparations: *Hong Kong 2009 – 2010* ................. 35

Chapter Seven: Hong Kong to Singapore: *Nov – Dec 2010* ....... 39

Chapter Eight: Thailand: *Dec 2009 – Jan 2010* ......................... 47

Chapter Nine: Thailand to The Maldives: *Jan – Feb 2011* .......... 51

Chapter Ten: The Maldives to Muscat: *Feb 2011* ...................... 55

Chapter Eleven: The Omani Coast to Salalah: *March 2011* ....... 61

Chapter Twelve: Salalah to Aden: *March 2011* ........................... 65

Chapter Thirteen: The Red Sea: *April 2011* ............................... 69

Chapter Fourteen: The Suez Canal to Turkey: *May 2011* .......... 77

## PART TWO

Chapter Fifteen: The Mediterranean Sea: *2011 – 2012*.............. 99

Chapter Sixteen: The Atlantic Crossing with the ARC:

*Nov – Dec 2012* .................................................................. 115

Chapter Seventeen: Grenada to Panama:

*June – Sept 2013*.................................................................. 125

Chapter Eighteen: The Panama Canal: *Sept 2013*........................... 135

# PART THREE

Chapter Nineteen: The Eastern Pacific Crossing:
*18th June 2014 – 1st Aug 2014* ........................................... 157
Chapter Twenty: Exploring the Marquesas: *Aug 2014* ..................... 169
Chapter Twenty One: The Tuamoto Atolls: *Sept 2014* ..................... 175
Chapter Twenty Two: Bora Bora: *Sept 2014* ................................ 181
Chapter Twenty Three: The Grand Reunion Papeete and
Society Island Cruise 1: *Sept 2014* ................................... 185
Chapter Twenty Four: Year Two in the Pacific Ocean and
Society Island Cruise 2:
*June – Oct 2015* ....................................................... 191
Chapter Twenty Five: The Western Pacific:
*May – Dec 2016* ........................................................ 207
Chapter Twenty Six: New Caledonia to Australia:
*Nov 2016* .............................................................. 237

# PART FOUR

Chapter Twenty Seven: Bundaberg and Hervey Bay,
Queensland Australia: *May 2017* ...................................... 265
Chapter Twenty Eight: The Queensland Coast Bundaberg
to Cairns: *April – Sept 2018* ......................................... 273
Chapter Twenty Nine: Cairns to Thursday Island
*Sept – Oct 2018* ...................................................... 293
Chapter Thirty: Thursday Island – Singapore
*Oct – Nov 2018* ....................................................... 299
Chapter Thirty One: The Finale, Singapore to Langkawi
*Nov 2018* ............................................................. 321

*Glossary of Nautical Terms* ............................................. 327

CIRCUMNAVIGATION

# PART ONE

# CHAPTER ONE

# Beginnings

A love of being on the water came early for me when dinghy sailing with my father aged about six. I knew I enjoyed it but I never reached the stage of exploring the sport any further until much later, which is one of my great regrets. I explain this to myself as being due to my intolerance of the cold… who knows. John however got off to a much better start braving the icy waters of England and Wales sailing dinghies from an early age, despite having been born and brought up in Iraq where it does not get much warmer. He joined his school navy section of the CCF and added to his knowledge, including discovering he got seasick, but luckily this did not deter him.

We had our first sailing trip together on the Norfolk broads and we had a lot of laughs but little experience and this was the start of a learning curve that is still continuing along a steep trajectory… that is just one of the many attractions of sailing. Next was a Mediterranean flotilla holiday with the children; comfortable conditions for me and the children to finally learn basic sailing tactics in a dinghy on and in warm water. John had his first instruction in handling a cruiser and after the first week we were allowed out on our own in a 36 foot Dufour with the rest of the flotilla. It was magical and such

a lot of fun although I nearly ended a beautiful debut by accidentally jibing the boom and knocking John on the head luckily lightly
enough to do no damage.

Our great opportunity to sail finally dawned when we moved
to Hong Kong in 1992. I had visited before in 1978 and seen how
perfect it was for sailing, as well as many other activities of course,
but our minds were made up and we were determined to take full
advantage of living there to finally sail in earnest. First we had to
pass the local examinations in engineering, navigation and seamanship which we did in turns as we attended evening classes to prepare
and did not want to leave the children unattended early in our
changed modus vivendi. They had a new life to adjust to as well.
I did another dinghy sailing course, again beautiful warm weather
and water so a real pleasure. We passed the examinations so we could
now legally take a boat out on our own. We started by sharing a
32 foot Trapper with some university colleagues which certainly
steepened the learning curve as inevitably in an old boat things
were always going wrong. I now know that the age of a boat is not
a prerequisite for this!

We had many happy adventures in this tiny boat and frequently
sailed onto the mooring at Shelter Cove, the Hong Kong yacht club
and mooring facility, as the motor had stalled yet again. We explored
the east coast of Hong Kong where there are so many beautiful
anchorages and despite the concentration of people in Hong Kong
we usually had them to ourselves. We joined the Round the Island
race which is around Hong Kong island. This was our first race in
Hong Kong and it proved quite exciting as again the motor failed
and we had to tack up Hong Kong harbour in the dark getting
to Kellett Island about 10.00pm. What we had learnt about lights
during the examination preparation now became in very useful.

The children always came along on our regular sailing outings often accompanied by friends and we were on the water almost every weekend and public holiday, of which there are many in Hong Kong. The warmer but still seasonal climate allows year-round sailing, and we took full advantage of this. Raft ups with other boats were always very entertaining, often too much alcohol was consumed and lively discussions ensued and there was always the music. Our beautiful and loveable black and white cocker spaniel Poppy adapted to life on board easily and enjoyed swimming and walking and being an important part of the family fun. She was often with her friend Bracken a placid brown cocker spaniel and between them they dreamed up and played many naughty tricks.

We decided we could now handle a boat of our own and the offshore adventure was on the horizon something which we could not have undertaken in the Trapper. So after a trip to the Southampton boat show John sealed a deal for a new Westerly Oceanranger 38foot and a comparative giant! She arrived in 1994 and was christened "Baringo" after the rift valley lake in Kenya which we visited so often when living there. A place of great natural beauty and tranquillity and John also liked the "go" at the end of the name. We sailed further afield to Macau in the Chinese New Year races which we did several times, then the great challenge came for us to do the San Fernando race to the Philippines in 1995, about 600nm across the South China Sea. The preparation to get Baringo up to the category 1 standard required for an offshore race was truly monumental with both of us doing full time jobs and looking after the children we were certainly stretched to capacity. The list of jobs was endless, the money flowed out extremely fast, and it took several weeks of struggle to get ourselves onto the start line. We were very fortunate to have the assistance of a true expert in offshore racing and sailing Hugh Rose without whose help we could not have done it. We were also supported by a very enthusiastic crew including the children. This was a real adventure into the unknown but with the umbrella cover of the race organisation at the Royal Hong Kong Yacht club some anxiety was eliminated but still what was left of our nerves was on edge. I could not imagine being in a small boat in the open sea for five days. What did you do? How did you eat? What did you see? How, where and when did you sleep? So many unknowns… but we had a marvellous voyage, entirely under sail, my questions were answered and the die was cast.

Then I began to read some books by circumnavigators of which "Dove" was the first written by a young Canadian who tried to sail around the world, next I was introduced to Myles and Beryl Smeaton's fascinating story and read their sailing adventures. Beryl became my heroine and the idea that it was possible to go around the world in a small sailing yacht took root and germinated. Over the next few years much changed in the cruising fraternity with the advent of improved weather forecasting, navigation technology and communications. As a result world cruising, encouraged and enabled by Jimmy Cornell, became a reality for many more aspiring sailors rather than a dream. Over the next few years we did several more South China Sea and San Fernando races adding to our experience, all were very exciting and each one different but none ever quite had the sense of plunging into a void as that first one had.

Once having decided that a circumnavigation was our next challenge we had to wait until we could finish work and the children to at least finish school. So we used the intervening time to read, observe, watch, and continue with the offshore races, Macau races and a Hainan race to build up offshore practice and experience for the "big trip". One conclusion we came to was that a round the world voyage might be more comfortable and maybe safer in a larger boat. Many piles of Yachting Worlds and Yachting Monthlies later and after a lot of investigation and research we felt a pilot saloon was what we wanted mainly for safety as there had recently been a nasty collision between a small tanker and a sail boat while the solo on watch crew was below doing navigation and had not seen the vessel. The outcome of that was totally disastrous and so it was a pilot saloon for us. At that time year 2000 there were few around of the size and price which suited us but at least this narrowed the choices and after viewing the only three on the market at the Southampton boat show our decision was unanimous, it was the Wauquiez 43 Pilot saloon. I only know now what an excellent choice we made. She arrived in Hong Kong in July 2001 accompanied by a typhoon. It was such an exciting moment to greet her alongside at Kellett Island, RHKY unscathed and brand new and then suddenly realising that she was ours. We continued with the name Baringo as so far this had not brought any bad luck. The first Baringo we sold to friends, and they still are friends, they wanted to rename her anyway and today she is still much loved and enjoyed and afloat.

The commissioning of Baringo was not all that smooth, starting with the fact that all the names of the bits were in French and the job was being done by an Australian who did not have a dictionary so several items were wrongly installed. Another mishap occurred on the test sail when we went into Hebe Haven yacht club to drop someone off and while reversing to turn around and leave the rudder hit the bottom with a sickening thud, a very unpleasant moment indeed. Luckily the problem was not serious and the necessary inspection was carried out without any major disagreements. We could then start enjoying sailing her and getting used to a larger boat. Hong Kong is perfect for that with no tides, good navigation marks, good weather forecasting and lots of places to sail to and anchor.

# CHAPTER TWO

# The First Voyage

*2002 – 2003*

## Hong Kong to Thailand

We were still considering a round the world trip but thought a trial run sailing around Asia for a year seemed like a sensible option. Our route would be Singapore, Thailand, North Borneo and back to Hong Kong via the Philippines. Fortunately we both managed to arrange a sabbatical year from work and after a lot of reorganisation… home, money, family etc. we were free to go. We had made some additions to the boat for long term cruising, a water maker being the most important, we already had a generator so by October we were almost ready to go. The optimum seasons for sailing away from Hong Kong are spring or autumn to avoid the typhoons in the summer and the strength of the North East monsoon in the winter. We had decided to leave with the Hainan Race in October as this gave us a deadline and we would have crew for the first leg. I realise now that one is never really ready to leave for a voyage so without a deadline we might have spent the year in harbour getting ready! The start was on 16.10.2002 a predictable downwind run and we were away with the gun with four of us on board heading SW but typically despite normal prevailing NE winds we sailed into a SW head wind which took us off course for several miles. We arrived three days later and were led in by a sampan and anchored, it seemed to have passed very quickly compared to the Philippine races but the shorter distance was the explanation. We enjoyed the usual post race festivities but once the race support structure came to an end it was an abrupt departure escorted to the boat with our provisions and fuel by the Chinese police. We had to go ready or not. No time to worry about being just the two of us away from land for the first time, we were summarily dismissed.

Luckily we had already decided where we were heading, to Tioman Island, East Malaysia. It was late afternoon as we left so we had the traditional Baringo cocktail as the sun set and China slowly disappeared. The first night out is always accompanied by a tinge of anxiety and it was particularly so on this our first night out alone. We had set up a radio schedule with another vessel going to Thailand from Hainan island and we had a dear friend Jane McKelvie in Hong Kong with whom we had twice daily radio chats which were wonderfully psychologically reassuring. Our first storm experience came on the fourth night, unheard, unseen and unfelt and very quickly in the dark! All four hands were immediately on deck to tame the wild beast that is our oversized boom which without its topping lift (which had been removed during the race) was wilder than normal. There was rain and lightning and an increasing sea, all very exhausting but as we now know all storms come to an end and we recovered shaken but not deterred, in fact encouraged that we had managed to come through it. Our regular radio skeds. with Jane were an invaluable support, hearing her soft reassuring voice twice a day and the knowledge that she knew where we were was more than comforting. We realised later that we were able to see the storms as threatening black patches on the radar screen but despite this useful information trying to steer a course to avoid them proved impossible as they seemed intent on following us. But we learnt the trick of using the radar at night to warn of impending storms which are invisible by sight, but easy to see with a working radar on board so at least we knew they were coming. Perfect conditions then followed, light breezes from the right direction… heaven again! We sighted land as predicted in the Pilot book, the historically famous peak of Gunung Kahang and later we anchored easily in Telek Teluk, Tioman island, as recommended by the SE Asian pilot book by Stephen Davies and Elaine Morgan. This book is an invaluable, essential, enjoyable and interesting companion for any voyage around Asia.

We had made our first offshore passage alone and enjoyed the challenge so we both felt exhilarated and satisfied but never over-confident, the sea is too unpredictable, moody and powerful to allow a moment of that. We enjoyed a few days of walking, cycling and exploring this beautiful island. On 1st November we had a narrow escape when en route to the shore our dinghy was struck at high speed by a water taxi. We had not seen it coming as it was hidden behind a nearby vessel in the anchorage but truthfully I don't think we were looking out very carefully either as we were not expecting such a high speed vessel to come by. Somehow or other we instinctively bailed out over the side of the dinghy at lightning speed and much to my surprise we both surfaced unscathed. Maybe because the dinghy painter had become entangled in the taxi's propeller and efficiently stopped it in its tracks. We had not taken the laptop that morning luckily but our rucksack floated unscathed as we had done but we had to dry our money and passports in the sun later, and the camera and mobile phone were a little sad. The dinghy had capsized and the outboard had gone underwater with it so we had a few problems to solve but it really could have been so much worse. The water taxi driver helped us and was fleetingly apologetic so we rowed back to the boat to recover from the shock and start planning the next steps. We had lost phone and camera and the outboard would need some help after a salt water dowsing while running and we had two broken floorboards in the dinghy. There did not seem any likelihood of getting much done in Tioman so we left and continued with our itinerary to visit Rawa island which we had visited many years earlier with the children on holiday from England. On that visit we had found some sweet fluffy white puppies there exactly matching the colour of the sand, we all adored these sand puppies and they proved never ending playmates for the children. Sadly they were not there this time but it was nearly twenty years later! The island was as unspoiled as our memories recalled so there was no disappointment, it was as beautiful a tropical island as ever. By now the weather was starting to deteriorate with the strengthening of the NE monsoon and we had a few rough nights at anchor off Rawa but we were using the anchor buddy, an additional lead weight attached to the anchor chain to improve holding and reduce swing. We did not drag but whether we really needed to put in the extra effort to deploy the buddy we will never know but it seemed like a nice belt and braces idea. Rawa island was not a very well protected anchorage so there was a significant swell and we did not get much sleep while there. Our shore excursions were limited by the weather as of course we had no outboard motor and it was too far to swim.

We were beginning to realise that we had to get to Singapore with the strengthening of the NE monsoon and the need for repairs so more island hopping along this coast was not feasible. We left Rawa at dusk in order to arrive at the crowded junction at Horsborough light at dawn where the world's shipping converges to enter the busiest harbour in the world. We were trying get to Sebana Cove on the east side of Malaysia but were uncertain about the depths in the river approach so after we had enquired from several sources and hailed a bystander off Tanjong Pengelhi to confirm that we could safely enter the river... he reassuringly waved us on... we motored very slowly up stream for what seemed an exhausting eternity. We were very tired after several disturbed nights at anchor off Rawa and a squally vessel strewn passage to Horsborough light. The heat intensified as the morning progressed and we only saw an interminable muddy mangrove covered shoreline... did Sebana Cove really exist we wondered but several cups of coffee later an attractive mirage appeared which then proved to be the Sebana Cove golf club with marina attached. It was 6th November and we had arrived. It was an elegant American style club house, perhaps slightly faded, situated in the middle of the jungle apart from the sculptured golf course attached. After the usual formalities we decided lunch and a cold beer were in order followed by a siesta which lasted until the following day!

The ferry runs from here to Singapore so essential tasks like buying a new phone and camera and provisioning were easy to do. The dinghy and outboard repairs were finished there and we enjoyed the delights of the club which although beginning to deteriorate seemed luxurious enough to us. In 2003 we were using internet cafes for communication throughout the whole year away, an experience of extreme frustration and discomfort and although the advent of Wi-Fi and 4G has improved this somewhat, from a cruiser's viewpoint e-communications are still far from easy.

Our next stop was Raffles Marina on the west side of Singapore an interesting trip through the enormous tanker park and into the chic (and expensive) marina that is Raffles. Friends from Hong Kong Jane and Houng joined us for a few days sightseeing and eating in Singapore but by 20th November it was time to tackle the Malacca Straits.

We did all the usual jobs, refuelling, refilling gas cylinders, cleaning the boat, provisioning etc and then it was off to Pulau Pisang a small island and the first stop going north up the Straits and recommended by the trusted pilot book. There are night stops along the length of the Malacca Straits so we planned to use them all and avoid night sailing, we had been warned about the presence of hazardous large logs impossible to see at night. The first night out at Pulau Pisang, really only a tiny rock, proved sleepless due to a storm with incessant lightening about which nothing can be done except hope; although we did dangle lengths of anchor chain, attached by bulldog clips to the shrouds, into the water in the vain expectation that they might conduct any stray electricity away from the boat directly into the sea. Miraculously we were not struck nor did we drag. A dawn start and onto the next stop the Water Islands, all the anchorages are clearly described in the aforementioned Asian Pilot Book and everything proved to be as described. Admiral's Marina was next where we formally entered Malaysia in the town of Port Dixon and a bureaucratic delay forced us to enjoy the facilities of the pool, restaurant and the computer (?) for two extra days. We met "Theta Volantis", a Dashew designed sailing vessel who was just completing its circumnavigation so we had long and informative discussions with them about their experiences. Then it was an anchorage off Port Klang, the port for the capital Kuala Lumpur, into which we were swept by the straits tide pushing us along at 9kts. The tides change like clockwork every twelve hours in the Straits so an even spread of for and against while traversing them but for us the adverse current was never really strong enough to warrant waiting out the adverse tides. John had luckily opted for a larger 70hp Yanmar turbo engine which proved its worth on this and many other occasions.

On ever north west to the Sembilan islands which look like muffins in the sea but we decided to anchor off nearby Pulau Pangkor which is a small, pleasantly scruffy tourist resort where we hired a motorbike and had a wild ride around the island. Pangkor Laut a small adjacent island is an exclusive resort with a de-luxe hotel but no landing permitted for cruisers who might lower the tone. We had the usual intermittent rain storms which are the year-round weather of the Malacca straits but never long lasting and it always remained warm and as we were not on a very tight schedule when possible we had the time to sit them out on board which was for the time being very dry and cosy. We were trying the local cuisine everywhere, one of the great pleasures of travel by any mode, and provisioning was always an entertainment rather than a chore. Baringo regularly found a challenge for us with something to repair, fix, replace or invent a solution for at each stop and underway as well, so we were becoming masters of ingenuity! Two brains tended to be better than one we decided.

During our stay at Lumut Yacht Club a step further up the Malacca Straits we took the opportunity to explore the Cameron Highlands home to Colonel Forster's black and white traditional English style houses which look rather unusual in a Malaysian forest. We had been before with the children on holiday from England but had found the mountains cold, damp and grey so had retreated quickly but this time the same climate was a very welcome respite from the tropical heat at sea level. We borrowed/hired an ancient car which barely made it up the hills but we stayed in one of Colonel Forster's houses, now a smart hotel and enjoyed the contrast of life on land for a few days.

Next was Penang where we had arranged to meet some Hong Kong friends now living there. We might not otherwise have visited as anchoring is difficult there so we were very glad to be met on the water with some help as it took at least five attempts to get the anchor to hold, all in the sweltering midday heat. Once safely secured the unpleasantness quickly evaporated as it always does so it was seamlessly onto enjoying seeing Penang with our friends and tasting delicious meals there. Our next sail to Bass harbour, Langkawi was overnight but we had a strong NE wind and made such good speed that we arrived too early to enter so we passed the night hove-to outside doing alternate watches, but it is actually more difficult to stay awake drifting slowly than when on passage but certainly a preferable option to a night entry into unknown territory. We have continued to adopt this policy and have studiously eschewed night entries into strange places. The wind was still strong the next day, always rather unwelcome when trying to get alongside in a marina but all went smoothly and we tied up at the Royal Langkawi yacht club overlooked by a statue of a giant eagle. "Langkawi" means beautiful eagle so quite appropriate for it to be there dramatically dominating the harbour. Langkawi is a duty-free port so this was the time to replenish stocks especially with our planned Christmas in Phuket with the family and several friends from Hong Kong.

We then sailed into Thai waters and island hopped our way to Phuket which was so pleasant with many strangely shaped rock formations in the sea and a wide choice of anchorages. The weather was the usual mixed bag of rain and strong wind and relaxing calms, and we were becoming accustomed to the large number of fishing vessels working day and night moving erratically across the water. Some were lit at night but many were not, which did not make for easy watches although we were not doing much night sailing at this juncture, and we were nearly there! We passed through the two famous Phi Phi Islands (pre-Tsumani) all very scenic and then finally into the Yacht Haven Marina in Phuket. We had done our first significant off shore passage and we were still here and we had enjoyed it, a definite feeling of exhilaration and achievement.

Christmas came and went in a flurry of friends and family; eating and drinking and having a huge amount of fun. We decamped to Bangtao Lagoon Bungalows, far from luxurious but quite adequate and very relaxed and friendly. Between us all we filled the hotel so we had the run of the place. Sadly the following year on 26th December the tsunami hit Phuket and of course Phi Phi and the Bangtao bungalows were destroyed as was much else with tragic loss of life… if the timing had been different our lives would almost certainly have been changed. But we were lucky this time but so many others were not.

# CHAPTER THREE

# Thailand to Borneo

## *January – May 2003*

Christmas and New Year festivities were over and everyone departed to the four corners of the globe and we also had to leave Thailand as our visas were expiring. So we sailed overnight in haste to Langkawi for two days and then returned to Phuket this time into the Boat lagoon where the entry is through a narrow channel which a vessel of our draft can only do at high tide and even then we touched the forgiving sandy bottom three times on the way in. We had the usual mix of repairs to do while waiting for friends to join us for a short but very pleasant cruise around Phang Nga bay famous for its strange rocky outcrops of limestone which rise dramatically out of the sea. It was full moon so the seascape was eerily magical with the rocks bathed in moonlight. Swimming and snorkelling are a delight here, such clear water and so many small islands to choose from to explore, each one with its own restaurant producing delicious Thai food, always such a treat. Later more friends arrived from UK, this time of year is optimal for cruising Phuket waters so we contin-ued exploring the area going over to Krabi, island hopping with ease sailing eventually out to a diver's island paradise, the Similan islands. The cruising guide was very accurate and one is spoiled for choice in this superb cruising area. Unfortunately we received bad news while staying at the Similan islands; John's sister Maggie had lung cancer and was having surgery to remove it and we obviously wanted to be with her in London over that period so we returned to Phuket quickly leaving the boat on the hard for a month to go back to London in February. The operation went smoothly and we returned to sail back down the Malacca straits and back to Sebana Cove where we left the boat for our planned trip to the UK for the month of April to see the children for Easter and obviously Maggie as well who was by then thankfully making an excellent recovery.

On 5th May we rejoined Baringo who was in good order despite her month of neglect. We had electrical problems to solve, no cabin lights and no VHF radio and also the anchor chain metre markings needed to be repainted. We found sediment in the engine fuel filters to add to the list, these took a whole evening to clean and the cause was dirty fuel and the so-called diesel bug. We subsequently invested (and they are expensive) in a Baha filter which we now use when filling the fuel tank and we have never had the problem again so presumably the investment has been worth it. The filter removes all contamination including water which provides the medium for the bacteria to grow in the fuel. With all jobs done we finally left Sebana Cove for Borneo on 12th May hoping to make it to Sarawak first then Sabah. We had to cross the main Singapore shipping channel to get further south, always a potentially hazardous exercise and this was before the marvellous AIS (Automatic identification System) which today removes most of the anxiety attached to these manoeuvres. The large vessels move at 20kts so approach very quickly although from a distance their movement and speed is very deceptive so judging it can be tricky. AIS has certainly improved all that by eliminating much of the guess work.

Three days after leaving we had our worst storm. We could see it gathering on the south side of us, and there was a very heavy premonitory atmosphere with dark clouds building on our starboard side and bright sunshine and clear skies on port. A marked contrast with the temptation to look one way and hope the other way would miraculously improve. That was not to be and we had a prolonged serious storm with all that that means. We lost course having to sail with the elements and by the time conditions had calmed 48 hours later we had missed Sarawak altogether and decided not to turn back. Our weather forecasting was less sophisticated at that time; we now have grib files and a wonderful private weather forecaster Emmanuel who I am sure would have foreseen all this and we could have avoided it, although it was just a local system so who knows but nevertheless it was quite big enough for us. The small jib tore and the Malaysian flag disappeared and foolishly we had not stowed things all that securely in preparation for a serious storm so below deck was chaotic to say the least. It also became surprisingly cold during the storm worsened by not eating very much as we were too busy surviving. We suffered the usual left-over sea afterwards as we headed towards the north coast of Borneo and we were relieved to read in the Admiralty pilot book, another essential companion, that we could anchor anywhere along the coast of North Borneo, just drive in and drop the hook in the mud in front of the mangroves. Of course there was an uncomfortable swell but for us this was almost total tranquillity after the storm and we were now able to enjoy the usual frisson of being in an unknown deserted anchorage.

After recovering from the battering, us rather better than the sails which would need sewing, we sailed towards Brunei and then to the Malaysian island of Labuan where we had thought we might find a marina but it had been demolished in a storm and not replaced. We sat out another storm at anchor there and did not make it ashore at all. Pulau Tiga quite a well-known anchorage was the next stop, another tropical island paradise which seemed deserted but we learnt later that there was a hotel around the corner in another bay. However as we had now both recovered our energy we decided to clean the fuel filters again as the red jelly had reappeared. In retrospect not a good idea as one of our vital tools broke, the fuel leaked and we produced an airlock so there we were on what we thought was a completely deserted island with no engine. I vowed never to undertake major repairs unless help was nearby and I felt we might be stuck there forever! Masterfully John pulled out the best of his engineering brains and by midnight we had a functioning engine again, we were learning fast. We arrived at Kota Kinabulu Marina in Sabah the next day to find it well suited to our needs, a luxurious hotel on each side, all the pontoons sound and facilities clean and tidy. It was as pleasant a place as possible to carry out the very unpleasant task of emptying the fuel tanks of diesel and cleaning the whole system, an extremely smelly and filthy job but essential. The sails were repaired easily; in fact we have found you can usually get most things done in unexpected places. We met up with another Hong Kong boat "Touch of Class" who had made the same journey from Singapore and hit the same bad weather system and not enjoyed the conditions either. It was fun to catch up and enjoy some Hong Kong gossip although news from there was not good as the territory was in the grip of SARS. John would have been in the thick of it at work in the Prince of Wales hospital which had several patients and doctors ill with SARS so a lucky escape for him.

Our friends from UK were arriving to cruise the north coast of Sabah with us but they sensibly stayed the first two nights in the hotel to recover from their journey and prepare for the rigours of a sailing voyage with us! We accompanied them in their short luxury sojourn in the hotel and enjoyed the change. It was a leisurely sail around the north west coast as there is a well marked passage through the reefs with no shortage of beautiful anchorages so we slowly made our way through with a mixture of sailing and motoring. We visited Turtle island Pulau Seligaan where we had stayed previously with the children on holiday from Hong Kong and seen the extraordinary laying of the turtle eggs and hatching of the baby turtles and their immediate crazy dash for the sea at any price. It was no hardship to see it again! Janet with whom I was at school has the distinction of being the only crew who has fallen overboard and that was while at anchor in calm conditions! How did this happen? Well it still remains a mystery but one morning Janet slid elegantly down the beautifully sloping stern of Baringo and effortlessly entered into the sea as if she was testing the adequacy of the stern as a water slide! Unfortunately although Baringo's stern was unscathed Janet's leg was not and a large colourful black and blue patch appeared some time later. Luckily recovery was speedy and uneventful. We sailed along the North Coast of Borneo but Sandakan yacht club was as far as we could go on this trip. They gave us a very warm welcome when we arrived and the gift of a club flag which decorates the saloon to this day and has become something of a good luck mascot. Captain John presented the prizes for a junior optimist race during our stay and we all relaxed and enjoyed the surroundings. Janet and Dale flew back from Sandakan after a surfeit of snorkelling and swimming in colourful coral and sparkling clear waters and we had certainly enjoyed the same.

We were back in Kota Kinabulu by 18th June but before going to Europe for the summer at the end of June we snatched a quick trip inland to Danum valley where there is a biodiversity research centre looking mainly at the effects of logging on what is left of the jungle flora. On the road into the centre through the jungle we passed many massive lorries carrying enormous logs so they have a lot of studying to do! We experienced our first leech encounter here, we were advised to buy leech socks, which covered ankles to knees, when we went walking but despite this precaution the leeches still found a way in. Their bite is painless so either you see their bloated bodies clinging on or you see a trickle of blood. They seemed almost indestructible and looked very prehistoric.

By the 22nd June we were ready to take our flight to Europe and Baringo was left in the water this time alongside in the marina.

# CHAPTER FOUR

# Borneo to Hong Kong

## *September – October 2004*

After our European trip we returned to Kota Kinabulu to find out what problems the stay in the marina had produced. Always a surprise and this time it was a punctured oil container stored under our bunk which had leaked…a nasty mess but at least it was clean oil. The propeller was gummed up but did eventually turn and the engine cooling fan had to be replaced. These were the most important things needing attention but of course there was the usual "bouillabaisse" of small difficulties to solve that is the boating life! Henry and Vanessa and a friend Alex were arriving the next day for a holiday, but Vanessa had arrived at the airport in London with the wrong passport and thinking she was well on her way, I had gone to the swimming pool without my telephone so missed all her distress calls. A very stressful time for her but all that vanished when she finally arrived and we sailed out of the marina to explore the adjacent tropical paradise. We swam, snorkelled and sampled the local resorts and their food, drink and music which proved to be an excellent holiday. At the end of September universities called and we were left on our own again but planning to sail for Hong Kong very soon. Sadly Maggie was not well and so we felt we needed to curtail our cruising to get back to Hong Kong quickly so we could get to London to see her. Mike from "Touch of Class" agreed to come with us on Baringo for the ride, a third crew is always such a help and 2+1 is certainly more than three in this situation. We left the marina to a gun salute on 30th September hoping for a quick passage with only a short stop in the Philippines which Mike knew well. He suggested Halley harbour for our first stop after two nights at sea and it was so peaceful, not a ripple on the water and very beautiful indeed. We stopped again at Maya Maya to make the final preparations for the crossing to Hong Kong; provisioning, weather checks, and refuelling but there was no diesel in the marina so we had to fill the jerry cans in town which was much more of a mission. I don't think we actually formally left the Philippines this time but it does not seem to have made very much difference to anything.

We left for Hong Kong on 7th October and had quite a rough passage with a mixture of most sailing conditions, wind from all directions of varying strengths, squalls and heavy seas. We arrived on 11th October sailing along our familiar route past the Ninepins and into Shelter Cove. Our experiment was completed successfully and our ardour not dimmed in the slightest.

Very sadly Maggie died a few weeks later and we had not been able to get back before with our work commitments. A truly devastating blow to our already small family. While planning this voyage we had tried to think of and mitigate every disaster... but in the final analysis when disaster struck it came from a totally unexpected direction. Maggie was not the source of upset that we had imagined in all our anxious crystal ball gazing when we were planning the year.

**Leaving party RHKYC bar, 2002**

**Hainan Island**

**Tioman Island**

**Sebana Cove**

**Sunset at Water Islands Malacca straits**

**Sailing in Phuket**

**Phang Nga bay**

**Baringo at anchor off sandakan yacht club**

**Avian hitchhikers in Borneo**

# CHAPTER FIVE

# The Interlude

In the aftermath of Maggie's death we wanted to be closer to the children so we decided to return England leaving Baringo in Hong Kong as we had not given up our plan to attempt a circumnavigation when the time was right. We both found employment in UK and some dear friends Sam and Gillie McBride looked after Baringo in Hong Kong. Our departure was executed smoothly and we left but we definitely said au revoir and not goodbye.

We stayed for five years in England and made the most of our time there seeing friends and supporting the children as best we could. We visited Hong Kong every year to check Baringo, not that we were concerned about her; she was probably in more capable hands than those of her owners! Our main job was to biocide the precious water maker which was never needed for local cruising but to maintain this important item for our next journey this had to be done annually. We tried to visit during the often dreary month of November in UK but a very pleasant month in Hong Kong so we just about managed to keep our nautical hands in with some local sailing. The years passed, not unpleasantly and by 2009 we were planning our return to Hong Kong and the circumnavigation with eager anticipation.

Our return was by train from Chamonix to Hong Kong via Beijing as Henry was now working there. A very much more interesting journey than the usual longhaul flight. Indeed it did prove to be fascinating and actually quite luxurious as we chose the luxury option of a cabin to ourselves with our own ablution facilities. We left Chamonix station on 26th September first to Paris for a few days then to Berlin for another few days all very pleasantly spent. Then the trouble started when we saw that the train from Berlin to Moscow travelled through Belaurus a country for which we had no visa. This was not an oversight because John had discussed the train route with Deutsche Bahn on more than one occasion and they had confirmed the route was not through Belarus only Poland. Obviously there was no time to act then, the train was pulling in and we had to get on it. After some discussion with the train attendant and most of our nearby fellow passengers no solution could be found so it had to be wait and see. When the train stopped at the Belarusian border at 04.00 the guards in their grey communist style cold war uniforms and peaked hats marched into our carriage to check the visas but despite our best excuses we were escorted from the train. We had the impression that we were on a film set as we had seen many identical scenes unfold on cinema screens. We were abandoned in a room that was devoid of anything except us and some benches. We waited in the lurid glow of the single light bulb for what seemed like a long time, our passports had been taken and we had no idea what was going to happen. What did was a curt instruction to get back to Biala Podalski in Poland and buy Belarusian visas. It proved in the end to be an enjoyable and interesting excursion thanks predominantly to the good will and courtesy of the Poles who could not have been more helpful as we spoke no word of Polish, had no Polish money and no map of Biala Podalski. We found a map in the town and discovered too late that it was almost impossible for a train to go from Berlin to Moscow without going through Belarus... if only we had looked at a map earlier! The visas were very expensive but we were not the only ones who had made the mistake so we looked around the town often encountering the same visa searching souls. All was accomplished by close of business and it was back onto the train and through Belaurus without a hitch this time. The next morning we were woken by the "providenista", a lady who takes care of the passengers in each carriage and there is one for each carriage. We were passing through a huge conurbation so now we had a map we could find out where we were, we decided it must be Smolensk and went back to our bunks for a few hours until we were to arrive in Moscow. Oh no, the providenista was knocking frantically again, we had to get off the train immediately... we had arrived in Moscow! This did not seem to be the perfect start for two aspiring circumnavigators.

Having visited Moscow before when Gorbachev was President we found the "new" Moscow was seriously uninteresting so we were glad to begin traversing Russia through the interminable but pleasant forests which are peppered with the most gigantic industrial towns harking back to the industrial revolution in the UK. There were occasional stops but one alighted from the train at risk of missing it and being stranded in rural Russia but we did risk it occasionally and often just to get some exercise walking up and down the platform. Our first formal stop was Irkutsk which is a historic Siberian town near lake Baikal the biggest fresh water lake in the world so a very worthwhile stopover. After Russia it was Mongolia with a stop in Ulaan Bator and an excursion to stay in a "gur" or "yurt" the latter being the Russian word which is no longer popular for obvious reasons. The highlight was certainly not the food, fermented mare's milk and mutton being the staples, but riding the small but strong Mongolian ponies across the infinite steppes was.

We arrived in Beijing on 16th October where Henry met us and we stayed for a few days before another slightly more luxurious train to Hong Kong.

# CHAPTER SIX

# Preparations

## *Hong Kong 2009 – 2010*

On 7th November 2009 we moved back onto Baringo as she would be our home for the year that we were preparing for the circumnavigation which was fast becoming a reality. She was still moored at the Shelter Cove branch of the Hong Kong Yacht Club. John worked part time at Chinese University and I was a boat girl. We had time to prepare and to push us along the way we entered the South China Sea race, a race always galvanises you into action as the inescapable deadline of the start approaches. Many things had changed and it proved significantly more difficult and stricter than our experience of previous years but once started an unstoppable process unrolled and we were on the start line ready at the appointed time. Unfortunately it turned out to be a miserable race with no wind at the start so we were dollying around Waglan Island just outside Hong Kong harbour for the first 24 hours. Later it was the other extreme with too much wind followed by a night arrival in Subic bay when we nearly hit an unlit buoy. It was not a happy voyage but probably our last as super fast racing yachts have gradually phased cruisers out of the race.

The rest of the year we enjoyed staying for long weekends in the peace of Double Haven as John always had a long weekend with his well-organised part time work. Of course we enjoyed many of the other marvellous anchorages in Hong Kong but for us Double Haven takes the prize.

We had several visits to Europe during the year and through-out there was continuous progress towards achieving our goal. We would need to leave Hong Kong in the autumn before the NE monsoon kicked up the South China Sea too roughly so although we had no race this time there was the deadline of the elements. Shelter Cove was a blissful place to live, waking to such a view every morning was a great pleasure. Luckily a colleague of John's had lent us her car for the year which made life so much easier as Shelter Cove is not easily accessible by public transport and we appreciated the extra storage for our dinghy clothes to get on board dry. It saved us having to carry it around all day.

Luckily there are plenty of experts in Hong Kong so bringing Baringo up to date with all the new technology that had developed since we left was very efficient. We got new sails, a state of the art chart plotter in the cockpit as well as at the navigation table and the wonderful AIS system. The latter two have both enhanced our safety and security enormously over the journey, no boat should leave land without them. The mast came down for inspection and the rigging was all changed, as Baringo was a surprising 10 years old now. We began to hear news of pirate attacks on our route across the Indian ocean towards the Red Sea and so decided to join the Blue Water Rally one of the emerging enterprises that helped cruisers around the world but we only wanted to join for the Thailand to Turkey section as that was where the danger lay. Apart from that we did not want to be restricted by a group but rather go at our own pace. We were to meet the group in Thailand in December then sail with them until we got to Turkey or at least the Red Sea. For this safety net we had to pay quite handsomely but as the situation with pirates was worsening as the months went by we felt it was money well spent. There were many other administrative and technical tasks in addition to which we had to sell the car we had been using, a condition of the loan. This began to look increasingly unlikely as our time got shorter and there was no interest until by word of mouth around the live aboard fraternity at Shelter Cove we sold it to the owners of another boat there and we were delighted it went to a good home and did not have to be scrapped.

Every time we crossed something off the list of jobs it was replaced by another not always one for one either so the list expanded and contracted randomly over the remaining few days. We left the mooring on 9th November to be alongside for the last few days making loading provisions amongst other things easier. We had the engine "super serviced" hoping to prevent any breakdown or failures off shore and spent time getting our weather forecasting organised. We now had an iridium satellite phone another very reassuring piece of new equipment to have as we could have e-mail contact through it as well as occasional phone calls to keep in touch we hoped, rather than in an emergency.

Our final departure was planned for Sunday 14th November and a few friends were coming for a shore party to give us a send off... any excuse for a party in Hong Kong! Sadly it was a disappointment as we realised we had not done the exit formalities at the Marine department being used to just doing it at the airport before catching a flight. Forty eight hours later we had checked ourselves and Baringo out of Hong Kong and there was only one way to go... into the South China Sea heading for Singapore about 1000nm away. We were waved away by Ah Kow one of the boat boys at Shelter Cove and we were on our way past the Lima islands where we had a last phone call from well-wishers; our grand scheme had started.

# CHAPTER SEVEN

# Hong Kong to Singapore

*November – December 2010*

The weather started well with sunshine, a light breeze and a flat sea as we sailed through the Lima islands but it all strengthened once we lost any shelter provided by the land. We had 30 knots of north east wind and were sailing downwind so we only needed the smaller solent jenny for the night. Not having the main up always makes life simpler and the South China Sea was as expected under the influence of the fairly strong NE monsoon but despite these conditions Poppy the autohelm worked tirelessly and reliably. We had christened the autohelm Poppy in memory of our wonderful cocker spaniel who was also totally dependable regardless of circumstance. We had been warned Poppy might fail us when faced with the strong NE monsoon and the swell it could create but on this occasion she did not. Downhill helming is the most demanding both on crew or Poppy but if there was a competition for best helm there is no doubt who would be the winner. There was surprisingly little shipping in these coastal waters I think because the fishing regulations had been tightened in Hong Kong which had been seriously overfished so this made for an easier passage in the first few days. The expected squall arrived on the evening of the third day with the usual uncomfortable accompaniments. We had difficulty keeping course as this now meant sailing dead downwind (DDW) which is difficult without a spinnaker; we only had the two jibs and a cruising chute so we had to sail off course for the time being and eventually we were blessed with some calmer seas and we hoisted the cruising chute in perfect conditions and were able to make course again.

We had discovered that the engine was no longer charging the batteries but we had the generator so all was not lost at this stage. John tried to diagnose the problem but could not until it all came clear when motoring on the windless morning of 23rdNovember, the alarm suddenly screeched signalling the engine was overheating. The cause... the fan belt pulley had sheared off taking the fan belt with it! It had not been secured with all the four bolts required but only with two. We were 400nm from Singapore and the prospect of going through the shipping lanes and tanker park without a motor was not appealing when afloat on the dark waters of the South China sea. We asked ourselves why we had done the "super service "on the engine at vast expense just before we left... we had thought it would prevent problems but the opposite was now the result. This was our first big challenge and the first reflex to maintain mental courage and avoid panic is to realise that the problem could be infinitely worse so solving the present crisis would be possible and not too difficult.

We found some suitable spare bolts in our sanctuary box for random oddments but they were too long so we had to hacksaw through them to the correct length and attached the pulley with them. They all sheared once we started the engine so we had to try again. We were not spoiled for choice... we just had to continue until we had a working engine again. Daylight arrived, always very welcome and a light breeze had picked up so at least we were sailing at about 2knots towards our destination. Amazingly another 4 bolts were found in the sanctuary box and this time they held but the arm of the pulley had been distorted by the abnormal stresses before it had finally broken so we were by no means certain how well and how long our Heath Robinson repairs would last. We were very lucky that a perfect wind helped us along precisely on course for Horsborough Light using a mixture of the chute during the day and big jenny at night. The big jenny is easier to furl away quickly if conditions dictate so we always revert to this at night rather than continue with the chute. By Friday 26th November we were approaching Horsborough Light at dawn as we had hoped but a nasty squall spoiled our arrival and broke the wind indicator at the top of the mast. We had managed without the engine most of the way which was a relief as we wanted to save it until it was absolutely needed. We sailed as long as we possibly could through the parked tankers until the tide turned at mid day and our speed dropped to 1.5kts and we had a deadline to do immigration before we went into the marina. We had chosen to use One Degree 15 a new marina on the south of Sentosa as it was more directly en route than either Sebana Cove or Raffles. We had visited Singapore to see Henry when he had had a meeting there from Beijing and we had used the time to assess the merits of the various marinas and yacht clubs and had decided on One Degree 15. It was new and had excellent facilities, central Singapore was easily accessible, and it was a change from the previous voyage. When we were unable to sail any longer John gingerly started the motor, it sprang into life but we dared only use minimal power, just enough to get us to the immigration anchorage near the marina entrance. After a radio call the customs vessel came alongside, offered a fishing net into which we put our documents and then disappeared with them for about 20 minutes. They were returned to us by the same method, we found this quite quaint for such a sophisticated city as Singapore but it worked. It was dusk by now and the tide was full strength and we had to get into the marina through a narrow entrance which was a sharp turn to port from the main channel which was also quite narrow so had very fast flowing water. We were speeding downtide in the small channel so to make the 90 degree turn to port into entrance would require skill and judgement. John was easily man enough for the task and by skilful ferrygliding with the strong tide we successfully gained the flat stationary waters of One Degree 15 and tied up.

We had a good night's sleep but were exhausted for the next few days while trying to repair the damage of the trip. For me this was the most exhausted I have ever felt after a voyage but maybe I have become more accustomed to the mental and physical stress of passage making as our journey continued. We had the usual ups and downs with the engineers but managed to get all the repairs finished. Internet services had improved considerably since our last time in Singapore on the boat seven years ago so communications were much less frustrating and we enjoyed all the modern new facilities, pool, gym, laundry and restaurant. A friend from Hong Kong was visiting Singapore while we were there and we joined him for lunch at the Singapore Cricket Club, a very traditional British style private club so we could not have gone independently so a special treat.

After parting with quite a lot of money for all the repairs and doing some sightseeing in Singapore which was much changed since 2003 we left for the third voyage in the Malacca Straits. We had the usual fishing net exchange at the immigration anchorage and then out into the Malacca Straits, but it was into the teeth of a storm, we wondered why we had not waited but it was too late by then. The rain can be extremely heavy in these squalls so visibility is almost nil, undesirable in these busy straits but after about two hours the sun was out again and we could dry off very quickly, and although the temperature drops with the rain it never seemed to get too cold. We had met a catamaran in One degree 15 who suggested we could do the Malacca straits non -stop to Thailand so we thought we might try this as we had done it stopping twice before, as it would only be more of the same we decided to try and see. Unfortunately squalls came regularly and the sky looked particularly menacing especially at night and the wind was on the nose where it should not be and we had not refuelled in Singapore relying on the NE monsoon to take us smoothly NW. The nights were proving quite threatening and unpleasant, with always a squall, so we decided to have a nights rest and dropped the anchor outside Port Klang. This was not the pleasant empty anchorage it had been in 2003 as there were many oil rigs and associated hazards one of which we only just skimmed by in the dark but we anchored before midnight with some relief.

We refuelled from the jerry cans in the morning with what was left of the fuel on board and while it was calm. It is always a messy job despite our best efforts not to spill diesel on the deck it always gets there somehow! The squalls continued relentlessly as we headed north west to the Sembilan islands and with the wind and for 12 hours the tide against us we were using the motor much more than we had anticipated. The skies were black and looked much as one might imagine hell with monster clouds and sheets and streaks of lightening and regular squalls often quite large as judged by the size of the black blotches on our radar, so although we could see where they were at night it did not alleviate any anxiety. As always it is the lightning that is the major worry. We were making so little progress with wind and tide against, there was no sign of the expected North

East monsoon yet so not being over full with fuel we decided to wait and anchor in the shelter of the Sembilans. Our depth meter had broken which did not of course facilitate this task. We tried four times to anchor in various places and finally ended up cheek by jowl with what seemed like the whole fishing fleet of Malaysia all taking shelter. We were still not happy with our position so close to so many fishing boats so we moved again in the evening and again had three shots before we finally settled, no more attempts were possible anyway as the anchor windlass had given up as well! A good night's sleep improved us all including the windlass so we could raise the anchor the next day. Many of the fishing fleet had departed signalling that the weather might have improved even if only temporarily so we weighed anchor planning to reach Langkawi hoping we could sail and not use the motor. We had more trouble with the alternator, rather annoying as we had bought a new one in Singapore but we did at least have the NE wind now in addition to surrounding squalls which we were learning how to avoid with some success but we could not help remembering our last voyage along this route which had been so much more pleasant and made a mental note that the Malacca Straits are better sailed in stages with night stops. We continued past Langkawi as conditions allowed and then anchored for the night off some of the many Thai islands on the way into Phuket. It is a magical sail even in bad weather as the limestone rock shapes are endlessly fascinating and provoke the imagination into finding something familiar that the shape resembles.

Our anchorage off Koh Petra remains firmly in our memory to this day as the worst anchorage we have ever had. We chose the south west side to anchor as we were in the NE monsoon season although that evening the wind was actually blowing from the SW, we assumed it would change but it did not and by morning the wind had strengthened and the waves were pushing to the vertical shore and rebounding back onto us with a vengeance. The rolling was so uncomfortable and at every roll the hull windows were underwater and it was impossible to lie, sit or stand with any ease. The crashing of the cupboard contents was exceptionally irritating in its regularity as everything moved with each roll so we turned to our other wonderful resource the Dashew sailing manual, a gift from Sam and Gilly McBride, in the hope that it would have a solution. Their description of our situation exactly matched our own experience and in addition was very amusing but the solution was a flopper stopper which we did not have. After an exasperating morning we could stand it no longer so even though we were worried that the buddy and anchor might hit the bow when coming up in such a swell we just had to get going. No damage was done in the process and the next night we anchored off Koh Ngai on the side of the island sheltered from the SW wind and oh how peaceful it was, no sign of the prevailing NE wind yet. It was squalls all the way to Phuket and we arrived in Ao Po marina on 12th December, another new marina since our last visit. We realised what a different journey we had had this time and now know to always overprovision and overfuel as journeys are always unpredictable. The fuel tank was under a quarter full, not the best management but we are a sailing boat so should not have worried!

# CHAPTER EIGHT

# Thailand

## *December 2009 – January 2010*

The family and other friends from Hong Kong were coming for another Thai Christmas. Phuket was changed and restored after the tsunami of 2004 but It had also become much more crowded. We had signed up with Blue Water Rally to get through the pirate area more safely so we went to meet the other Blue Water Rally boats who were already there in the Yacht Haven Marina where we had stayed in 2003. Because we were going to spend the next three months sailing with them and friends and family were coming for Christmas we only made the briefest of acquaintance with them assuming we would have plenty of time to acquaint ourselves on the forthcoming voyage.

We had a quick weekend in Hong Kong to meet friends and enjoy the annual Winter Christmas party and buy some decorations for the boat, it is easier in Hong Kong as we know where to go. We somehow missed the BWR briefings which were over this weekend as we did not receive any communications about them so not entirely our fault although we were later to receive the blame. The children arrived and we all stayed in the Andaman Bangtao Beach hotel very near the now sadly destroyed Bangtao Bunglaows. They had been totally demolished in the Tsunami the year after we had stayed there in 2003. Christmas and New Year flew by in a flurry of eating, partying, beach massages, swimming and snorkelling and thoroughly enjoying ourselves. We had a day sail on Baringo with about 10 people on board and we discovered that the anchor windlass was not working. Luckily that day there were enough hands on deck to pull the anchor up without the windlass and we returned to the marina only to be hit from behind by a strong squall which none of us had seen creep up because we were too busy chatting ! The children and their friends went off to Phi Phi for a few days after New Year before returning to the UK. Vanessa and a friend stayed a few days longer hiring a motor bike and exploring Phuket. We contacted BWR to say we might be late leaving for Sri Lanka as we would have to get the windlass fixed and chandleries along with other marine services worldwide as well as in Thailand were closed for the Christmas and New Year holidays so it was going to be impossible to get ready in time. This news caused our instant dismissal from the group along with complaints that we had not socialised with the other boats while we had been in Thailand and had rushed off to Hong Kong rather than join the briefing, about which we had known nothing. It was a military reprimand with a vengeance and we were upset and annoyed but the main problem was how were we going to traverse the pirate zone. We had paid a substantial sum for the privilege of the protection of BWR but they did return this to us in full.

News of the pirate attacks had been gradually worsening over the last few weeks so we could not attempt the journey alone. The search for a new windlass continued unabated we visited the chandlery daily to review options for different types of windlass and if they could fit easily into our deck fittings, how quickly we could order one from abroad and from where... so many unanswered questions which took up a lot of time. A miracle happened on our fourth visit to the chandlery, just as we were beginning to give up hope... the very helpful Australian assistant in the chandlery had been asked by a catamaran owner if he knew anyone wanting his old windlass! Even better it was a Lewmar windlass the same make as ours and only just one size bigger and it slotted onto our deck windlass fittings exactly. It seemed too good to be true but for a change it wasn't and it is still in excellent working order to this day. We still had the problem of the pirate infested waters to cross safely but again good fortune favoured us. Our neighbours in the Ao Po marina Samasun who had been planning the same journey but after an unpleasant experience in the Indian ocean when they had lost their steering and been badly damaged by a rescuing boat coming alongside to help them in rough weather, had decided to wait and recover suggested that we take their place on the Thailand to Turkey (TTT) rally. We immediately took the opportunity and made acquaintance with Rene the leader of the TTT and the other boats in the group and decided to join and for a much more reasonable cost than our original BWR. We now had a working windlass and a group to transit the pirate zone with, it was extraordinary how all our problems which at times had seemed insurmountable and looked as if they might prevent our circumnavigation early in the adventure had all resolved. We were ready to go!

We sailed to Nai Harn bay in the south of Phuket to meet the TTT rally boats and receive instructions. We had been advised by Puerto Segura a South American boat in the Ao Po marina also joining the TTT that it was very likely we would get fishing net caught around our propeller during the journey and we should get an oxygen cylinder, regulator and tube so John could dive underwater and disentangle the mess if needed. Phuket is a diving centre so it seemed a good place to find the equipment which we did easily and it has been very useful although we did not get seriously entangled on the journey mainly thanks to the efficient rope cutter on the propeller shaft.

We checked everything and stowed all our provisions; the trick is to remember where things are of course! We left for Sri Lanka on 16th January 2011, our recent distress with the anchor windlass and BWR now a distant nightmare.

# CHAPTER NINE

# Thailand to The Maldives

## *January – February 2011*

We had initially thought to go straight to the Maldives as we were becoming increasingly worried about the pirates who this year had captured several large commercial vessels and were using these as mother ships to cross further east from Somalia against the wind which they had previously been unable to do in their small skiffs so their range had increased substantially as a result. We did not feel much like sightseeing we just wanted to get through the pirates and into the safety of the Red Sea as soon as possible. However, Puerto Seguro suggested we should go en route to Sri Lanka with them so we changed our minds and headed for Galle on the southern coast of Sri Lanka. The group was only loosely connected at this stage and boats were meeting either in Galle or the Maldives. The start of the voyage was very pleasant we flew the cruising chute during the day for the first few days but a storm came on day four so it was snuffed but we could not lower the mainsail fully as a screw on the front of the mast had worked loose and stuck out in such a way that the mainsail car attachments could not run down freely, the best we could reduce the mainsail by was to two reefs but we could not get rid of it completely and it was too rough to climb the mast comfortably... if it is ever comfortable... to remove the screw. The weather changed as it always does and once calm, I tightened the screw and we could drop the mainsail now and sail with foresails alone always much easier downwind which we were. The moon was spectacularly bright on this voyage more so than we had ever remembered and we learned later that it was unusually close to the earth at that time, it certainly made night sailing much easier with all the light it shed. By 24th January we were in sight of Galle, we had slowed up slightly to arrive at dawn and we anchored in the waiting area for our inspection by the Sri Lankan navy which involved lots of paperwork and an exchange of wine and snickers bars. We could then enter the port and found we had to tie up to a very flimsy bright blue plastic floating pontoon which was very wobbly and which in any strong wind would have disintegrated.

We walked the city walls and explored the old town and then hired a car and driver to go north to Nuwara Elya. We treated ourselves to dinner at the Hill Club there and this was truly a trip back to the British Colonial times, soup served in tureens, waiters in white gloves serving out the main course with silver spoons and carrying starched white napkins. John had to hire a jacket for the occasion but he had his own tie. We returned through Ella a beautiful small town in the hills and back to the reality of the pirate problem. Many of the TTT boats had arrived and also many independent sailors who were considering their options. The talk on the plastic dock was only of pirates and where the latest attack had been and how to make the safest decision.

To our surprise the Galle literary festival was in full swing while we were there so we were able to hear Jang Chung and her husband John Halliday in a question and answer session about their recent book on Chairman Mao which was so interesting and standing room only. The festival was well attended and very lively so it was difficult to get into any other events they were all so popular and for us it proved a welcome relief from the pirate chatter and the rumours circulating around the pontoon. Rene our leader held daily pirate briefings for all the yachts whether they were TTT or not and gave the information he had regarding current pirate attacks but rather surprisingly we learnt later that a Danish boat who had attended the briefings decided to cross the dangerous area with their teenage children and were taken hostage. They were released some months later after diplomatic negotiations.

The next stop was the Maldives and we left Galle on 1st February and would meet the rest of the TTT boats there. Several members of the group had decided against the voyage as being too risky and opted to put their yachts on transport vessels or wait for another year or go via South Africa and the cape of Good Hope so the group was now only about twelve boats rather than the twenty or so that had gathered in Nai Harn in Phuket. We had a rough start on the passage to the Maldives with 40kts of wind and big seas for the first twenty-four hours and it was difficult to sail on course as we really needed to be more downwind to reduce the stress on Baringo and Poppy and indeed all the steering gear including ourselves. It all changed before we had to alter course and deviate from our goal which was the island of Uligan in the Maldives which is the yachtie stop. This is not the luxurious resort island conjured up by the name Maldives but a rather poor rural outpost with a mainly Muslim population. The generator stopped working on this trip but luckily after several attempts in the last few ports we had managed to get the engine alternator working again, in fact we now had two engine alternators and so we could at least charge the batteries without the generator so we felt lucky the two problems had not occurred simultaneously otherwise there would have been no power. We arrived in Uligan on 4th February to find a crowded anchorage as this was decision time for everyone, the last stop before the pirate attacks were going to be a serious risk. Many kind and well-meaning friends did their best to dissuade us from joining the trip but we felt that if we did not do this leg we would never be able to complete our circumnavigation which we had only just started. We attended daily meetings with our leader Rene and the remainder of the TTT boats and looked at where the attacks were happening which Rene could find through a Dutch naval link and we finally agreed that we would go north up the Indian coast to Pakistan and then cross to Muscat. Theoretically we would be under the protection of the Indian navy at less than 100 nm off shore and as they shoot pirates before asking questions the pirates might keep clear of this coast. The increasing anxiety amongst the boats did not bring out the best in people and several sub groups formed who all had secret radio chats to make their plans. Some BWR boats were there as well but they had no leader to co-ordinate them so they broke into different factions so we were very thankful that fate had put us with Rene and TTT. The water surrounding Uligan was a clear turquoise so we did enjoy some relaxation, swimming and snorkelling while making up our minds. We finally agreed it had to be the Indian coast route, we were now only six boats so five of us: Alondra, Puerto Segura, Skylark, Lizza Forte and Baringo all left on 12th February heading north into the prevailing wind which luckily was never too strong throughout the journey. Two French yachts Apsara and Oukiok had already planned to visit India anyway and had missed the Maldive stopover .Lyra the German boat had gone ahead of us.

# CHAPTER TEN

# The Maldives to Muscat

## *February 2011*

The wind was light so not too difficult to sail into and it was pleasant weather heading up the Indian coast about 100 nm off shore near enough to get protection for the Indian navy should we need it. Our generator was not working so we needed to use the engine to charge the batteries but as there was quite a lot of motoring to be done this did not present too much of a problem. We had to decide which side of the Laccadive Islands to pass and agreed on the east side closer to the mainland for safety. We had a daily radio sked. with the other yachts and on the second day Alondra had to go to India for repairs to her engine and Lizza Forte accompanied her which was just as well because they had to tow her into port. On 15th February we a had a surprise call on the iridium from UKMTO with whom we had been in contact about the pirate passage several times before so they knew what our plans were, they were just checking if we were still on course but declined to offer any assistance. They also enquired about the nationality of our fellow sailors at which point we realised we were the only British citizens so John managed to gloss over this in case we ever needed help. At this stage none of us were quite sure exactly what we were going to do, call in at Mumbai, go to Karachi Yacht Club (affiliated to RHKYC) cross early to Salalah, lots of decisions to be made. Puerto Segura and Skylark had to go to India anyway to get water and fuel which they did successfully but of course they were far behind us now and Lyra was far in front of us so really the original group had now disintegrated. Karachi Yacht club was ridiculously expensive with so many different fees and that was given the thumbs down by every-one, so the major decision was when to turn west to Muscat. We were much further north than Puerto Segura and Skylark so they considered turning north west heading directly towards Salalah and we would go west to the Omani coast and then sail south down the coast to meet them there. However, we felt very unsure about doing this as we had got quite far north by now, and after all we were trying to avoid the pirate area. We had heard nothing from Alondra, complete radio silence. We agreed to talk again the next morning and make a final decision. We had a sleepless night wondering what to do, we did not like their plan but did not want to break up the group by continuing northwards on our own trying to catch Lyra. The next morning the decision was taken out of our hands because Henry sent an e- mail telling us of the pirate attack on a Blue Water Rally boat in exactly the area we had considered passing through, a very timely message. The decision was made for us, so we all contin-ued north up the Indian coast now planning to turn west much later towards Muscat. Just after this news we finally caught up with Lyra so we were no longer alone and we sailed with her, she can go at about the same speed and angle as us whereas the other two were slower and could not sail as easily to windward. We felt a huge sense of relief that we had quite serendipitously been dismissed from Blue Water Rally because of our broken anchor windlass which with hindsight now looked like divine intervention rather than the immensely frustrating equipment failure it had seemed in Thailand.

On 20th February conditions became much rougher with strong winds and large waves so we dumped the main sail and carried on with jenny alone and after thirty-six hours calm returned. We had marked our turning point with an X on the chart and we were now getting close. John had fallen in the cockpit and hurt his back so was not his usual mobile self but with lots of tablets he could manage. We finally heard Alondra was in Cochin doing repairs and planned to meet us in Salalah all being well rather than Muscat so we just hoped they could get across the Arabian sea safely. We heard that the crew on the Blue Water Rally yachts that were captured had been killed which sent a chill down our spines. Once again we gratefully thanked our old anchor windlass for breaking down.

We were quite far north now and still close to the Indian coast so we felt our position should be secure. We had lost Lyra again but were hoping to catch her before making the turn west across the northern Arabian Sea to Muscat and we finally found them on 24th February and then made the turn. We were overflown by a fighter plane (probably Omani) so low between our two boats at the level of the mast followed by a"Top Gun"style roll up into the sky. So much noise but nice of them to let us know they were around. On 26th February at dawn we sighted land, the dry treeless sand of the Omani desert and were greeted by a pod of dolphins herding fish. We sailed on towards the Muscat Marina in the company of Lyra only to find we have to take the yachts to Sultan Qaboos port 4.0 nm away to check in. Commercial ports are inevitably difficult for yachts as they are designed for large vessels and we had to tie up against a very high concrete wall for four hours to complete immigration. By then the wind had increased blowing us onto the high wall so we had to spring off which was not easy and we damaged the guardrail on the bow in the process, all very annoying but at least we had arrived safely. We returned to the marina and were glad to be finally secured after some skilful manoeuvring by the skipper getting Baringo into place in a strong cross wind.

We met the French boats Apsara and Oukiok who had visited India and discovered to our amazement that they both lived about 15 km from us in France, quite a coincidence. There was a lot of work to do on the boat as well as getting the guard rail repaired but we were waiting for the other yachts so had some time. There was a very good swimming pool at the marina largely unused until we arrived and a quick swim always made a healthy and refreshing break from working on Baringo. On 2nd March we hired a car and driver to visit Nizwah the old capital of Oman where there was a wonderful souk with lots of fresh fruit and vegetables and the most succulent dates we have ever tasted. We also visited the Jibrin Palace which was more like a fort and very Arabic in style, the roads were all excellent not a single pot hole. Sam and Gillie McBride who had looked after Baringo in Hong Kong during our absence but were now living in Ras al Khaimah, were coming to see us for a few days so we were delighted. They had done lots of cruising and a few ocean crossings with us and had looked after Baringo while we had been working in the UK. They arrived on 4th March and we had a very enjoyable few days touring Oman over the mountains and into the desert wadis, visiting the local luxurious Shangri La Hotel which Sam and Gillie knew well to enjoy sumptuous food and good wines and we did some hiking to work it all off! Before they left, we went to the local Carrefour and did the largest shop for provisions of the whole trip because we did not think there would be much between here and the Mediterranean so it was a huge help having their Landcruiser to carry it all back to the boat. We said farewell on 7th March and continued preparing for the journey down the

Omani coast to Salalah where we hoped to meet Alondra. We had ordered some parts for our Fischer Panda generator which had to be collected, Puerto Segura and Skylark had arrived and the engine had been serviced by the yard as John's back was still painful. We had the skippers meeting for the passage and some unwanted lessons about how to make Molotov cocktails from the newly arrived ex-army crew on Puerto Seguro. We all departed on 10th March and luckily as we were several yachts the authorities came to check us all out in the marina rather than all the yachts sailing to Sultan Qaboos port, a great relief.

# CHAPTER ELEVEN

# The Omani Coast to Salalah

## *March 2011*

The first night was quiet and we stayed in close convoy using walkie talkies to communicate. The next morning to our delight and amazement Alondra were on the radio despite our best efforts at radio silence but we had Rene our leader back which was a relief as the ex-army officer had tried to take over his role which none of us wanted. So, it was back to normal now but unfortunately that night Lyra and Skylark both got caught in fishing nets and had to go into the sea and cut themselves free. It is a well-known hazard along this coast as Puerto Seguro had warned us, and although the nets have small floats on them they are difficult to see by day but quite impossible at night. The conditions were fairly calm some sailing and some motoring but there were a few skiffs around but so close to the coast they were unlikely to be pirates and were only fishermen. The coastline is very harsh and barren and we needed to go at the speed of the slowest boat which is Puerto Segura the smallest in the fleet. On 14th May we neared Al Hallanyah and as we passed in land of the island the wind picked up and we had to sail freely, the convoy separated as we made our different ways between the island and the coast but we were keeping our lights low so it was a sleepless night trying to avoid any collisions. At dawn with the light we found each other easily and reformed the convoy as the wind had died. We arrived in Salalah that evening at 20.00 and followed Alondra like ducklings into the commercial port to anchor. It was now that our anchor windlass did not work again so we had to let the chain out manually and wait until daylight but with it came a huge sandstorm, the anchor alarm went off and we were dragging. We saw some of the other yachts moving as well, in fact several had dragged because the holding was very poor so Rene somehow arranged for us all to go into the inner harbour. Meanwhile John had found some corroded wires to the windlass and having cleaned them and reconnected them we now had a working windlass in the nick of time as we were dragging ever closer to the harbour wall. We moved in to the inner sanctum and moored stern to and slept for the rest of the day.

Refreshed after an uneventful night the next day we hired a car and spent the day at the Crowne Plaza Hotel where we enjoyed the beach and the pool but no internet. It was the dry season when Salalah is not at its best, and it wasn't, it was like one huge building site with half constructed houses and apartment blocks everywhere, roads dug up and blocked off and almost no pavements to walk along, all covered in dust and very scruffy. There were some shops and I managed to buy some frankincense as this is where it grows in the wet season when the desert here turns green. We drove along the coast one day to see the Al Mugsail blow holes and then we spent the next day relaxing at the Hilton. We met a few of the Blue Water Rally boats who had suffered the loss of the yacht in their group in the pirate attack. They were all understandably very trau-matised and depressed and they had all agreed to put their boats on transport ships to return to the Mediterranean rather than sailing there Of course this gave us second thoughts about the wisdom of continuing but if we did not a circumnavigation would be beyond our reach and we had confidence in Rene as leader of the convoy and no-one else was deserting so we tried not to converse with the Blue Water rally sailors and kept to ourselves. We had a restful and lazy day at the Hilton Hotel and then an evening drive to Job's tomb in the mountains and saw lots of camels. We left Salalah on 21st March after we had taken the car back, done more shopping at Lulu's the local supermarket, loaded the provisions and waited for clearance. At 18.00 everyone was ready to leave but apparently we had not been cleared out and we were instructed to re-anchor but instead we all went alongside Alondra, eight boats on one anchor but not for long and we all moved off at 20.00.

# CHAPTER TWELVE

# Salalah to Aden

## *March 2011*

The weather was calm the first night but three yachts got stuck on fishing nets, we just prayed we would be lucky and that our rope cutter on the propeller shaft would work and either we did not hit a net or the cutter worked, we never knew. We crossed the big bay from Salalah rather than closely following the coast and had a night of free sailing round the cape but again tiring watching out for the other yachts with their dimmed navigation lights. We saw no-one in the dark but we were all within sight of each other when the day light revealed our positions. We regrouped in the light of dawn and continued in convoy down the coast. Skiffs were always approaching our convoy and under the instructions of Rene when one was sighted we all closed tightly together and kept low in the cockpit. None of them became truly threatening, either they did not want to tackle a convoy of yachts or they were only fishermen but they all looked the same with their heads swathed in turbans holding long sticks which might have been fishing rods or rifles. We all stopped once every twenty-four hours usually around 15.00

to check engine oil and refill as needed, we were all doing a fair amount of motoring so it was a wise precaution. Two other yachts got stuck on nets but the weather was fair and the sky cloudless and the coastline harsh but beautiful.

On 24th March we enter Al Mukalla a port in Yemen to the shouts of demonstrators in the streets! We anchored just under the town which looked like an Arabic version of a Cornish fishing village but no sooner had we settled down to tea than the authorities asked us to move to the commercial harbour as it would be safer. We did not manage to get our anchor to hold there so in the end as it was getting dark we rafted alongside Alondra and it was a good excuse for a drink with them. Early the next morning we were asked to go ashore, it was a big rush as we were asleep but Lyra took us over and we waited on shore in a big concrete yard inside a wire fence watching hundreds of goats being off loaded from a Somalian ship. That was the morning's entertainment and we were then told we could not go ashore so back on board and then the skipper's briefing at 17.00. Finally permission for us to go ashore with our shore passes arrived and we all went in a bus to a local restaurant, a Yemeni version of Kentucky fried chicken but there were other choices on the menu and we had a good meal and were bussed back. The atmosphere in the town felt very unstable with many soldiers with guns so it was with some relief we returned to the boat.

At 06.00 we left Al Mukalla for Aden travelling in convoy as usual, we all have our own positions with respect to each other further apart when there is no sign of danger and closer when anyone sees a skiff and Rene instructed us all by VHF radio to try and avoid collisions. The Yemen coast is dramatic with black mountains rising vertically from the sea and perhaps I was admiring the scenery too much as I ran over a fishing net that afternoon creating a nasty noise from the propeller which woke John up pretty quickly. Baringo did not stop so presumably broke free but John went down with the cylinder and checked and found only a small fragment of net still left on the propeller, luckily it was daylight and warm so not too unpleasant. It is always surprising to find the fishing floats so far off shore and in such deep water. On 28th March we arrived in the haze off the peninsula on which Aden stands. It is an amazing natural harbour of bays within bays and in such a strategic position, no wonder the British commandeered it. Those days were long gone and it was barely a shadow of its former self.

We followed Alondra in and anchored in a rather drab harbour with the so called Baby Ben looking over us, a replica of the big one in London... Once anchored securely , we launched the dinghy to go ashore but not before struggling with the outboard, the mixture was too rich because of evaporation, but we finally got it going and after quite a walk in the heat found the most dilapidated customs house. Everywhere was untidy, littered and completely lacking in any maintenance, broken roads and pavements, chipped and worn paintwork all looking tired and sad. We took a taxi to Lulu's for provisions and we did not like the rather threatening angry expressions on people's faces and hoped we would not have to stay too long here, it felt like trouble was brewing. I had noticed that many men seemed to have large swellings in their cheeks so wondered if parotid tumours were common here but it turned out they were all chewing balls of Kat or Khat which contains cathinone a drug causing euphoria as well as excitement and has been a custom in Yemen for thousands of years. Judging from what we saw around they certainly needed it now. We were still struggling with the generator and even Rene could not fix it, we will probably scrap it when we get to Turkey as it has not been reliable throughout the voyage. That evening we all went ashore to the small town At Tawahi and had an excellent meal eating the food on enormous naan breads and then eating our plates as well. The group took a city tour the next day but we did not feel inclined to join them so wandered round At Tawahi, collected the laundry, bought Yemen T-shirts and met an elderly Indian gentleman in the garden of the Unknown Soldier. His father had been brought here by the British and he was now stuck here rather than living in his home country and had no way of returning. He had really drawn a short straw at the hands of the imperialists, a very sad story and probably not the only one that might be heard here. We all went to the refuelling dock in our dinghies transporting as many jerry cans as possible and waited in line for diesel but that all went smoothly and later Rene not to be deterred by anything returned and finally fixed our generator. We had the skippers briefing the next day at 08.30 about our plans for Eritrea and we left later at 15.30 the same day. We had picked up another boat in Aden because the German skipper's wife had been in hospital in Aden after a heart attack but had been flown back to Germany. He did not want to continue single handed so a spare crew from another yacht joined him and he continued with us in the convoy.

We had a quiet night apart from me losing my bearings in the convoy, confused by fishing boat lights I had inadvertently changed positions but no major adverse consequences fortunately and tye to the next after noon we approached the Bab el Mandab strait the narrow entrance into the Red Sea with rising anticipation and excitement.

# CHAPTER THIRTEEN

# The Red Sea

## *April 2011*

We passed through the Bab el Mandab strait between Perim Island and the Yemen coast the narrower of the passes but the one recommended in the pilot book, the wind picked up and we all raced through so happy to be out of the pirates reach now. Rene came over the VHF loud and clear "Welcome to the Red Sea, ladies and gentlemen." Something I will never forget. We had great wind pushing us along and we were making 6 knots with only a handkerchief of jib and enjoying a great sail after all the tension of recent days. We crossed the shipping channel to the western side, the Eritrean coast. Yachts are not allowed to land on the Saudi Arabian side of the Red Sea. We rounded Fatma Island and anchored off Lalaheb Deset sheltered from the waves but not the wind. We all celebrated our safe passage through the pirates with a few beers on Alondra and much thanks to Rene.

The next morning Lyra called for medical help for a local fisherman who has an infected area on his foot so we went over with our collection of medical instruments, dressings, bandages and drugs and

I managed to lance the infection and he seemed to be much happier. We left him dressings and antibiotics and some T shirts and at follow up the next day his foot was much better. We wandered over the low-lying island in the afternoon and saw some flamingos and enjoyed the emptiness and peace. We left next morning, Lyra had already gone ahead alone as the pirate risk was no longer and we all left by 11.00 into the 40 knot breeze but it was behind us. We were going north to Ras Darma Deset and today we made 6.0 knots with no sail at all. We anchored in the strong breeze, annoyingly we were having trouble with our anchor chain not flowing out easily which meant that Baringo moved a lot before the anchor hit the bottom so we did not end up where we had intended. We had tried untwisting it many times but the problem always recurred so anchoring in a group we often had to anchor twice as we ended up too close to another yacht. The wind blew all night and the anchor chain was horizontal and the anchor buddy visible just below the surface, but there were no waves, this is anchoring in the Red Sea! We left on 4th April and during the afternoon as the weather was fine we discussed with Rene about sailing overnight., We had a nice wind behind and he agreed so we all continue, we were making 7.00 knots without any sails! The wind pattern in the Red Sea is simple, in the south the wind is from the SE and at some point about half way up it changes to north west and so sailing is into a headwind the rest of the way. Each year the point of change varies but this year we got it at 03.00 on 5th April and it was quite sudden, from cruising along smoothly downwind suddenly the sails flapped and the wind was in front in a matter of seconds! There it stayed until we reached Port Suez! We tacked into Anfile Bay later in the morning and on arrival there a skiff approached Oukiok, just as we thought we were safe, but it was the Eritrean navy! It was a quiet night near a rather featureless landscape but quite an interesting terrain of shells and coral and lots of birds. The day ended with a beach bar-b-q but we had omitted to leave a deck light on Baringo so spent some time searching for her in the black night. We left again next morning and during the course of the day Alondra had engine trouble and needed to be towed by Lizza Forte and Rene thought it was best to go directly to Massawa rather than anchor for the night when he had no engine. Obediently we all followed our leader and anchored outside Massawa at 03.00 on Friday 8th April.

Massawa is a war-torn city with bombed buildings full of bullet holes and on the verge of collapse everywhere. The damage is left over after the war between Eritrea and Ethiopia. All this destruction has almost removed the last vestiges of the Italian presence here in the nineteenth century. There were hardly any cars but we found beer and restaurants among the ruins. I also found a hat as my Australian Byron Bay hat had not survived the Red Sea wind and we had parted company. On Sunday 10th April Rene had organised a bus to take us to Asmara the capital in land and uphill and we stayed for two nights in this very Italian capital in a very Italian hotel. We checked in at lunchtime and settled down on the Italian style terrace to enjoy lunch. The waiter appeared with a large leather bound volume which was the menu and we read all the possibilities carefully in order to make the perfect choice. We gave the waiter our orders, no they were not available today, back to the leather bound volume and we made two more choices, these were not available either so we then asked what was available ... only chicken and chips or omelette! Perhaps this could have been written in a slimmer volume. There were some beautiful Italian buildings in Asmara all well preserved as well as excellent pizza and ice cream. We did the Lonely Planet city walk passing all the elegant houses, it was really one of the pleasantest and cleanest African capitals we had seen. We visited the Tank Cemetery the next day where acres of war detritus are piled up, old aircraft, Land Rovers, tanks etc, not a pretty site and a grim reminder of the war. We returned later that day to Massawa and back to the boating life. We left on 13th April and now we were heading into the wind and would be for the rest of the Red Sea voyage. The next stop was Khor Narawat and the wind angle allowed us some nice sailing most of the time varying from NE to N to NW so always close hauled but the sea was quite flat. We gave the Sudan Eritrean border a wide berth. Sadly Alondra's repair in Massawa was short lived and she was being towed again by Lizza Forte but we made it into the anchorage behind Ras Istani in time for breakfast on 15th April. The island is the usual pancake providing little protection form the wind but we had nice snorkelling off a reef there. The plan to leave the next day was thwarted because the skipper of Lizza Forte was ill, we were called in but fortunately found nothing serious so we had another day swimming, walking and relaxing. We were ready to move on to Trinkitat on 16th April, the sailing was very pleasant and after anchoring in the harbour we had a visit from the Sudanese navy who checked our documents but we all pass muster. Suakin was the next stop a curious town made of coral which had a heyday as a 14th century port but was now very dilapidated and the entrance was rather tricky up a narrow channel and with a small island partially filling the centre of the bay inside so not leaving a lot of space for our group of yachts and in addition it was rather shallow.

We decided to leave the group the next day as we wanted to press ahead faster than they were so we said fond farewells and departed at 07.00 so we did not see much of Suakin.

The great beauty of this coast of the Red Sea is the large number of marsas which are bays and inlets which make perfect anchorages. They are all described in detail in the Red Sea Pilot by Stephen Davies and Elaine Morgan, in fact this is not only a cruising guide but a work of literature full of historical anecdotes and even his own charts of safe passages through the reefs in places. The Red Sea has had no recent surveys so much of the information on the charts is hopelessly out of date and very inaccurate often putting Baringo on land when the GPS position was plotted on the chart when she was at anchor in the middle of the bay! It is an invaluable book for any Red Sea sailing excursions. Our next marsa on our own now was Marsa Fijab on the way to Port Sudan and it was a rather barren place with a rather desolate naval base on the shore and we had a lightning storm that night but no damage done. We always put the computers in the oven and disconnected the SSB radio during any lightning storm. The next day we were unlucky with a strong headwind so were obliged to motor sail into it this time through a marked channel in the reefs but all the marks were present and easily visible. We passed Port Sudan, contemplated going in to shelter there but decided against, commercial ports are usually not pleasant so we sailed on to Taila Islets which are a small group of reefs with some sand on about 2nm off shore. They stop the waves but are so low lying make no difference to the wind. We stayed there the next day while the wind was strong and on the nose, the islands were very beautiful with amazing colours and breaking waves on the opposite side, a picture perfect refuge. We were just enjoying the enforced inactivity of waiting for the wind to die down when we found the bunk room very wet possibly because the hatch was not tightly closed so all the sheets had to be changed and the mattresses dried out which at least was easy in the strong warm wind but not exactly a rest. Later some fishermen came and we traded T-shirts for some fish which we ate for supper.

On Friday 22ndApril the wind dropped so we left the Taila Islets and followed another marked channel through the reefs admiring the wonderful colours created by the breaking waves on the coral.

We had a little wind for an afternoon sail but we lost it before arriving at Khor Shinab which was a magical marsa to anchor in. We found out later that it was everyone's favourite. The entrance is hard to find so much so that the pilot book recommended using radar which we did and we entered this amazing inland waterway and had the bay to ourselves which added to the surreal nature of it. The desert met the sea and there were high exotically shaped mountains towering over us and the only green spot was a single tree growing on an islet in the middle of the water. It was Easter weekend, there were no eggs here, but plenty to compensate as we swam and had ideas of climbing the mountain but the strong wind prevented that. The scenery was so extraordinary and we kept looking at the lone tree wondering how it got there and how it survived in such a dry windy environment. We left on Easter Sunday into a strong wind and we had lost the protection of the reefs so the sea was very choppy, a short chop which is rather unpleasant and Baringo slammed her way through it shaking everything on board at times. The angle of the wind was head on but a slight change either side enabled us to sail for short periods and the strength was variable but not bad enough to stop us moving ever northwards.

We stopped at Port Ghalib on 27th April, we were now in Egypt and we noticed there was much more illumination along this coast compared to Sudan. This marina is well organised and professionally run so we could check in first, refuel and then go to our berth. There was good internet, several cafes and restaurants and the staff were very friendly and excited because this was the time of the Arab spring and they were hoping their country would soon be a democracy. We now know their hopes were dashed. After the leak into the bunk room we still had a lot of cleaning and drying out to do but the weather made this easy and we got all the laundry done at the near-by Crowne Plaza Hotel. We even looked round the laundry because the father of John's friend Alan had a laundry in Scotland and we had looked round that so we could make some useful and interesting comparisons. I remember well that it was the only laundry that was able to remove those tenacious brown stains that get onto clothes on a boat and are impossible to remove. We enjoyed the resort facilities, pool, gym, bars, television and internet but there was not much useful provisioning for sailors. We left on 31st April but had a horrible night out with strong headwind and lots of slamming in the short chop and the lights on land never seemed to move past us, we were only making 2-3 knots over the ground so not very fuel efficient. John's birthday did not dawn pleasantly and after a weather forecast from Claire on Apsara in Port Ghalib we decided to go into Hurghada as we did not want a repeat of last night and nor did Baringo, the banging of the waves shaking her hull had been horrible. We could go more off the wind to get to Hurghada and eventually got some shelter from the offshore islands and we got into the marina there stern to but we had no plank to get ashore! A kind German sailor produced one and we could get onto the land. The berths were just on a seaside walkway full of restaurants and bars as Hurghada is a tourist resort for diving and there were many dive boats around. It was quite lively and so we celebrated John's birthday in style in one of the restaurants. We had another day there and found the slightly scruffier part of town behind the marina but also fruit and vegetables and a small supermarket. A sandstorm was over us next morning, we had read about the occurrence of these in the Pilot book and dreaded being caught in one while sailing as all visibility disappears and the sand gets everywhere. Luckily this one did not last very long and we left by mid-day in 15knots of wind and a flat sea and no slamming, a welcome change.

Our final goal was Port Suez at the southern end of the Suez Canal and where we would organise our passage through into the

Mediterranean but we did not want another night out so stopped at Endeavour harbour in time for a swim and a calm night. We are now in the Gulf of Suez which is narrow and busy so we decided to anchor again at Ras Ghareb but it was too shallow to get proper shelter and the surroundings were becoming more industrial with more commercial shipping from the canal. We had to cross the shipping lane to the east side of the Gulf and today we had a southerly wind which helped as we sailed through lots of oil refineries and oil tankers. This made the area very polluted and the overcast weather added to the greyness and then brought a squall. We anchored in Ras Sedr that night now close to Port Suez but the wind prevented us leaving early enough to make it the next day so we had another stop at Qid al Tawila behind a reef 10 nm before Port Suez and with lots of large ships at anchor nearby. The wind blew strongly during the night but we were secure with the 60m chain we had let out. This is the minimum length necessary for off shore cruising. On 7th May we arrived in Port Suez, the end of the Red Sea but we felt we had had an easy journey up in comparison to some stories we had read of days of delays due to strong adverse winds and wild sandstorms. The Newport channel was buoyed to the Suez Canal Yacht Club at the southern exit/entrance of the canal and we finally got a berth with the help of Kar Kar whom Puerto Segura had recommended to us. The entrance/exit of the canal was very unprepossessing hidden behind a sand dune its presence only revealed when a huge vessel emerged as if by magic.

# CHAPTER FOURTEEN

# The Suez Canal to Turkey

## *May 2011*

Two days after we had arrived in Port Suez we visited Cairo while the administration for the canal passage was in progress. It was only a two hour bus ride away so we took the opportunity. It was empty of tourists because of the Arab spring uprising so we enjoyed the pyramids and the Cairo museum almost on our own. We found an excellent hotel with a mixture of Egyptian and French character run by a lady of the same mixture.

We had booked our canal pilot Ali and he arrived at 10.00 on May 11th and we entered the canal, first we were on our own and it really just seemed like a river in the desert, no sign of the hard engineering work that the French had put into it. It was built in the mid nineteenth century by the French under the leadership of De Lesseps and needed no locks and it was finished in 1869. The relative ease of the construction of the Suez Canal had encouraged De Lesseps to try his hand in Panama but this proved to be a different story and had finally defeated him. We eventually passed a large vessel coming south towards us, it seemed enormous passing at such close quarters but there was room. We fed and watered Ali the pilot but he did not speak very much English which was a pity as we would have been interested to know more about the day to day operations of the canal. We motored through Little Bitter Lake then Great Bitter Lake then the Deversoir by pass where there are two lanes and into Lake Timsah where we docked for the night at Ismaili. This stop is compulsory for small yachts but the commercial craft can go straight through without stopping. We had the company of a large German yacht "Absolut" that evening and as her name suggests the alcohol flowed and they were very friendly and hospitable. We stayed a day there because bad weather was forecast in the Mediterranean and we managed to get a land exeat from the authorities with a French boat to visit the town and do some shopping and have lunch there, this was strictly forbidden because we had checked out of Egypt in Port Suez, but our powers of persuasion and a gift worked. I suspect it had worked many times before! On Friday 13th April our new pilot knocked on the boat at 06.00 so we had to rush to get ready as we had not expected such an early start. The northern part of the canal seems more like a canal with man-made brick walls on the side rather than just sand and there was a smart bridge going over it which was quite new. We saw some evidence of the planned widening engineering works starting and we arrived in Port Said at 12.00. There are lots of beautiful nineteenth century French style port authority buildings around the entrance all looking slightly faded now but still elegant. It was now trouble started when a launch approached us and our pilot got off and another pilot dressed in full naval attire scrambled egg included got on to take us a few hundred meters to the berth for which he tried to charge us 50$US which was outrageous. At this point John had a sense of humour failure, he had been worn out by the continual demands for money we had experienced while in Egypt and a row ensued while we were approaching the basin to tie up. The wind was strong and blowing us off so it was difficult to moor up and several men stood idle on the side watching us struggle with only one man helping us, really infuriating so we had to shout for help and finally we tied up. We gave the "pilot" 20$US and he left but it was an unpleasant experience and it sullied the rather favourable impression of the people we had got when we had arrived in Port Ghalib. We had checked out of Egypt in Port Suez so we only needed a brief inspection in Port Said after which we headed out for the Mediterranean planning to anchor just outside in a spot Puerto Segura had told us about as the weather had still not settled. We anchored in the spot and were in the middle of our lunch when a loud screech reverberated outside the hull and we were summarily dismissed from Egypt by the authorities and expelled into the Mediterranean sea.

As expected from the forecast the sea was rough and the wind 25 to 30 knots as we wove our way through an oilfield in the dark, not a very auspicious start but we knew the forecast had been bad. Things improved when the wind dropped, the moon came out and we could sail on course for Turkey... or almost. We needed a NW course but that was directly into the wind so the question was, do we sail north hoping for a wind shift later or do we charge the batteries and motor on course? The generator took this decision out of our hands by not starting so we motored on course until the batteries were charged. Two avian hitchhikers landed on Baringo, one small feathered friend in the cockpit obviously very tired and a larger one under the vang behind the mast for shelter, we were very happy to give them a lift. In the morning the little bird died so we had a burial at sea using a beer can as a coffin. When they are so tired we could hold them in our hands and try and revive them, this was not the first time this had happened but we were never successful. The larger bird flew away at mid-day and we hoped we had helped his journey. The wind was occasionally westerly so then we made good course and did not need to land in Cyprus which we left to starboard. It was surprisingly cold but the sea was calmer the moon shone at night and we had pizza for supper. On 16th May it was six months since we had left Hong Kong and we sighted the land of Europe which if our navigation has not let us down is Turkey! A very exciting moment indeed but we did not count our chickens yet. We crossed the bay of Marmaris on 17th May and entered the marina and we decided to ask if we could fill up with fuel before going to the berth. We went into the basin, filled up the fuel tank and then when we tried to leave the engine did not start... how could this be after so many stops and starts coming across from Port Said. John had a look but could not solve the problem but here in a port we have the luxury of calling the Yanmar engine expert who fixed it quickly. A wire from the solenoid had fractured but he easily repaired it, rather lucky timing otherwise we might have been out in the Mediterranean sea for much longer. The Mediterranean is stern to style mooring territory so we must master the art although Baringo is not well designed for it with her backward sloping un-scooped stern and we did not have the necessary plank to enable us to get ashore but our kind neighbours found one for us.

We celebrated our safe arrival through the pirates and all the other hazards the sea can bring with a bottle of champagne and began packing Baringo up for a few weeks stay in the water in Marmaris.

**Leaving our mooring at Shelter Cove in Hong Kong**

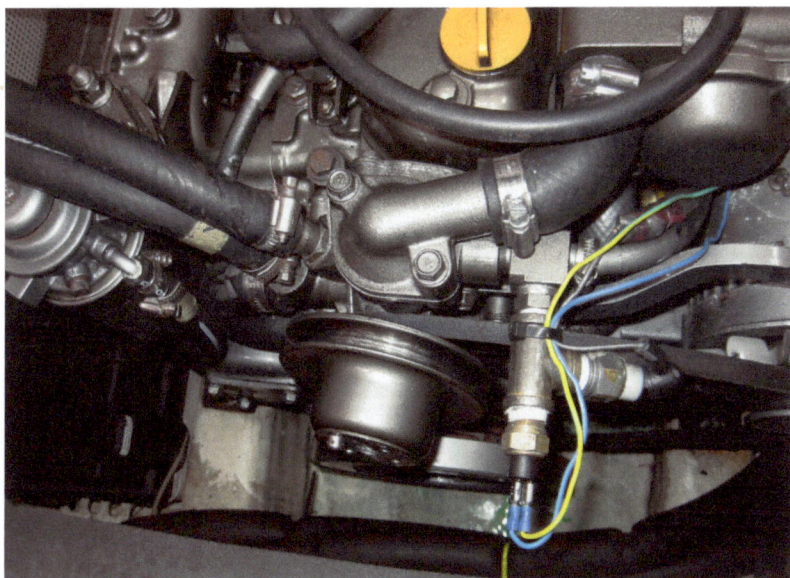

**Broken engine**

**Arriving in Singapore – casino still under constrction**

**Malacca straits busy with ships**

**En route to Phuket**

**Ao Pao marina Phuket**

New Year's Eve – Bangtao Beach hotel

En route to Sri Lanka – bright moon like daylight

**Approaching Galle Sri Lanka**

**Beach cafe near Galle**

**The hill club at Nuwara Eliya**

**Meeting in the Maldives**

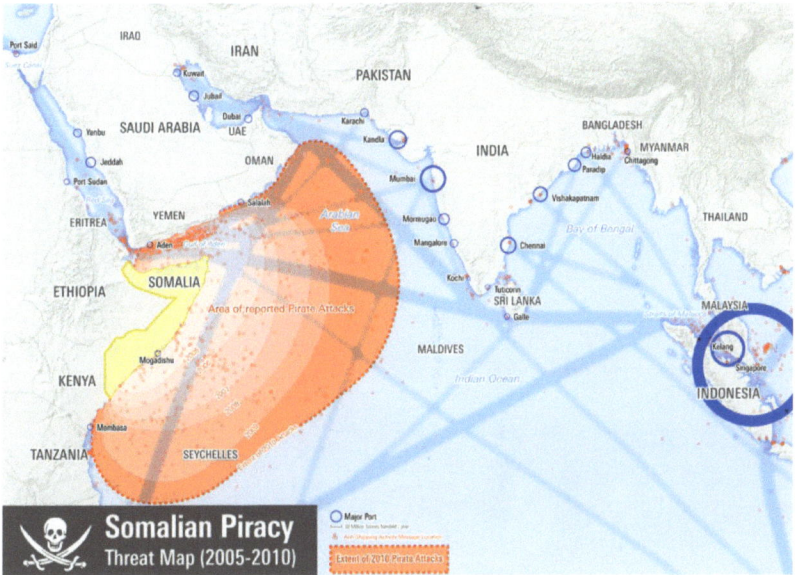

**Pirate**

**Anchorage at Uligan island Maldives**

**TTT convoy**

**Approaching skiff possible pirates**

**Convoy sailing Omani Coast**

**Mukala Yemen gun boat**

**Little Ben Aden**

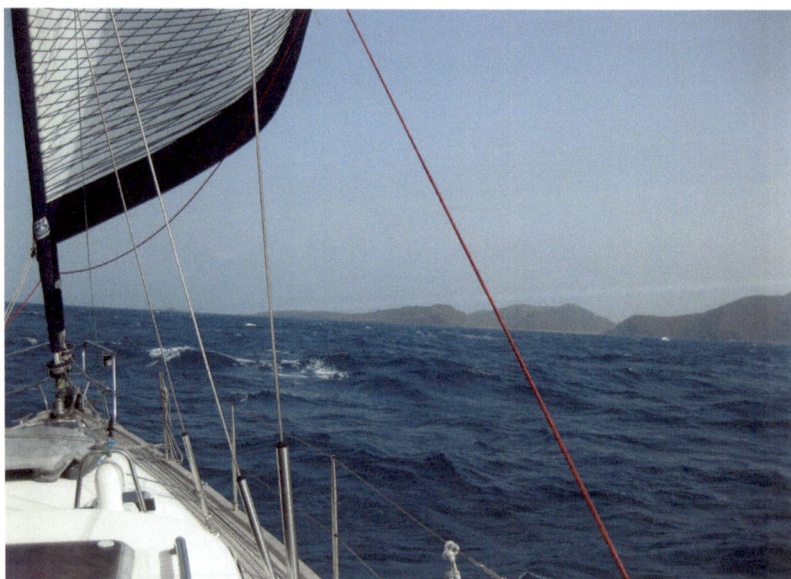

**Entering the Red Sea through Bab al-Mandab strait**

**Windy anchorage in the Red Sea**

**Flamingos in the Red Sea**

**Fisherman in the Red Sea**

**Albergo Italia Asmara Eritrea**

Lone tree in Quorshinab Marsa

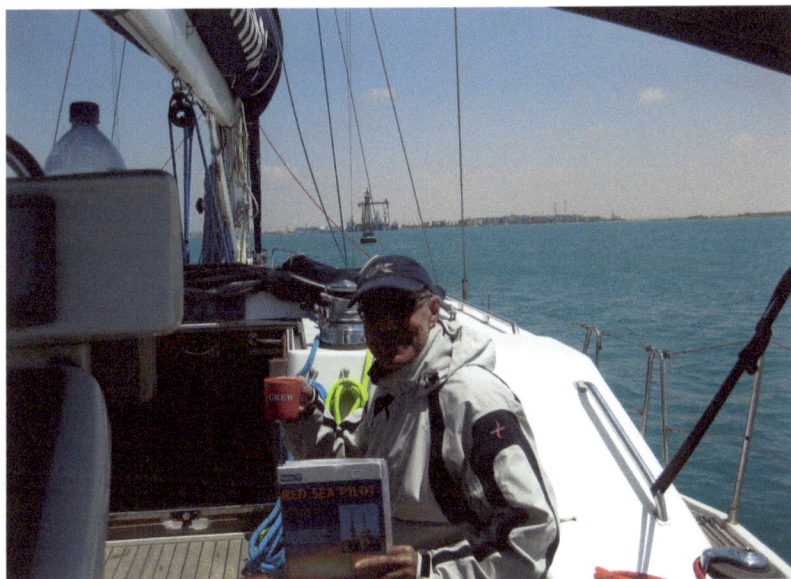

Port Suez end of the Red Sea thanks to RS Pilot

**Entry to Suez Canal**

**In the Suez Canal**

**Arrival in Marmaris Turkey**

# CIRCUMNAVIGATION

# PART TWO

# CHAPTER FIFTEEN

# The Mediterranean Sea

## *2011 – 2012*

## Summer 2011

After a break on land in Europe during June and July 2011 we had decided to postpone our Atlantic Crossing to the following year to give us some more time sailing in the Mediterranean. We spent the first summer season 2011 exploring the Turkish coast between Fethiye and Datca, enjoying beautiful anchorages, delicious Turkish food and lots of swimming. Several friends came to sail with us as well as Henry and Vanessa but after having unbroken sunshine all summer unfortunately for the week of their visit the wind and rain never stopped so we did not get beyond Gocek or the Gocek Marina. Henry and his girlfriend got cabin fever and left for Cappadocia but Vanessa stayed with us and was rewarded with one nice day's sailing. The Southern Turkish coast is very hard to beat for cruising as it is very irregular with many peninsulas and bays and therefore many anchorages.

We had decided to leave Baringo in Gocek this winter because we had met Rizza from Emek Marine who promised to help us with the work needed on Baringo, Rene had introduced us and he seemed sensible and spoke good English; how deceptive appearances can be as was more than proved the following year. Baringo was lifted out and we left for Europe on 21st October, we had already seen snow on the Turkish hilltops so it was definitely time to go.

# Summer 2012

After our return to Turkey we spent April 2012 in Gocek struggling to get the work done on Baringo. We had visited Baringo earlier during February to check some progress was being made primarily with installing the new Cummins Onan generator and thought things were going as planned. It was interesting to see a wintery Gocek in a very different guise, empty of tourists and cold. During the convoy we had damaged the turbo in the engine by having to motor more slowly than an engine with turbo units likes and it needed to be repaired. Also we had the injectors and fuel pump checked, valves replaced (probably unnecessarily), and the propeller shaft seal replaced. The rudder needed some attention related to the original accident in Hong Kong, along with various other smaller repairs.

This time in Gocek spent trying to get this all done was a very low period, we waited for days for workers to turn up, I think a total of seven in all, the work was done badly causing more problems than it solved and there were lies, phony photographs and huge bills. We were always within an ace of going to Marmaris but continued to give Emek Marine the benefit of the doubt, unwisely in retrospect. By 26th May we left, ready or not and very much poorer. We were now heading westwards to cross the Mediterranean through Greece, Sicily, Sardinia, Minorca and Gibraltar where we would leave for the Canary Islands to join the Atlantic rally for Cruisers (ARC).

We had only been out of Gocek for four days when the steering cable which Emek Marine had renewed broke. Luckily it was calm and the autohelm still worked as it attaches directly onto the steering quadrant so we went to the nearest anchorage and called Rizza. His father came the next day to repair it but the new cable they brought with them was only just long enough, another job badly done and no apology. We would have to replace it before the Atlantic but hoped it might last to Gibraltar and vowed that we would have no more dealings with Emek Marine ever again.

We had several friends joining us at various islands along the way and we were joining a Yacht Squadron Cruise in Menorca courtesy of Hugh Laing. The Greek islands we visited were all charming with very traditional in architecture, dress and cuisine and all a pleasure to sail into. We used the Mediterranean Bible of Rod Heikell to plan our route with all its detailed information about everything everywhere.

The following vignettes tell the story of the more interesting and sociable sections of our Mediterranean transit:

Sailing in Sicily

On Friday June 15th we finally left the island of Kithera, south of the Peloponnese with some sadness as this was our last Greek island; the island was very relaxing and we had enjoyed the company of our neighbours there. It was our first long passage for some time so there were some feelings of uncertainty but it was a beautiful morning as we sailed up the east coast of the island past the bays we had visited in the car. We had found rounding island capes in the Mediterranean to be very tricky because the land alters the behavior of the wind usually in an adverse way and our final Greek cape Tanairo proved no different. So after a brief attempt to sail, which the wind around the cape made impossible we had to motor sail away from Greece. As we left land behind the sea became rougher left over from the recent high winds and the wind was north west as well so we had to motor sail all the first night. With the sea state it proved quite uncomfortable especially for the skipper but by the following morning conditions had improved so we could finally sail on course for the next two days. We sighted Mount Aetna on 18th June smoking as usual, no flaming larva but nevertheless a dramatic and welcome sight as we sailed into Catania on the east coast at Sicily at midday.

We had arranged to meet Richard and Isabel Winter there, our rendez-vous was successful although we were a little late and they had amused themselves driving north to Taormina, but we all met for dinner that evening. The dockside of Catania does not have much to recommend it, but the city is one of enormous dark stone baroque buildings in a state of shabby disrepair which shrouded the city in mystery, making an unusual contrast to the jovial Sicilians carrying on their normal daily lives seemingly oblivious of the backdrop. The markets were fantastic, full of all kinds of fruit, vegetables, spices, cheese, meat and every imaginable edible product so provisioning was a treat.

After our mornings outing in Catania we set off for Syracuse having decided to avoid the Scylla and Charybdis of the Messina Strait this time. It was a pleasant sail south down the coast the land is quite flat and gently sloping in contrast to the steep sides of the Greek islands. Our arrival in Syracuse in the late afternoon sun was truly magnificent like sailing into a history book and we could tie up along a wall right in the heart of the old town. We had a wonderful time exploring the small alleys and shops of the old city the next day. The archictecture had a surprise at every corner and always a beautiful one.

In the evening we went to a performance of a play about

Prometheus in an ancient Greek amphitheatre just outside the old city. The play which although in Italian/Sicilian was very enjoyable, for those who have not been to Syracuse it is definitely worth a visit.

We started early the next morning to reach Marina di Raguza (about 60 nm around the SE corner of the island) before dark and had a good sail most of the day but the dreaded headwind started for the last 2 hours of the journey and we just got into the marina before closing and much needed help was there to get into our stern to position, always tricky in strong wind. We had a good last night in town with Richard and Isabel, a delicious meal, a Sicilian specialty of couscous and seafood accompanied by two bottles of Sicilian wine followed by a sweet wine tasting organized by Richard. Next morning's start was delayed for obvious reasons but we went to Raguza about 20 miles away by bus as Richard and Isabel had to get back to Catania the next day for their flight. Raguza is another old town built straddling a deep narrow ravine so the setting is rather more dramatic than the city itself which does not match up to the delights of Syracuse. We said au revoir to the Winters and took the bus back to Baringo.

The next morning we left for Licata further along the coast and arrived safely in the marina which is very modern and has all facilities although you pay for the privilege! There are few anchorages along this Sicilian coast so there is no way of avoiding the expense of the marinas. Here the walkway in front of the pontoons was the local venue for the traditional Sicilian "passagiato" when everyone comes out for an evening stroll. The girls are dressed up in their finest and John certainly enjoyed the spectacle! We had planned to leave early the next day but on rising we found a very strong wind and decided against moving so we used the day for John to do some work and have a look around the town in the evening and watch the Italian v England football match.

We left the next day for Sciacca and again by the afternoon a fierce head wind and rough sea came suddenly out of nowhere as often seems to happen so we battled the last two hours into it to reach Sciacca. The coastline became slightly more mountainous on this stretch and there were some dramatic white cliffs. It was gusting up to 40 knots and right on the nose so quite hard on the boat. As we approached a kite surfer came into view careering along at 30 mph becoming airborne as he went about, quite a dramatic sight especially as he came rather too close to us for comfort. Amazing to be out in such conditions. However, pride comes before a fall when he lost control and fell in the water! We were a little worried his wires might get entangled around our mast which would have been a disaster. We arrived undamaged and were welcomed into the marina very efficiently. Sciacca is another old city perched on a hill and famous for its thermal baths. The weather meant we had to stay for a few days but there are certainly worse places to be stuck!

We were able to leave a couple of days later and had two more stops, the last one was saved for the best. A wonderful anchorage at Isolo del Marettimo the western most island of the Egadi group. We expected to be in another marina but as we approached we saw other yachts at anchor and decided to join them. We were under a vertical cliff face in clear water surrounded by beautiful birds and a very pleasant quiet night was passed. We dragged ourselves away reluctantly at mid-day after a swim and set sail for Cagliari in southern Sardinia. We had a very favorable wind, well worth waiting for and arrived after a peaceful overnight sail and anchored off the south coast in a large bay. We motored the last 14 miles to Marina del Sole in Cagliari the following morning.

The marina was rather shabby and not well protected and despite several e-mails requesting a month's stay and informing them of our ETA they seemed to have no idea about us and when we said we had arranged to stay for a month they promptly asked us to move just after we had moored up! We did move but to a much more protected marina which was less scruffy and more professionally run.

We flew to France just 4 days later and we planned to start sailing again all being well in august when we will be joined by our usual august crew Sam and Gilly McBride... happy days!

# The Sea and Sardinia

We left Cagliari on 6th August 2012 on our way to meet Sam and Gilly in Olbia on the east coast of Sardinia. The first night out we anchored in the same bay on the south coast that we had used on the way to Cagliari. It was much more crowded this time but John inspected the bottom of the boat only to find the oceoprotec copper based antifouling had not been applied properly in Turkey and there was growth on the keel ...it seem the problems generated in Turkey will follow us forever. We continued the next day motoring around the SE tip of Sardinia to make some progress up the east coast and had good anchorage in the small bay of Cala Pira, but here John was singled out by a jelly fish and stung. It was very painful and caused the usual swelling and inflammation but it had improved by morning. We learned from the pilot book that they are called sea wasps, not seen but certainly felt.

We continued up the east coast pleasantly and uneventfully with the usual erratic Mediterranean winds we have become accustomed to. It is a scenic coastline with beautiful red cliffs near Arbatrax. The beaches are unspoilt, there are very few buildings and all are low rise and designed to blend with the environment rather than dominate it. The anchorages are all only a day sail apart and all were straightforward. Further north there is Isola Taverola which rises vertically out of the sea and it is quite tricky navigation to get through the inland side of it while trying to look at the view as well. I think the chart plotter paid for itself that day! We arrived in Olbia to meet Sam and Gilly who were coming from Edinburgh that evening so great jubilation welcoming them on board again. After a jolly evening we set to work the next day preparing for our cruise of the la Maddalena archipelago. The islands are all very close so we had long days luxuriating in turquoise water of amazing clarity, swimming was a real pleasure. We decided to have drive-by to see Porto Cervo the Mecca of the Costa Smeralda (Emerald Coast) to see some outsize motor yachts and several other super yachts all very interesting and it certainly is a beautiful bay so not really surprising that it has been chosen as a playground by the rich and famous. After a week of island hopping we went to La Maddalena town to provision again. It was difficult to find a berth in the marina but eventually we did but in a rather awkward place.

Isola Caprera on the east of the group is home to a memorial museum of Garibaldi because he lived the last 27 years of his colourful life in a beautiful house on the island. He wanted to die looking at the sea. The house is now a museum and was interesting to visit. After reaching northern Sardinia we decided to try and see Bonifacio in southern Corsica. We stopped en route on the Isola Cavalloa a small island in the narrow strait between Sardinia and Corsica named in Italian but actually in France! We saw several other yachts at anchor in the bay on the island and decided to join them. The island appeared to be a holiday resort with some rather beautiful houses on the shore but we could not take a close look as we were not allowed further inland than the beach. We sailed to Bonifacio the next day with a dramatic final approach under steep white cliffs with a fantastic view of the old town perched on the top, sometimes rather precariously as the sea has eroded the limestone lower down underneath it. There is a long inlet into the harbour and despite our best efforts to get some help to tie up none appeared. The pontoons were very crowded so we just picked a spot. As so often seems to happen at the moment of tying up the wind was quite tricky but luckily with four hands on deck we managed to get tied up safely in the crowded harbour. The next day was sightseeing and a wonderful lunch in a tiny dining room overlooking the sea from the top of the old town. It was too hot for anything other than a siesta in the after-noon so by the evening we were ready for another delicious meal ...fish again accompanied with the local rose wine!

Our intended departure was delayed by a day of strong wind so we finally left on 28th August and found quite a heavy swell imme-diately outside the protection of the harbour. We were heading for Castelsardo a small marina on the north west coast of Sardinia as we had arranged to have the water maker pump renewed there. The journey was about 35 nm and the coast was much less populated than the Costa Smeralda, more remote and more natural. Castel-sardo was another town on a hill built by the Genoese as a natural defensive point. The marina was a working fishing port as well with slightly more normal sailing boats!

We could only have one night there because the weather forecast showed bad weather coming from the Gulf of Lyon the so-called tramontana so we left in order to make Menorca before it arrived. Luckily we had good wind and we arrived around 02.00 on 30th august anchoring in an easy bay on the east coast. We had the bene-fit of a nearly full moon but as nothing is ever that simple we had no depth sounder temporarily! A cold beer in the moonlight was very welcome and we were glad to have got across without any sign of the heavy weather.

# Menorca

After a refreshing swim the next morning we entered Cala Addidia on the NW of Menorca to find a well sheltered anchorage to stay during the coming bad weather. We provisioned quickly and by afternoon the wind had risen to force 4. We put out a kedge anchor and then as the wind strengthened a German boat behind us advised us to put out a stern anchor as well which he lent us. The dinghy provided most of the traumas; Sam nearly got blown away by casting off without the kill cord! Then in the course of laying the kedge anchor in the dinghy Sam and Gilly were seen rapidly disappearing towards the end of the bay (luckily not out to sea) when the outboard failed and one oar broke! They were rescued by another sturdier RIB. Then later when they were all back on board the dinghy flipped over twice during the night with the loss of the other oar, the pump and the bailer. The sea water dunking did little for the already parlous outboard function! It seemed we were up the creek again literally without a paddle. Once the weather calmed Sam and John gave the outboard a nice fresh water shower and this seemed to work the magic and after reaching the shore John bought some new oars and we were mobile again. Sam and Gilly left us and returned to land life in a rented flat nearby… already arranged not in desperation!

On the 5th September the wind finally settled and we had a lovely day out with Sam and Gilly exploring the delights of Menorca on land with wheels. The island is very well manicured with miles of beautiful dry stone walls and farms with curious curvy gates. We explored Alior, Cuitadella and Mahon over the next few days and had some excellent meals.

On 7th September the Peacocks arrived for the Royal Yacht Squadron rally the following week. We hired a car to meet them at the airport and then took them up the Torre, the highest point on the island where there is a magnificent view of the whole coastline.

We all had a very enjoyable farewell supper with Sam and Gilly as they were going to Majorca by air for a week's sojourn there on land. The RYS rally started the following day in Mahon so after two hours spent pulling the two anchors up we finally set sail for Mahon around the east coast to meet the other Squadron boats who gave us a warm welcome even though our own Squadron member Hugh Laing had not yet arrived.

The following week we made a circumnavigation of Menorca cruising in company with the boats in the Yacht Squadron rally and enjoyed some excellent dinners and cocktail parties arranged by the Squadron. All was perfectly organized, great company and wonderful cuisine to say nothing of the champagne and local wine sampling… Thank you very much Hugh! On Friday 14th September very early in the morning Vanessa finally arrived in Cuitedella having missed her flight connection in Barcelona. Her friend Kate Llewellin had arrived late the previous night on schedule but after a rest Vanessa recovered her energy and they explored Cuitedella, a truly beautiful old town of narrow alleyways and a magnificently restored church.

On Saturday we left Cuitedella with Vanessa, Kate and Hugh on board and sailed around the south west of the island and had a good anchorage that night, we had a nice supper on board under a starry sky after a refreshing swim…this is what it is all about! Hugh left the next morning and David Surman arrived to join us to sail to the Canaries in preparation for the ARC. We returned to Addaia again completing our circumnavigation of Menorca and were able to see the girls off from there and provision for the next leg to Gibraltar. The marina here is excellent the best since Turkey! We had thought of going to Port Leucate to assess the copper antifouling which had been badly applied in Turkey but one look at the weather and we changed our minds there was a strong mistral blowing again which made the journey north impossible. We finally left Menorca on 18th September heading for Gibraltar.

# Menorca to The Canary Islands

# September – October 2012

David Surman, the brother of our Hong Kong friend Giles was accompanying us to help and also find out if he would like to stay on for the Atlantic crossing which he did. It was a great help having another crew. We departed from Addaia around mid- day and sailed along the north coast of Menorca as the wind was more favourable but it faded with the light so we motored past the lights of Majorca which were welcome in the absence of any moonlight. The next day the wind picked up again to 30 knots and we made good progress with furled sails.

On Thursday 20.9.2012 we crossed the Greenwich meridian into the western hemisphere and as the wind continued it became progressively more roly-poly and the wind progressively increased. That night we were very thankful for the AIS system because at around 3.00am as we approached our waypoint off the SE corner of Spain it seemed many other vessels had chosen the same point and this small area of sea was very crowded. Of course it was a black night and the wind was by this time blowing force 9 and it was difficult for us to change course as any deviation into the wind would have been extremely rough. AIS to the rescue, we could identify all the vessels by name and we called up three of them and they all very cordially agreed to keep out of our way. Without the clarity of AIS it would have been a Christmas tree of navigation lights and being so rough holding binoculars to try and assess what all the vessels were doing would have been tricky if not impossible. So we turned westwards around the corner of Spain without colliding with anyone. Conditions abated and we had a calm journey along the south coast of Spain to Gibraltar.

There were many large vessels anchored along the coast and we sighted the Rock at 11.00am on Saturday 22nd September, a very exciting moment seeing it emerging through the haze. A few hours later we were entering the marina and were overflown by an easy jet flight that only just seemed to clear the mast! The marina was just next to the runway but despite that it was not too noisy.

On Monday 24th we took delivery of our new parasailor designed to take the pain out of downwind sailing and it was a great success on a sunny afternoon with a light breeze and flat sea! We had Thomas the expert from the manufacturer on board so we all learnt the technique from him. It only remains for us to practice. We had debated endlessly about buying this sail it was expensive and I was doubtful but John was keen and I was persuaded by Jimmy Cornell's endorsement of it but in fact it proved of almost no use as the majority of the time the wind was far too strong to use it and it was too complicated and powerful to use on our own.

The rest of the week was a continuous downpour which was disappointing but the sun reappeared in time for us to go up the rock and see the apes and the war time tunnels. We took advantage of the duty-free alcohol and bought vodka to put in the gills of any fish David was hoping to catch, it is supposed to ease the pain of dying which I hope it did. The town had a faded military air about it and apart from the Rock Gibraltar was not somewhere to spend a lot of time. We got the help we needed in the marina and renewed the steering cables. Both John and David fell in the water here while walking the plank that precariously linked Baringo's stern to the concrete wall and with the rise and fall of the tides was sometimes at an alarming angle.

On Monday 1st October we left for The Canaries an evening start to try and avoid the contrary currents through the straits. We spent some time calculating the optimum time and we were sailing in company with a catamaran who had decided on the same departure time but it seems we were all wrong as we both experienced an adverse current on the way through! We saw the lights of the rock fade away… the last glimpse of the Mediterranean and through the Pillars of Hercules so no going back now.

We tried the parasailor with some success but could not hold it for very long as the wind became too strong. There was a large swell but not in the same direction as the wind but related to a hurricane further out in the Atlantic so it was rather an uncomfortable sail. We had dropped the main early on because it was banging around too much in the swell and the light winds but that evening while trying to enjoy cocktails in the roll we saw the main halyard gradually ascending the mast having parted company with the shackle! There was no way anyone was volunteering to go up and get it in those conditions so it would have to wait for a calmer moment.

Our course was downwind and as the wind was light and the swell large we rigged the pole to control the large jenny and sailed very successfully for the rest of the way. We had the moon for this trip and had the great pleasure of an unusual mixture of moonlight and sunlight at dawn. On the night of 5th October what we had thought were fishing vessels turned into the lights of Lanzarote and we were nearly there. We went to the all singing and dancing Marina Puerto Calera and thoroughly enjoyed all the facilities. Shops, showers, and restaurants were all within a few metres.

It was here that I received the highest accolade from the skipper because I rescued the lost halyard from the top of the mast, a great relief and a fun experience. Having achieved that we had a day exploring the island by car and it was wonderful with an enormous and most extraordinary larva field which is unchanged since the volcanic eruption of 1730. I think it must be unique and is well worth a visit. We then moved on to Fuerteventura which was nothing like as nice as Lanzarote and is definitely not worth a visit. So no time lingering there but onto Las Palmas about 56 nm from the southern tip of Fuerteventura. We had the most fantastic sail which was much appreciated after some rather trying conditions. We sailed all the way without altering the rig as the wind and waves were steady all the way... such a pleasure.

We arrived in the marina in Las Palmas flying our ARC flag to find we were in good company with many others and tied up until the Atlantic crossing on 25th November. We had some time in hand before the race preparations started in earnest so we flew back to France on 17th October and returned on 11th November to start serious preparations for our first big ocean crossing.

# CHAPTER SIXTEEN

# The Atlantic Crossing
# with the ARC

*November – December 2012*

We returned to Las Palmas, Gran Canaria on 11th November and found all well on board. The marina was much busier now, many more yachts had arrived and all were preparing for the big crossing, a real hive of activity. The Atlantic Rally for Cruisers was started by Jimmy Cornell 25 years ago with only a handful of boats but this year the 25th anniversary there were over 200! His original idea was to enable cruisers to undertake their first ocean passage in company giving confidence and security and minimising the sense of loneliness that is inevitable crossing a huge ocean in a small boat. He certainly succeeded and the ARC goes from strength to strength every year. The organisation is excellent and there are many useful teaching events as well as all the fun social events. Of course the local marine merchants take full advantage of so many cruising and racing yachts in town for just a few weeks so unfortunately prices rise significantly. We had three crew joining us for the rally including

David who had sailed with us from Minorca to Gran Canaria and still wanted to do the crossing, his brother Giles from Hong Kong and an old friend from medical school Andrew Peacock. The ARC does have a racing division as well but that was not our scene in Baringo who is definitely a cruiser, but there was still competition amongst the cruisers for a variety of combinations, double handed, traditional yachts, catamarans, youngest skipper etc. We started provisioning early as we were five on board for probably three weeks at least so it was quite a gargantuan task. The local shops and market were geared up for the demands because all the yachts were doing the same and they delivered loads of shopping to the pontoons for everyone. We attended seminars on weather, nautical emergencies, and rigging which were all very useful. Most evenings there were gatherings for drinks and sometimes food so we enjoyed meeting other yachts and comparing stories and also exchanging tips.

Other activities included planting trees in the ARC forest on a nearby hillside much in need of them and It proved surprisingly much harder work than we had expected but certainly a worthwhile effort. We engaged Jerry the rigger who had taught us so much in his seminar to check our rigging which he did barely using the standard hoisting procedure on a halyard. He seemed to climb up the rigging with lightning speed like a ballet dancer sticking to the shrouds as if by magic while his apprentice tried to keep up with his ascent tightening the loose ropes, quite remarkable. We received Jerry the Rigger's seal of approval afterwards and he rapidly moved along the next yacht and was immediately aloft again. We heard Jimmy Cornell the founder of the ARC speak and prevailed upon him to sign the many books we had of which he was the author. We enjoyed an owner's dinner and the provisioning continued on a daily basis during these preparatory days. We hired a car for a day and had a welcome break from the boat preparations to explore the dramatic interior of the island driving along almost vertical narrow roads with breath-taking views. After this brief respite there were many visits to the chandlery and strenuous efforts to get the gas cylinders filled. This task had been a problem since we left Hong Kong as every country has a different filling system and different gas. We had already a rather fine collection of regulators and had acquired some excellent bottles as well but the bottles were always sacrificed because they were too large and too numerous to carry as spares, but our regulator collection continues to expand. International uniformity and simplicity sadly does not apply to gas cylinders and regulators around the world for yachties. So again it was new cylinders and another regulator all at a high ARC price.

On 19th November two of our crew arrived David and Giles Surman so we had lots of chat and catching up. They had sensibly decided to stay in a hotel until the start to avoid the inevitable chaos on board that came with working on the boat and storing the provisions. Their hotel was in the old town of Gran Canaria which has old fashioned charm and elegance and a some rather beautiful statues of the dogs (canes) which gave the name to the islands. The last member of the crew Andrew arrived during the masked ball on 21st November just in time to enjoy the party and the many and varied costumes and masks.

The start day was approaching now so everyone went their separate ways doing different errands, collecting diesel in jerry cans, collecting laundry, more purchases in the chandlery, refilling the fire extinguisher and meanwhile the excitement on the pontoon was building around us. The crew attended some of the symposia on such subjects as sextant use, downwind sailing techniques, navigation, heavy weather boat handling etc but the skipper did relent and permit Andrew and Giles some time off so they hired bicycles and had a day relaxing on the town beach. I wanted to

117

be one of the radio controllers for our group of about 20 yachts, all picked because we were likely to do similar speeds so be fairly close although not within line of sight, the ocean is too big! There were meetings for our instructions and information about schedule timing and radio frequencies so all very useful. We planned radio "skeds" twice daily and one controller led the two sessions each day taking positions, sharing any problems from the other yachts in the group and exchanging general chat and local weather information. They proved a twice daily highlight during the time at sea.

During the packing and stowing of the array of provisions the crew managed to sneak in a large iberico jamon to be sure they had some meat for the crossing but with the lack of space remaining in the boat it had to hang unceremoniously in the forward heads. Andrew had also brought some vacuum-packed steaks from Scotland which was definitely the provisioning trump card and lasted the whole voyage even though the freezer stopped working two days into the voyage. Lack of meat was not one of the problems we encountered!

We all enjoyed swimming in the Club Nautico pool usually before supper in the evening and the time passed swapping notes with other yachts, drinking cocktails and dining in various restaurants. Abstention from alcohol to prevent sea sickness was in continual postponement... manyana, manyana. On one afternoon we all had a pleasant tutorial with the parasailor in the Gran Canaria harbour with Thomas who had been through the sequence with us in Gibraltar but was happy to revise it with us and show Andrew and Giles the wonders of this sail. On 24th November it was the skippers briefing for all yachts just skipper and one crew from each yacht. We had been looking at the weather forecast along with all the other yachts in the ARC and everyone was and becoming increasingly worried as strong headwinds and storms were forecast for the start day and beyond which was not a pleasant prospect. Discussions were becoming increasingly more anxious along our pontoon as we departed for the final skippers briefing. It seemed the ARC weather experts at the briefing had the same forecast as us and one could sense the hearts of the ARC skippers sinking as it was delivered in words and graphic meteorological charts. The rising tide of foreboding was palpable when Andrew Bishop the ARC chief organiser stood up to speak but to everyone's amazement and relief, he decided to postpone the start by 72 hours for the cruising division, immediately the tension was released and the cheers went up! This had only ever been done once before in the history of the ARC. It was certainly a relief to us as we still had jobs left to do and we watched the start of the racing division which went ahead on schedule the following day. The weather was far from clement so a few yachts in the racing division just did the start and then returned to the shelter of the port to start with the cruising division in what we all hoped would be better conditions.

Tuesday 27th November…the start at last at 11.00 we were out of the harbour and across the line with over 200 other boats which was an inspiring sight. We were still straight into squalls so it was very wet, windy and cold until the following morning, but we were underway and there was a great sense of anticipation because none of us had done a long ocean crossing before and we were determined to enjoy the challenge and the experience. The next morning the day dawned with a clear blue sky and the wind dropped to an easier 25 knots but the left over waves were still giants. We had a rota that allowed one person to be on galley duty only for 24 hours while the others sailed the boat, and I had thought that the galley day would be the easiest and a chance for a rest and some sleep but how wrong I was! The galley was such hard work in the serious downwind roll in the huge waves staying steady was a fulltime job without trying to cook as well, sailing the boat proved a very much easier option. We were only using the two foresails as the risk of jibing our oversized main sail in the strong winds was alarming and indeed we inadvertently jibed the big foresail a few times as helming downwind in large waves and strong wind is particularly difficult and very tiring; the solent jib is self tacking/jibing but too much of this even on a smaller sail can do damage. Despite our best efforts the clew of the big jenny split with the forces and we could no longer use it. Luckily Skipper John noticed this before the clew parted company with the sail completely which might have been dramatic and difficult to manage but we furled it in time but could not drop it to repair as conditions were far too rough. We had to be content with just the solent jenny alone but managed 5 kts with that and the always useful spray hood. Squalls came and went but we had the full moon at night for these first few nights always so welcome. No other boats were in sight but we continued our twice daily radio skeds, and rolled along down the still sizeable waves rather wishing we could use the big jenny. After 48 hours Skipper John had the brilliant idea of adding the trysail to our rig, the big main was too much but the trysail would be perfect and preparing it and hoisting it would occupy the crew for the afternoon. Normally the trysail is reserved for big storms but any way of increasing our sail area would be advantageous, after all we were competing in our group. We still had 25-30knots of wind but the trysail looked very pretty and added some speed.

On Sunday 2nd December we changed our clocks putting them an hour backwards to make dawn arrive earlier. Waiting too long for the first light on the last night watch often seems endless. The next few days continued the same, squalls, strong wind and large waves but our spirits were high and we were enjoying the challenge. By the 5th December the wind decreased and we decided to hoist the mainsail otherwise we would really lose speed and we sailed a little less downwind to avoid jibing although Poppy was rather better than any of us at doing this. We always had one or two reefs in the sail as the wind was still quite strong and on 6th December David who was in charge of fishing caught a very large fish, a mahi mahi which I cooked for supper and it was truly delicious. On 7th December it was time to change the clocks again. We had lots of rain squalls which changed the wind direction through all points of the compass very frequently so there was lots of work to do on deck, but by now we were halfway across. The jamon had long since been eaten and the bony leg thrown overboard but Andrew's steak was still going strong and very popular. Our radio net companions all seemed to have gone further south than us and several had hit a hole and were motoring, luckily we still had wind and plenty of it so were the envy of the others in our group. On 8th December the first racing yacht crossed the finishing line so we decided to do the sweepstake for our own ETA in St Lucia the prize for the winner was to be a dinner out in St Lucia. At this stage we really needed to go further south ourselves but without poling out the big jenny, which we could not use anyway, a more southerly heading was very difficult. Even if we had been able to use this sail poling out in such heavy seas might have been tricky but we did not have the luxury of this choice and it was still impossible to drop the big jenny to repair it in the present conditions. We had very bad squalls over the next few days and accidentally jibed the doubly reefed main which we had exchanged for the trysail to improve our speed. It was very difficult to retrieve in 40 knots of wind so we had to resort to the motor to release the preventer and then drop the sail so it was back to the solent jenny alone until morning when we hoisted the main again but now with three reefs in it. The day of 12.12.2012 was an unusual date and we marked it by changing the clocks again, we were now on St Lucia time so nearly there. The next day the wind reduced and finally died and we went through a few hours of sloppy sailing with the waves emptying the sails because the wind was insufficient to keep them filled, certainly a change but not really a welcome one as we were so close now and everyone just wanted to arrive...after all the steak had finally finished. On 14th December we were becalmed and the crew swam in mid ocean apart from me and David...we were too scared of sharks. Once back on board we had to motor as there was no wind and no sign of squalls, what a change. We stopped for another swim in the calm conditions but a light wind returned later that day and we sailed again and spotted the loom of Martinique at 03.00 on 16th December and by dawn we could see the mountains of the island clearly. We were now about 60nm away and the sight of St Lucia quickly followed and we celebrated by flying the parasailor which had not been very useful until now in such strong wind. It looked very pretty once we hoisted it, but we needed three attempts because the tutorial with Thomas in Gran Canaria before the start had not surprisingly been forgotten! It was a pleasant sail in the light 12knot breeze and we rounded Pigeon Island towards the finishing line dropping the parasailor to go upwind to the finishing line on a beautiful sunny day and we crossed on 16th December after a voyage of twenty-one days. The photography boat greeted us and we anchored in the bay for a swim before going into Rodney Bay marina. It was wonderful having a daytime arrival and we all felt elated and rather surprised we had made it with relatively few major incidents. We learned later that we had indeed escaped quite lightly compared with some other yachts that had suffered serious damage and some who had lost their auto pilot. We swam, drank champagne and whisky accompanied by the Christmas cake Giles had brought, it was an unforgettable moment. We went to the marina before dark and were greeted by a steel band, rum punch and given a basket of fruit. We were all a little spaced out but enjoyed supper on land and a good night's sleep. We woke the next day to find the crew had disappeared into a local hotel! We opened the ETA sweepstake and Giles was the winner so we kept our promise and took him for an excellent supper in Marigot Bay.

On 19th December with our energy recovered we climbed the Gros Piton with two guides. They were not strictly speaking necessary as there is only one path to the top which luckily is tree covered as it was a very hot day. The reward was a magnificent view over the southern end of St Lucia and the Caribbean Sea. We then went for a swim in a volcanic lake followed by a meal in Soufriere which is perhaps not the most pleasant town in St Lucia. We all contemplated going to the Arc Toga party but after all the sailing and climbing we had done fatigue got the better of us. December 21st was the final denouement, the prize giving ceremony, with drinks and supper thrown in. We found we had come 7th in our class and 96th overall and all wondered again how much better we would have done if we had had the big jenny all the way across. We were awarded a bottle of wine for being radio net controllers during the crossing as well. There were many prizes awarded and so a very interesting and fitting evening to close the ARC event. Our long suffering crew departed home for Christmas and we continued organising and doing repairs on board and preparing for our first Caribbean Christmas with the Colvin family Iris, Stephen, Pippa, Jo, Natasha and Harry in age order who flew over from New York and Vanessa came from UK.

It was a lovely few days over Christmas and New year spent eating, drinking and enjoying the beaches. We took the whole family for a boat trip to Marigot Bay which for Iris (Stephen 's mother) and the oldest crew member was her first voyage in a sailing yacht but she thoroughly enjoyed it as we all did, with the usual swimming, lunch

and chat. Vanessa's friend Kate arrived for the New Year and we celebrated with champagne and an excellent dinner at the hotel where
the Colvins were staying, "The Windjammer" a beautifully restored
plantation house on the beach. The Colvin family left the next day
and we began preparing to sail south with Vanessa and Kate to leave
the boat on the hard in Grenada, just further south enough to avoid
the hurricanes. We left Rodney Bay Marina in strong winds trying to
get around the southern tip of St Lucia but it proved impossible with
the wind and the waves, once out of the lee of the islands the full
force of the Atlantic breakers is unleashed! We had no choice but to
turn back and sail up the sheltered coast of St Lucia and try and find
an anchorage but there were none! Night fell and saw us motoring
around every bay and inlet looking for anchorage spots but it was all
too deep and there were no available moorings either. Just as we were
giving up hope a man in a boat appeared and said he would take us to
a mooring which of course aroused suspicion and more anxiety but
in the present predicament we had little choice so we followed him
and he led us to a small deserted bay with an empty a mooring buoy.
Of course no sailor should take up a strange mooring but our friend
gave us plenty of reassurance and as it was this or the open sea we took
the chance and had a quiet night. We continued south via Mustique,
Carriacou and finally to Port Louis Marina in Granada. There Vanessa
and Kate left us to fly back to UK and the next day we had to get
round the southern end of Grenada to St David's Harbour and the
hard standing. It was again a very unpleasant journey against a 35knot
f head wind with waves to match always worrying if Baringo could
take the strain with so much slamming of the hull into the waves.
We got into the calm bay through a narrow channel in the reefs with
much relief. Baringo was packed away again on the hard and we flew
to Hong Kong to start work teaching in the Clinical skills centre in
the Prince of Wales Hospital.

# CHAPTER SEVENTEEN

# Grenada to Panama

## *June – September 2013*

On 20th June we returned to Grenada to find Baringo on the hard in St David's bay. Luckily there was a pleasant but basic hotel on the beach nearby where we stayed until Baringo was ready for the sea again. John had purchased a new Rocna anchor, but in placing it on the bow we had to remove the not so useful bowsprit we had been given in Turkey. The Rocna however more than proved its worth over the rest of the voyage. Despite not being completely ready, in fact in fact one rarely is, we were driven into the water (no travel hoist here) and then picked up a mooring in the bay to finish the rest of the work. We hoisted then furled the sails which had been stored in the forward cabin and put the repaired main sail cover back and of necessity tested the dinghy and outboard to get ashore. We serviced the winches here, we always tried to do this in a beautiful locations following the "maintenance in paradise" option and this was no exception. St David's Bay fits that description.

The next day we were ready to make a move to Prickly Bay a very well -known typhoon safe anchorage (at least for the moment) just below the magic 22 degrees south. Many yachts were there, they had stayed for the last few months during the typhoon season, including our friends Chris and Zara on their catamaran. We had met them first in Gibraltar then in the Canaries but they had not done the Atlantic crossing with the ARC but gone to Barbados instead. We had a grand reunion over a pizza and the next morning heard Chris on the radio fostering exchanges of any kind for anyone on the "Treasures of the Bilge" radio net which was rather amusing. We then went around the southern tip of Grenada back to the Saint David's Yacht Club where we had been with Vanessa and Kate the previous January as it was easier to prepare from here for the next passage. The weather did not look auspicious for a quick getaway so we hired a car and looked round the island which was tropical and pleasant. We visited the Grand Etang in the centre, a volcanic crater lake, we discovered Aggie's café for refreshment then the rather sombre Sauteurs where the locals had jumped into the sea to avoid being taken as slaves. All rounded off with an excellent meal in St George's the island capital. We decided that although we had not especially liked the little we had seen of the Caribbean islands Grenada was the top of our list. The next day we visited the campus of St George's university which is widely advertised abroad for medical training we think maybe for students who can pay but for whom it is not first choice.

Departure was imminent but the process was very slow, Caribbean style, but we were underway by mid-afternoon on 1st July sailing with the poled-out jenny with a 16 knot ENE wind heading for the Dutch Antilles, the ABC islands (Aruba, Bonaire and Curacao but not in that geographical order. They lie off the northern Venezuelan coast. We make good progress if a little off course to maintain the rig of the poled-out jenny and not use the main sail but with the current with us we were making 7-8 knots. Sailing is about changing; adapting the sail plan to the conditions as they present themselves and by the third day we furled the jenny, dismantled the pole and jibed, unfurled, furled again to hoist the main and then unfurled so plenty of occupational therapy, as if it were needed! The first reefing line snagged so it was full sail or two reefs until the next port. We changed again to a goosewing rig until the wind became too strong and we needed to make a diversion to avoid the Aves islands off Venezuela which were considered dangerous at the time. Bonaire was in sight by early next morning and we were greeted not only by dolphins, a great pleasure but also a squall, the latter not such a great pleasure. The south east of Bonaire is salt flats so little protection from the wind initially but as we approached the capital Kralendjik conditions calmed and we picked up a mooring just in front of the town. The water was crystal clear and the town very relaxed and simple but all the basic necessities were there, restaurants, cafes and immigration where we found a Cantonese speaker… a surprise in this tiny Dutch outpost but it is a rare place indeed which the Chinese have not discovered! The mooring was so convenient just in front of Kralendrik with the clear water and swimming lanes as well, it was quite unusual, but we had no idea we had to pay until we found a curt message in the cockpit threatening removal if we did not, but it was well worth the small sum.

We hired motor bikes to explore the island, very empty over the salt flats which used to be the main industry using donkeys imported especially to carry the loads. Since the demise of the salt industry the donkeys were just left to wander but now there is a lovely sanctuary for them including a hospital which we biked around. We were very happy to see them enjoying their well- deserved retirement in peace. We had a few maintenance jobs as usual but after that we tried bicycles to explore and exercise and we took the dinghy floor boards to be repaired in the small industrial area and a bonus was finding an

Ikea store in there. Fresh provisioning was so easy here as there were several fresh fruit and vegetable stalls along the front with produce from Venezuela. We decided to try a car next to explore the national park in the north of Bonaire which is very dry and volcanic. We found a perfect spot in the park for lunch by a beach and as soon as we started to eat about twenty large Iguanas appeared and fought ferociously over a piece of tomato John gave them, an unpleasantly primitive battle colourfully enhanced by the red flesh of the tomato. We quickly retreated to the car only to watch another family make the same mistake and retreat equally speedily. We used the car again the next day to return to the Soroba Hotel which we had found on our bikes. It was situated on a beautiful turquoise lagoon, where we relaxed for the day. We collected the dinghy boards on the way back and the next morning used the car again to provision in the local supermarket which was surprisingly good for a small island. We had found the Soroba Hotel had excellent internet, a rare commodity elsewhere on the island so we returned again this time on bicycles, it was nice to have an excuse to go again.

We left Bonaire on 14th July early in the morning as it was only a day to Curacao and we anchored there in Spanish Water using the new Rocna for the first time. Spanish water is a huge bay with a narrow inlet on the south coast of Curacao and a very popular well sheltered anchorage. We were preparing for Sarah to arrive by air for a short cruise with us to Aruba the next and last ABC island. While waiting for Sarah's arrival we hired a car from a local hotel The Limestone conveniently located on the shore of Spanish Water. We drove to Wilhemstadt a large and noisy capital, quite a contrast to Bonaire but with some attractive typical Dutch houses of varying colours looking rather like a toy city. There was a curious swing bridge, the Queen Emma, over the estuary linking the two halves of the city and we saw it in use while lunching at what proved by chance to be the premier restaurant in town according to Lonely Planets. We had our first experience of a water boat in Spanish Water, we had to book a fill up and the vessel appeared the next day and filled our water tanks from a huge vat. We had not yet started the water maker as the inter-island passages were quite short. By this time Sarah had arrived and was getting used to life on board, and travelling to and fro by dinghy which became a little more precarious after it got stuck under the pontoon at the hotel and we had difficulty extracting it late at night, it subsequently leaked more than desirable. We all explored the island, which is much larger than Bonaire and more industrial but we visited the Amsterdam fort, the museum in Wilhemstadt and sampled a few restaurants as well. Of course the must see was the Curacao distillery although it was rather dingy and rather disappointing. We then moved to Pescadero Bay further along the coast to divide the journey to the western-most end of the island from where we wanted to leave for Aruba to avoid night sailing. We then took a bus back to Wilhemstadt to check out and this time the Queen Emma bridge was open for marine traffic so we took the ferry across. The next stop was overnight in Santa Cruz Bay at the southwestern end of Curacao which enabled us to reach Aruba in one day with an early start.

We left before dawn on 23rd July and had a good sail with both jennies goose-winged but it proved more eventful than anticipated as we had the big jenny poled out with a sacrificial sheet and I had foolishly tied up the lazy sheet which tightened when we started to furl the sail and it was impossible to undo the lazy sheet or furl the sail! It took John's masterful knot tying (the very useful rolling hitch) to secure the end of the lazy sheet to a winch and finally winch the knot undone, luckily we had plenty of sea room and the wind did not pick up so the only casualty was the loss of the marlin spike we were using to try and undo the knot. We arrived at the Renaissance Marina in Aruba only to find we could not check in there but had to sail about 5 nm back the way we had come to check in at Barcardera. We suggested a return by road would be easier but this was not permitted. Barcadera is an industrial port not designed for yachts and we had to go alongside a steel fishing vessel and then clamber over the vessel in the extreme afternoon heat to get ashore to the office. Luckily the fishermen were on board to help with our lines and the clambering. It was then back to the Renaissance marina in Oranjestad the capital of Aruba and we finally moored stern to in a 35knot wind with some help. Unfortunately the voyage had done nothing to ameliorate Sarah's sea sickness so after some consideration a move to the hotel attached to the marina was considered the best solution. The internet was very poor here and as we were having problems with the flat in London with new tenants it was particularly frustrating and eventually we gave up and handed the problems to the agent and we could then begin to enjoy the island. The other facilities at the Renaissance marina and hotel were very good with the small Renaissance island only a ferry ride away with a beach and sea swimming pool and resident flamingos. We hired a car to explore the island with Sarah who was now feeling much better on land. The south east coast is very developed in an American way with large hotels and apartment blocks so the Dutch culture was submerged to extinction but we visited the appropriately named California lighthouse at the northern tip. The north west coast was untouched and rugged and we found the Arikok national park in the centre with its interesting pink rock formations and caves with old rock paintings. We always managed to find a beautiful beach somewhere to finish the days exploration with a swim, and there was a wonderful choice of restaurants for supper. Sarah's stay ended but we had to wait for the generator technician to fly in from America as the water pump was not working and the generator was still under warranty. We were entertained in the meantime by Captain Jean Claude (not the owner) of a 67foot catamaran which had a broken forward cross strut which he had held together with "string" and was waiting for repairs. An enormous machine with the luxurious interior all under wraps awaiting the owner's arrival. Jean Claude gave us lots of advice about the Pacific which did not mean much at the time but after our voyages there we seemed to have visited most of his recommendations!

Carlos arrived as planned and fixed the generator's water pump and we could now use the air conditioner for which we needed the generator here as the American shore power is incompatible with our European electrics. This would not be the only time we encountered this problem and it was lucky we used the generator as the next thing was a diesel leak, but with Carlos still captive on Aruba he came and fixed that as well. Now it was time for departure preparations and we left for the Santa Marta marina on the north coast of Colombia on 7th august but not after checking out at the infamous Barcardera in the wrong direction, into the wind and the waves, and a near miss with the bow roller up against the same steel vessel.

The passage to Santa Marta was the usual variety of strong wind and no wind but this time accompanied by lightning but we were spared a direct hit on this journey of three nights. We had the usual changing sail combinations in an effort to maintain the best course along the coast. We saw the huge mountains of Colombia loom and we managed a well-timed dawn arrival in Santa Marta. We had an unwanted encounter with the unfendered pontoon getting alongside in a strong tide and the incident left its reminder on the GRP. We intended to leave Baringo in the Santa Marta marina and do some land travel in Colombia as anchoring in deserted bays along the coast was not recommended. We needed an agent to check in here which costs but removes the hassle and so we soon set off inland by overnight bus to Bucamaranga and then on to Barichara via St Gil.

We had chosen Barichara from Lonely Planets and were not disappointed, a beautiful place, very Spanish and almost no tourists. We returned through St Gil where by chance we saw a carnival with costumes and lots of music. The Colombian buses are very comfortable with reclining seats and uninterrupted film viewing if required. We returned to Santa Marta to meet Jeremy Vevers who was arriving to sail with us to Panama, but not before we had all visited Cartagena and the Tayrona national park by land. First was Cartagena by bus, a beautiful old city full of history and we stayed in a very central traditional Spanish style courtyard hotel owned by an engineer from Manchester. The highlight of the visit was the barber in the square in the old town. The young barber was just on the street with an electrical lead coming through the window of his house to his barber's chair on the pavement. He worked so elegantly it was like watching a ballet so of course Jeremy and John had their essential hair cuts. We wandered the streets all day absorbing the historical atmosphere and sampling the local restaurants. We returned to the boat briefly and then it was a taxi to Tayrona National Park on the north coast and the amazing Barlovente hotel with the open ocean and crashing surf on one side and a flat silent lagoon on the other. Our bedrooms were open to the sea and the air so although dramatic it was also rather noisy with the relentless breaking surf just outside the open window. We spent the time walking the coastal path in the national park with wonderful beaches some with lagoons which made swimming possible and enjoying the hotel which had deservedly won an architectural award when it had opened. Jeremy had plenty of material for his drawing here and it was indeed a magical place to explore. Luis the owner of the hotel drove us back to Santa

Marta as he wanted to see the boat.

On 26th August we were ready to leave for the San Blas islands a group of picture-perfect tropical islands off the coast of Panama. There are 365 islands but only 49 inhabited by the Guna Indians. The first night out was very stormy with almost continuous lightning and the wind came and went as we tried to dodge the worst of the storms. The unsettled weather accompanied us for the whole journey and on the third night out we felt we were struck by lightning as there was a huge flash and the electric wind indicator went berserk, circling randomly at great speed and then ceased to work. We arrived the next day at El Porvenir Island in the San Blas group but waited for the weather to calm before anchoring off in the late afternoon and we planned to check in the following morning. We had no wind indicator and no depth sounder either! The next morning the ladies boat came over selling bracelets and molas the colourful decorated cloth pictures which are irresistible, hence we bought rather more than we should during our stay. We went ashore but had a nasty surprise on checking in as the cost of our visit to the islands was rather higher than expected, $100 per person to enter, $193 for the cruising permit and another $5 each for the local permit! We recovered from the shock and only hoped some of the money made its way to the right place. We had an excellent pilot book with google maps overlaid on the charts, it was very expensive but essential for cruising these islands giving us the best chance of avoiding the numerous reefs. We started by sailing to Chichime island but found it too crowded so decided on Banedup and found a good anchorage just before a storm broke. We were asked for water the next day by some islanders and as we now had a working generator to power the water maker we could oblige. We had thought the islanders lived there permanently but we later learned that they rotate visits for about six weeks and then go home to the mainland

and the next group come out. It was an idyllic sandy palm covered island setting and we thoroughly enjoyed relaxing and swimming although there was usually a storm with lightning in the afternoon. We moved to the East Holandeses cay next and having thought we had found a deserted spot we were disturbed in the early evening by several noisy motor boats with loud music and blazing lights. These islands have certainly been discovered! John and Jeremy set to and repaired the leaking dinghy, the bottom of our trusty Avon now looks like a sealed colander but it is still afloat. The next day the crowd departed and we had peace and quiet for the day while we swam and snorkelled at leisure until the motor boats reappeared that evening. Our cruise continued in the same vein visiting several cays, meeting the local people, buying more molas, swimming in the clear water, snorkelling, eating and enjoying lots of interesting chat over the evening cocktails. We returned to El Porvenir on 5th August to check out and refill the fuel tank from the jerry cans and then oh dear! I accidently dropped the plastic top of the biocide bottle into the fuel tank. I blamed my oily fingers! There was nothing we could do there so we had to leave hoping that the plastic cap would not block the fuel pipe and render the engine useless. We stopped one night in Green Turtle Bay and were very relieved to arrive the following day in Shelter Bay Marina just inside the breakwater that marks the entrance to the Panama Canal. Jeremy's time was up and he left for Panama City airport to return to the UK. We had enjoyed his company and always interesting conversation. Now we had to tackle the errant plastic top.

# CHAPTER EIGHTEEN

# The Panama Canal

*September 2013*

There are serious penalties for breaking down in the Panama Canal so while in Shelter Bay Marina we serviced the engine and checked what we could to prevent any breakdown in transit. The boat had to be professionally measured, the measurer came from southern China but dropped his tape measure in the water, it can happen to anyone! We eventually found help to find the lost cap in the fuel tank, quite a task as the fuel had to be drained and the access hatch opened but it had to be done. Now it was the turn of the fridge / freezer to give up but we have another fridge so would just manage with that for the moment.

After a few days of dedicated boat work we decided to go to Bocas del Toro by air for a short break, we had met a catamaran owner who had been hit by lightning up there so thought it better to leave Baringo in the marina where there was competition for the lightning strikes from other vessels. We flew up from Albrook Airport on 14th September and enjoyed a pleasant few days there exploring beaches and walking along the coast which was quite unspoilt, we felt we were having the real Robinson Crusoe experience trekking along this wild deserted coastline. We returned to Shelter Bay on 17th September and the next day Janet and Dale arrived to join us for the Panama Canal transit. We decided to meet them in Panama City as the Shelter Bay marina is in the middle of a forest on the Colon side of the canal and there is not much to see around Colon which is the antithesis of Panama City, very squalid and with a reputation for robbery and muggings. We took the famous train from Colon to Panama City; without this railway line the canal could never have been built so a rather historic ride. The transit was booked for the 24th September so we had a fun few days exploring Panama City the new parts of which are very modern with a skyline reminiscent of New York but there are two older versions of the city as well so many contrasts. We braved it to a salsa dancing club where everyone except us was a wizard dancer but this did not deter us from having a go.

Transit day arrived, the line handlers arrived and then we moved to the waiting anchorage just in front of the first lock and after three hours our pilot arrived and we entered the first of the three Gatun locks curiously behind a container ship from Hong Kong. Luckily we were tied to a tug so not a huge size differential between us which is what can make for difficulties in the locks. This is what we had hoped for as there were no other yachts doing the transit at this time for we were late in the season. The majority of yachts do the transit in the spring in order to make Australia or New Zealand by the same autumn but luckily we were not in such a hurry. We passed through the three locks easily and safely without too much turbulence from the water although when the large vessel ahead put the engine on we received some severe wash in the confined space of the lock. The linesmen on the canal side throw the ropes with monkey fists to land on the boat for us to catch and swiftly tie the attached warps on to our cleats, and we had no mishaps. The boat is pulled along into position by "donkeys" small canal side engines on rails and the men on the canal side take up the slack on the ropes as the water rises or let off as the water falls. It all seemed to work like clockwork and round the clock. We moored up in Gatun Lake for the night and cooked supper for us all except the pilot who departed, we would get another one early the next morning. The second pilot arrived at 06.15 and we crossed the lake at dawn, so very calm and peaceful. The canal then goes through the "cut" which was the most challenging part of the canal to construct as it is hewn out of solid rock although today it just looks so normal with no evidence of the immense struggle to complete it. Next there is the Pedro Miguel lock, going down, then two Miraflores Locks and we were in the Pacific Ocean as if by magic. We delivered the line handlers and the pilot to their respective launches and anchored in the Panama City municipal anchorage for the night.

We moved to the Flamenco Marina the next day which was expensive and had very few facilities. Janet and Dale took a break in a hotel as we had the same electrical problem as we had had before with US incompatibility so could not use our air conditioner. We found the remarkably industrious Edgar to repair the fridge /freezer which he did after many days of toil.

On 30th September we tried to go to Taboga Island 7nm away, we had a late departure waiting for a storm to pass but arrived in a beautiful bay and anchored overnight intending to go to Las Perlas Islands the next morning. This was not to be because the anchor windlass was not able to generate enough power to raise the anchor as the voltage dropped away as soon as we used it. We managed to get the anchor up but felt discretion was the better part of valour and returned to Flamenco Marina to get it fixed. We examined the power switch and the relevant circuit and could find no problem and it all seemed to work so it was back to Taboga island and the same anchorage again. After some electrical brain storming John realised it was a problem with the service power switch which is rarely switched on and off once we were on the boat for the season. It had become gummed up and after a few wiggles electricity flowed once more and the windlass worked well. We had erroneously blamed Edgar the poor hard-working fridge engineer but we learnt to always wiggle the switch regularly from then on. We spent the day wandering on Taboga Island and then headed for Las Perlas Islands the next day. The islands were almost completely empty but very tidal so we really needed the San Blas pilot book which also covered these islands as there are many reefs covering and uncovering and it required great care in navigation and a close watch on the tides to avoid a collision with an underwater reef. Large chunks of land appeared and disappeared with the huge tidal range of about 6 meters. John and Dale did what proved to be a marathon swim at the height of the tidal current and in her enthusiasm to swim as well Janet jumped off the dinghy too early and had to be rescued and towed back to the safety of Baringo! It was an extremely strong current. We returned to the Flamenco marina on 7th October and on the last day of Janet and Dale's stay we went to the Miraflores visitor centre to see the canal from another angle and hear some of the history. They left the next day and Edgar had returned and was still struggling with the fridge, he was certainly not a quitter, and luckily we had agreed a fixed price for a working fridge not an hourly rate. He did repair it and it never failed again.

We had noticed over the last few weeks that the steering was becoming very stiff so decided we needed to haul out Baringo and have the rudder examined. This was expensive in Panama but the marina found an excellent person to do it and he arrived with the cleanest neatest set of tools I have seen. His meticulous work matched the tools and the rudder came out covered in tiny barnacles which we knew we had picked up in Santa Marta as we had gradually cleaned the same ones off the hull while in the San Blas islands. We were not allowed to stay on board for the night the boat was on the hard so after one night ashore Baringo was back in the water and we returned to the Flamenco marina with the steering now featherlight and we decided to stay there until we left for La Libertad in Ecuador where we planned to leave the boat until the next year. Although the municipal anchorage was free and had plenty of space, getting ashore was a death trap at worst and at best a recipe for a broken limb. It consisted of landing in the dinghy then getting into two successive plastic bath tubs that were on the verge of overturning with any movement and the final straw was climbing out onto stones which made an ice rink seem sticky. I felt avoiding this danger especially loaded with shopping and laundry was worth the $100 per night at the marina. We were now ready for the next voyage, the last of this season, to La Libertad, Ecuador. We planned to go via Bahia de Caraquez to break the journey which we knew was going to be difficult thanks to the adverse Humboldt Current and the prevailing wind.

We left Panama on 17th October, after the usual formalities from which there is no escape and we stopped the first night at Isla Bona about 20 nm away just past Taboga. We went quickly with the tide but little wind and It proved a magical night with a full moon and the beautiful bay to ourselves. We had earlier enlisted the services of Emmanuel for our weather forecasting; Claire of Apsara in the convoy had used him to give us all forecasts and we had engaged his services since we left the Mediterranean. He advised us to wait until Saturday to leave so we stayed as instructed for two nights and left with the tide at 04.30 on 19th October in the full moon. This journey proved one of the worst we had with the Humboldt current and the prevailing wind both against us. We had continuous squalls and lightning and had great difficulty making the course. The size of the waves and the strength of the wind were up and down but always against us. We had a lucky break when we discovered during the rig check that we had been taught to do by Jerry the Rigger of ARC fame that the main halyard and topping lift were twisted around each other as they exited the top of the mast so once conditions permitted we lowered the main and untangled them. Undoubtedly if we had not corrected this chafe would have broken both of them with undesirable consequences; we learn as we go.

On 24th October we crossed the equator at 00.07 and did our best to honour Neptune, it took some effort but we must have passed muster as we reached Bahia de Caraquez at dawn the next day. The Puerto Amistad yacht club which has a group of moorings and anchorage spots was up a river and we needed a pilot from the yacht club to guide us up at high tide so we had to anchor in the so called waiting room just off the estuary mouth quite far off the coast with no shelter and again the windlass was not working. We had to anchor despite the windlass problems and later we received a call from the yacht club to say Pedro the pilot would be with us at 06.00 the next morning to guide us in on the high tide, so it was overnight in the waiting room. Fortunately it was a quiet night and Pedro arrived as planned to not only navigate us in but help us get the anchor up without a windlass which he did with good grace as he was not really expecting that. The ride in was tense with the depth down to 0.7metre under the keel and perilously close to the beach it seemed. We arrived unscathed and anchored as there were no moorings available and had a welcome rest after a very tiring voyage.

Bahia de Caraquez was pleasant enough with good provisioning in the local market and an adequate supermarket but $100 notes were difficult to use in the supermarket! Of course we had to tackle the windlass and received help from another sailor an ex truck driver who suggested by-passing the power switch on the negative electrode and having done that it all worked again…the mysteries of marine electrics! We took a trip to Monte Cristo the true home of Panama hat makers and came away with two hats. We had to leave Bahia de Caraquez at 14.00 on 2nd November with the tide and with Pedro, once far enough out at sea Pedro jumped on the launch (which had accompanied us out) to take him home leaving us with the swell and the wind. We headed south passing the Manta peninsula which gave some shelter from the waves and the next day we anchored off Isla Salonga and managed to get the big jenny folded away to save time in la Libertad. We stayed there for two nights and there were lots of birds here, they always provide plenty of entertainment. The next day we were in La Libertad by 12.30 where first we anchored off, radioed in our presence, then we were asked to move onto fore and aft buoys while the lengthy administration was processed. Finally we were lifted out at 17.00, luckily just managing without taking the backstays down but it was a close run thing and Baringo ended up on land with a fore-aft tilt as a result. We were planning to travel around Ecuador with Vanessa next and needed to buy air tickets and book hotels but without internet this was tricky and finally we resorted to a travel agent in town. We had to get the main sail and little jenny packed away and discuss the necessary work to be done in our absence with Jeremy the marina manager who seemed helpful.

We had an excellent time travelling by land in Ecuador first with Vanessa and then on our own. It was very varied and so easy and cheap to travel by bus. We returned to the boat to leave finally for Europe on 14th November taking the autohelm with us to be serviced in France and hoping Baringo would be safe in our absence.

St Nicholas island Turkey with McBrides

Turkey visit by Janet, Dale and Kate.

**Anchoring Turkish style in Tomb bay**

**Broken steering cable after previous replacement**

**Volcano on Nisyros island Greece**

**Approach to Syracuse**

**Gibralter berth**

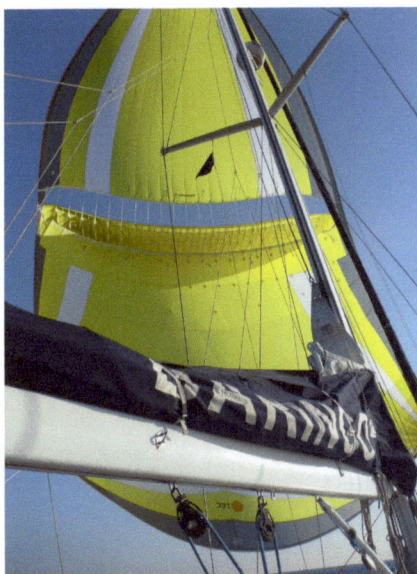

**En route to canaries flying parasailor**

**Tree planting Gran Canaria**

**Crew for ARC**

**Trisail in use during ARC**

**David's catch**

**Crossing the finishing line**

**Approaching St Lucia**

**Grenada island, Caribbean**

**Salt pans Bonaire**

**Donkey sanctuary, Bonnaire**

**Swimming with flamingos, Renaissance Aruba Resort**

**Aruba with Sarah**

**Jeremy hair cut in Carthegna Columbia**

**Hotel Barlovento Tayrona Columbia**

**An island in San Blas Panama**

**Gatun locks Panama canal**

**Miraflores Lock opening into the Pacific**

Pelican in Panama

Crossing the equator homage to King Neptune

CIRCUMNAVIGATION

# PART THREE

# CHAPTER NINETEEN

# The Eastern Pacific Crossing

## *18th June 2014 — 1st August 2014*

We returned from Geneva to Guyaquil, Ecuador via Madrid accompanied by the autohelm in our hand luggage. The autohelm had created some interest at the security check points but was allowed through. We took a taxi from Guyaquil to La Libertad and found Baringo where we had left her but minus the wind vane because despite a rather Heath Robinson deterrent at the top of the mast the large local boobies had chosen it as their resting place while we had been away. Our first night on board on the hard came to an abrupt end when the taxi driver arrived at 06.00 and woke us, we had actually asked him to come at 18.00 but our Spanish had obviously got rusty while we had been in Europe and Hong Kong! We reorganised during the day and then the taxi driver did arrive at 18.00 to take us back to Guyaquil for a flight to the Galapagos islands. We were to meet our pacific sailing crew Malcolm and Glynis Gibson on the flight there if all our organisation had been successful. The plan worked and we were all aboard and spent an interesting few days exploring the wild life on a few of the islands by boat. We had considered taking Baringo to The Galapagos but after negotiations with an agent who is compulsory there was far too much bureaucracy and too many restrictions to deal with. The other problem was that we could not cruise the islands independently in Baringo so we would have had to leave her at anchor as there are no marinas in the Galapagos islands and our insurance did not permit this for more than 24hours. So if we were all to see the Galapagos it would have been a very long stay. The guided tour proved very satisfactory and the birds and the beasts were marvellous and totally unafraid of us allowing very close observation

We flew back on 27th June to prepare for this the longest crossing of the circumnavigation and it was all made so much easier and more fun to have our crew with us. We all stayed in a local hotel Costa del Oro, which from the number of comings and goings probably served another function as well, but nevertheless was adequate and we all boarded Baringo once she was in the water a couple of days later. Work started in earnest but with four people took half the time and of course was much more enjoyable and interrupted with watching the world cup football matches. The 1st July was provisioning day quite a task for at least a three week voyage with four people. Malcolm and John tackled the drinking provisions and Glynis and I the food. The supermarket was pretty good and when we joined trolleys at the check-out Malcolm had certainly provisioned our drinks for the possibility of a very prolonged voyage. There were countless boxes of Clos red wine, which we had approved during tastings over the previous few days and deemed acceptable. The large supermarket trolley was barely able to contain its alcoholic contents and I had serious doubts about being able to stow so much wine on board in addition to at least twenty one days of beer and tonic. A very surprised and a wide eyed American lady shopper asked what it was all for and John replied for a sailing trip and she replied "some trip!" The storage space in Baringo proved to be more than up to the job, she is French after all so designed to carry enough wine for long voyages, and everything was stowed by the end of the day. In fact we seemed to find boxes of Chateau Clos as it became known hidden away in strange places for several months afterwards when the pacific was a distant memory! We had organised a new transom for the dinghy, we knew from other sailors that the dinghy is a lifeline in the pacific as marinas are rare so it is the only way to reach land for the necessities and possibly emergencies. We enjoyed some interesting restaurants during our preparation time, the food in Ecuador is generally very good and tasty. Jeremy the yard manager was very helpful and advised us where to go and even took us out for lunch one day and gave Glynis his special cerviche recipe.

On Thursday 3rd July at dawn we left La Libertad for a shake down sail back to Bahia de Caraquez and had a good sail after motoring for the first two hours. We were going north east with the south east trades so a good wind angle but we had to round the Manta peninsula again which meant a slight course change but the main hazard this time was unlit vessels. We were greeted by a large school of dolphins who changed course to sail along with us and then a pod of whales about 200meters away one of whom broached to entertain us. The annual whale migration goes up and down this west coast of South America when the humpbacks come north from Antarctica to breed in the warmer water during the winter. It is an extraordinary sight to see such huge creatures heave themselves out of the water but also rather alarming as they could do serious damage to a yacht and her crew. We had asked a whale expert in Panama about the dangers as we knew we would be amongst the migrating whales and we were reassured they were no threat although we had heard tales of yachts overturned by whales but not along this route so maybe these whales are better behaved and have learnt yacht etiquette.

We arrived at the Bahia de Caraquez "waiting room" off the beach at 02.30 the next morning and anchored in the same spot as before but this time the swell was much larger so it was quite a roly-poly night. At 06.30 we radioed Puerta Amistad Yacht club and were told that Pedro was already on his way as apparently there was another yacht waiting to come in which had been left at anchor all night but unlit as we did not see it until day light. The Swiss / Ecuadorian skipper (as we discovered later) came out with Pedro and we surfed in following him with Pedro on his yacht. We knew from our first experience it is a tricky entry through breaking waves in shallow water but much to our amazement the other yacht ran out of fuel just as we approached the river mouth! Dollying in the surf in shallow water waiting for him to refuel his outboard, (which surprisingly was all he had) was a little stressful but we made it safely to the club and anchored. There are many Americans in Ecuador, a pleasant place to retire, $US currency and cheap living so there were lots of 4th July celebrations underway in the club but we did not join in preferring to watch another football match. The final preparations were well underway but Malcolm and Glynis could not miss a trip to Monte Cristo to see the Panama hat makers and while they were away we met with Chuck and Linda from Jacaranda whom we had met the previous year on our way to La Libertad. Chuck is a mine of information on all aspects of sailing he gave us some useful tips for the voyage and we were to meet them again in the Pacific islands. We sampled nearly all the restaurants in Bahia and were continually searching for internet before we left, always rather frustrating and slow. Because we were at anchor loading fuel and water was more difficult than in a marina so we had a lot of dinghy trips and heavy lifting to do. We were hoping to leave on Thursday 13th July but we had a serious hiccup with the bureaucracy because one of our papers we were told was a copy and not the original which we had given to the agent in La Libertad and should have received back. We had not thought to check and not surprisingly $200 solved the problem, almost certainly a scam but we had no choice but to pay otherwise we would all still be in Bahia! There was therefore some uncertainty surrounding our departure time which had to be with the tides and with the documents but we thought positively and Glynis and I went to buy the fresh provisions at the market in the hope of leaving as intended that day. In the end Pedro appeared around 12.00 with all the papers and passports and led us safely out into the ocean.

The voyage from Ecuador to The Marquesas was the longest on our circumnavigation 3,000 nm and once en route there is no turning back as the strong SE trades and accompanying waves simply make it impossible. We said a fond farewell to Pedro who had been wonderful, so pleasant and helpful and we motored west until we caught the wind once we were out of the lee of the Manta peninsula. It was quite rough and we all felt a little queasy especially me which was very unusual and John had to do my watches on the first night, but we all settled down by the third day and the boat routine established itself. With four of us the watch system was very much easier. We progressed westwards with the trade winds varying between 20-25knots from the SE and it was rather overcast and cloudy for the first few days. We had to check the weather reports from Emmanuel and the grib files John had set up and carry out the usual water making and battery charging on a daily basis. We did not have LED navigation lights so with Poppy our autohelm steering and navigation lights at night the amps soon disappeared. On the third day we were passing the Galapagos Islands to the south of us, we had to keep out of the prohibited zone around the islands but there were lots of birds flying near the boat always a pleasure to see and a delight when they decide to hitch a ride with us. That night

Poppy started to make a funny noise, not welcome so soon after the start of such a long passage, the prospect of hand helming for 3000nm was not mentioned, but John descended into the aft locker, not easy as everything had to be removed and replaced for access but he found that the vital nut had worked loose and after tightening it Poppy was back on form again. We had seen one other vessel so far and during the whole journey we saw only anther two so the Pacific is truly empty, with only Alaska to the north and Antarctica to the south and a lot of sea in between.

We were making good speed with 1knot of current with us and we were in full trade wind swing. Occasional squally clouds passed by bringing with them temporary wind shifts requiring sail changes and continual reefs in and reefs out manoeuvres. By day 5 we had a trade wind as described in the pilot books 15 knots from the SE, steady and with the current we were making 8 knots in fine weather but it was still quite cool. We shared the food preparation fairly between us and enjoyed a cocktail every evening in the Baringo tradition and the Chateau Clos was going down very well but only one glass each night. While in Puerto Amistad Chuck had warned us about goose necked barnacles and showed us photos of them looking particularly nasty; pink, fleshy, ugly creatures that cling to your boat while crossing the Pacific despite moving along, but the answer is floating a line from bow to stern on both sides for about two hours each day and this prevents them clinging on. We did this daily when possible and never picked up a goose necked barnacle, so worthwhile occupational therapy while sailing along. On day 7 Malcolm caught a dorado and he and Glynis did the necessary in the cockpit to make it edible while we sailed the boat and we all enjoyed if for supper. We saw another vessel on day 8, rather a surprise as we had seen only one other since leaving, it was a fishing vessel piled high with nets but we could not identify its origin. The rest of the dorado was eaten that night and we continued ever west-wards getting used to the ceaseless rolling movement of downwind sailing with the large waves coming from behind. So far they had not been as large as the Atlantic rollers so may be the Pacific does deserve its name, but I am not making a judgement too soon. The trade winds were steady in direction and speed about 20-25knots from the SE and all the systems were working: generator, water-maker, Poppy, fridges, heads and lights, long may it continue. We had good e-mail connections with the iridium phone so we could all e-mail our children and Emmanuel for the weather. Despite being so far from land we had a beautiful white bird with us flying grace-fully around the boat every morning, an uplifting sight but how they manage the complexities of survival in the ocean is miraculous. We now have a watch system of three watches during the night and two during the day between Malcolm and Glynis as one and John and me as two, three hours watch at night and six hours during the day so every third day was a day off for someone which allowed for rest, ablutions and reading. We needed more fish to eat but day 10's catch got away taking the lure with it so Glynis made patties with a rather lurid purple vegetable possibly taro or an Ecuadorian sweet potato which we felt because of the colour must be highly nutritious. Largely thanks to Malcolm we were eating well and not losing any weight.

By day 11 we were over half way so we make an arrival time sweepstake and put our guestimates in a secret envelope. This was to be the exact time we dropped anchor in Atuona harbour to avoid any disputes on arrival. Malcolm caught an enormous fish that day it filled the stern of the cockpit behind the wheel and took a lot of patience and skill to get it on board but our resident experts managed it masterfully. Once organised and refrigerated it lasted for three delicious suppers. John and I felt rather guilty about our lack of contribution to the fishing while still tucking into the tasty suppers and lunchtime sashimi which Glynis made but we felt in the interests of conserving the other provisions we should eat the catches and it was impossible not to enjoy the meals although we did not like the death throes. We used a strong dose of vodka into the gills which we hoped eliminated any suffering.

The wind strengthened to 40 knots on day 13 and we had to dump the jenny and put the third reef in the mainsail, later it eased and we added a tiny handkerchief of jenny as we made 6.5 knots in 27 knots of wind, we could not go any further downwind to reduce the apparent wind without heading north west. With the stronger wind the waves became larger and the rolling increased with occasional unpleasant lurches as one hit Baringo at an awkward angle. In order to get the main down we would have to turn into the wind which is extremely difficult crossing large waves broadside and increasing the apparent wind speed enormously so as long as we could manage with the much reduced sail plan we carried on as it was not a storm only very strong trades. Galley activities were cut to the minimum as everything rolled around once out of the cupboards and indeed even opening a cupboard on the "wrong" side of the boat often led to the contents emptying. On the next day we did get what remained of the mainsail down and went with a furled big jenny alone which made life much safer, no jibing risk, and much calmer. It seems to me a lot of tension leaves the boat when the main is dumped in strong conditions but there is always a natural reluctance to drop it because of the reasons above and also the difficulty of hoisting it again if the sea remains choppy after the wind has died.

On day 14 we crossed the "crease" which we had made by the necessity of folding the chart on the chart table but it meant we had not been able to see the whole journey, only up to the crease and as the scale was small our daily runs looked very short so to keep spirits high we could see the crease approaching faster than the Marquesas. However, when we turned the chart over after reaching the crease the rest of the journey looked comparatively short which was a pleasant surprise. We now had the jenny poled out to enable a more downwind course and we could furl and unfurl without needing to adjust the pole significantly. It was getting warmer as we were further south but we still had the occasional rain storm but could usually see them coming so could be prepared. The skies were amazing at night better of course without the moon, a source of endless fascination and awe. Rather surprisingly we still had the company of some birds who came and went… where to is a mystery… but they usually paid a daily visit. It may be a sign we are getting close to some land now but by our calculation we are still a few hundred miles off but "closeness" is all relative given the size of the ocean.

At this stage Baringo temporarily became an employment agency with Malcolm being head hunted by e-mail for a job in Sydney, Henry applying for a job in the Financial Times and Justine waiting for exam results and a particular job hanging on it. Tense times indeed in addition to the steady rolling downwind in 25 knots with the poled-out jenny. All applicants were successful so Baringo proved her worth in another role.

With such a long passage we had changed the time by one hour about every 4 days, usually once the dawn became too late and the night watches waiting for a dawn that never seemed to come became too hard. This meant an extra hour of watch on those days but as a democratic boat the hour was always split usually around the middle of the day. On day 15 we sighted the third vessel of the crossing, a Japanese fishing boat. Malcolm's fishing trophies had fed us most of the way across but on day 17 another fish got away and the loose line blew into the wind generator and wound around it pretty fast. It was impossible to untangle it in the swell so we had to tie the wind generator off and move the fishing rod to the other side, something we could possibly have done sooner, but no fish for supper that night. Obviously the fresh provisions were running low but I had been making yoghurt all the way and we had become quite imaginative with our cuisine just making up dishes with what we had and the cocktail hour was always fun with some heated discussions and Chateau Clos was definitely not running out, Malcolm had made sure of that. Day 18 was Vanessa's birthday and day 19 Henry's but with the wonderful technology which makes ocean sailing a possibility for us we could speak to them both and wish them Happy Birthday! Emboldened by our good progress and some reduction in the wind strength we decided to use the para-sailor, a large downwind sail with a horizontal slit about a third of the way below the top to allow wind to pass through. With such a competent crew we managed it well and the boat was more stable downwind than with the other sails, but it has a narrow window of use between 12-18knots for us at least although more courageous sailors seem to have ridden out much stronger winds, the slit apparently enabling this, but we never put it to the test. It stayed up until dusk, we did not want to manage it overnight but we flew it again the next day, raised it at dawn and it seemed to attract some dolphins and more birds with its bright yellow colour. We flew the sail for the whole day but doused it at sunset and replaced it with the reliable poled out jenny which was just as well as the rain came that night bringing increased wind. The wind stayed strong the next day so no more parasailor, we removed the pole, rather tricky in the rough conditions but just tied it to the deck and went further downwind to make course for the Marquesas and on day 22 Malcolm sighted a small bump on the horizon... a Marquesa! Great excitement added to by Malcolm catching an enormous sailfish. A few more

166

Marquesas came into view and as it was going to be a night arrival we did not want to go into the main Atuona Bay on Hiva Oa so we found Puamao Bay on the chart, clear of hazards so somewhere we could drive in an drop the anchor safely in the dark which we did at 20.30 local time! We celebrated our safe arrival in traditional style with a bottle of champagne and Glynis cooked the sail fish or "swordette" as Glynis preferred to call it because it tasted like its namesake. Perhaps the special flavour was enhanced by our delight at being in the Marquesas after 3000 nm of downwind rolling.

It was Saturday 2nd August when we woke to a magnificent bay surrounded by high verdant mountains which we had not really noticed in the dark. We swam before breakfast, such a pleasure to stretch our legs and we saw a school of dolphins herding together to catch their breakfast. We then motored round the headland to Atuona Bay to anchor and check in. After so long in unmeasurable depths the depth sounder was not working and we found the bay surprisingly full of yachts some of which looked as if they could not make it to the next bay never mind sailing 3000nm or more of Pacific Ocean, but they must have done. The depth meter sprang into action in the nick of time as the anchor dropped and the first task was to open the secret envelope with our arrival guestimates, Glynis had won with her estimated time within an hour of our actual arrival! We had a delicious supper of more swordette and now more than one glass of Chateau Clos.

# CHAPTER TWENTY

# Exploring the Marquesas

## *August 2014*

The Marquesas are five main islands, and several smaller outliers, all volcanic in origin apart from one, Motu One, which as its name suggests is a sandy coral reef, they are some of the remotest islands on earth. There is a northern group and a southern group and we planned to visit those we could in the time available. The original Polynesians came to the islands from the west around AD100 followed by the Spanish and finally the French who gained control in 1870 and are still there.

The day after anchoring in Atuona was a Sunday so no offices would be open so there was no rush to get ashore. Malcolm used the time productively to put some U bolts in the dinghy transom so we could hoist it rather than pull it over the stanchions onto deck. Dinghy theft is everywhere so it was too risky to leave it in the water overnight. The Gibson lift as it became known proved its worth many times during the rest of the voyage. Our neighbours came over with a very welcome melon, a Canadian couple in a cute boat called "Hannah Rocks" and they gave us some local knowledge as well as their warm welcome. They had sailed from Canada and were planning to work in a marine biology laboratory in Tahiti and we met them on several subsequent occasions as our journeys coincided. During the afternoon a very ragged boat arrived with no boom, only a small outboard motor and hanked on sails, we discovered it had taken 55 days to sail from Colombia but given its appearance had been really lucky to make it at all. We took a shore party in the afternoon and walked to Atuona town about 30 minutes away and watched a fiesta over a few beers feeling rather strange to be on land again. Monday dawned bringing with it the prospect of checking in but we were pleasantly surprised by the lack of paperwork and exchange of money in Polynesia, a sharp and welcome contrast to our experience in South America. We found the Paul Gauguin museum with very true copies of most of his paintings there, the originals are all over the world in different galleries and later on we found his grave, but it was time to head back as we needed to eat a pizza for supper on the way.

We hired a Toyota Hilux, the standard Polynesian vehicle, for a couple of days and discovered beautiful bays, pretty villages, amazing churches, some supermarkets and superb views. We explored Puamoa bay where we had anchored the first night and it was more lively than we had expected with a village and shop and an interesting ancient archaeological site. Jacques Brel is the other famous name associated with The Marquesas so we found his grave and a small museum of photographs and his restored aeroplane "Jojo" so we wandered around with his songs playing in the background. We sampled most of the island's restaurants and restocked the provisions and discovered that the islands are all supplied by a roving provisioning ship the Aranui all very efficient and likely at the French tax payers expense. On Thursday 7th august we were on the move again a short hop to Tahuata island to the south west, a fast downwind sail and into Baie

Hanamanao a beautiful palm fringed beach with turquoise water to go with it. After a couple of days in this paradise island inhabited by one man and his two piglets we set off for another bay on the island, Vaitahu, but the wind was very strong and enhanced in the bay by katabatic winds of up to 40 knots falling down the high mountains making anchoring very hard with Baringo swinging wildly on the windlass before we could get the snubbers on. We woke the next day to the church choir singing; church events are the bedrock of life in most parts of Polynesia and the Marquesan churches were the most beautiful with local artist's wood carvings illustrating and decorating the religious story and embedding the local style on the pews, alters and fonts. We went ashore in rotation as we were concerned in the strong wind to leave the boat unattended but we all met the very friendly local villagers and returned laden with fruit, mainly pample-mousse, which are large grapefruits which keep very well because of their thick skin and although hard work to prepare because of this are delicious to eat.

Malcolm and Glynis had brought Bananagram, a fast type of scrabble, with them to keep our brains working. We spent many evenings at anchor playing this for the rest of our voyage, it was great entertainment and very competitive.

We left the island of Tahuata at 21.00 on Monday 11th August for an overnight sail to Fatu Hiva to find what was reported to be one of the most dramatic anchorages in the Pacific the renowned Baie de Vierges apparently originally named Baie de Verges (penises ) after the phallic rocks surrounding it but the name was later changed by the missionaries to Baie de Vierges in the interest of religious propriety and correctness. We could not miss a bay with such a story. We knew it was an upwind sail and would be hard work but we had eschewed the advice to land there first to avoid this as we could not have checked in there and we might have been fined for landing before checking in. Although tough on the boat it made a change from the downwind roll but just on arriving at the Baie de Verges the big jib fell down because the tape on the top of it had chafed through, luckily not the halyard itself. Its descent was quite a surprise! The bay is certainly dramatic, high sided with the phallic peaks surrounding it but it was narrow so not much anchoring space and room was restricted even more by an abandoned vessel in the prime location. Luckily another yacht was just leaving so we took their spot and had a quiet night with the help of the anchor alarm as we could not afford to drag very far in the confines of the bay. The scenery was indeed striking and the next day Patrick, who lived near the dinghy landing in the bay and also sold fresh baguettes, arranged for a boat, a local "tinny" to take us to Omoa the capital. The plan was for Malcolm and Glynis to hike over to Omoa in the morning then we would meet there with the tinny. We would hike back while Malcolm and Glynis returned in the boat. It was a wonderful walk and the plan worked perfectly. The Marquesas are well known for their beautiful wood carving and strolling round the environs of the bay we found several artisans at home carving stunning pieces. Of course we should have bought much more but the tiki and bowls we have are a wonderful reminder. We needed to pay in kind, and wine was requested by the craftsman but when we brought him a bottle we had he asked why we had not brought Chateau Clos, obviously we were not alone in our choice in Ecuador. The day after the hike was rainy so I mended the jib, luckily there was some spare tape and it was a good job which lasted until the end of the season!

We left Fatu Hiva island at midnight on 16th August to return to Hiva Oa to Baie Ta'aoa to the west of Atuona and then sailed around the east coast to Hanaiapa Bay which we had seen when we drove around and had particularly liked. It more than lived up to our expectations, no boats there, a very clean and tidy village with perfectly manicured gardens and full of flowers. The hull had become quite dirty during the voyage rather surprisingly considering how clear the water was so we spent a lot of our swimming time cleaning it. Malcolm and Glynis returned from one of their forays on land with news of a local yacht club so we went to find it and met William the commodore who showed us round his small but clean club where many other sailors had signed his visitor's book. We reluctantly left Hanaiapa bay at 03.00 on 20th august for Ua'Pou which has the most dramatic mountainous coast line with spiky unusual shaped peaks. Malcolm caught another dorado on the way over so we enjoyed sashimi and cerviche for lunch. We anchored in Hakahau Bay and relaxed again. The French influence is never far away and we could find croissants, baguettes, and a restaurant run by a retired French military man where we had dinner one night once the dorado was finished. We decided to visit Plage aux Requins (Shark Beach) for a picnic and swim but it was further than we thought so had to hitch a lift there in the school bus with all the children in the back of the Hilux truck. Just as Glynis was about to enter the pristine water the beach lived up to its name and the shadows of several sharks came close to the water's edge. Glynis made a hasty retreat even though they are all black tipped sharks which are not dangerous but they still look frightening. We all managed to swim later as the sharks kindly swam out of sight, we had the beach to ourselves, almost always the case in The Marquesas and enjoyed a picnic before the long walk home. The villages were all so clean and neat each with a splendid church with interesting wood carvings, a real pleasure to visit. After a couple of days there we moved to an adjacent bay Hakahetau where we met up with the guy who had given us a lift to the Shark beach and we visited his house and met his mother who was making rather marvellous hats. We were given lots of fruit, mangoes and pamplemousse and were then invited to a baptism party. The last island to visit on our travel itinerary was Nuku Hiva, the largest one of The Marquesas and that took about 6 hours but it was rough and windy so we had three reefs in the main and a very small jenny. We anchored in Baie Taioha'e, a large space and a few other yachts but it was by no means crowded and there were all facilities there, laundry, cooking gas and bananas. We explored the island by car again so beautiful and empty but each small village had a café and a church and here there was an ancient archaeological site. It was interesting for Malcolm and Glynis as New Zealanders to see the almost identical cultural style of the Maoris here with similar tikis and carvings and the people who are the same as Maoris but speaking French. We hiked in the central mountainous area picnicked and found wild horses!

We needed to get the repaired big jib up before sailing to the Tuamotus and we needed calm water to go up the mast to get the halyard so we moved again to Hakatea bay for more shelter. John rescued the halyard then we hoisted and furled the sail and we left.

# CHAPTER TWENTY ONE

# The Tuamotu Atolls

## *September 2014*

The Tuamotu atolls are a chain of eighty islands and atolls still in French Polynesia so we did not have to check out before leaving The Marquesas. An atoll is a thin rim of coral often with gaps in but containing a lagoon. The coral gradually acquires sufficient sand and then coconut palm trees so the reef enlarges providing enough ground to live on and to build homes and a few of the more substantial ones even have resort hotels and airstrips. Where the reef is larger and more substantial it is called a Motu. From the sailing point of view the atolls present a challenge because to enter the lagoon a pass has to be navigated and the water flow through these is tricky to read and can be very fast. Sea water enters the lagoon more easily than it exits because when the waves are large, which is most of the time, the water goes over the low-lying coral rim of the atoll. This water then has to leave through the pass, the only exit because the lagoon inside the coral rim is calm with only tiny waves which don't reach over the reef. So when the tide falls the lagoon sea water can only rush out through the pass and therefore the falling tide lasts much longer than predicted on the tide tables because the force of the outflow is greater than the force of the incoming tide. Entering the pass is safely done with the water going in on a rising tide and exiting when the water is coming out on the falling tide but timing is everything. We eventually discovered a marvellous calculator in the Admiralty Pilot book using several factors such as moonset and the tide tables to arrive at a propitious moment to enter or leave any atoll.

The journey from the Marquesas to our first Tuamotu was very mixed, changing wind speed and direction, several rain showers and quite a heavy sea but after four days we arrived at the pass into Kauehi atoll at 08.00 and as the water looked smooth and it was a rising tide we went nervously in to find that our speed rose quickly up to 8 knots in a whirl of eddies and we were carried rapidly into the lagoon. In the extreme this can make the boat very difficult to control but the pass was not long and we were then in the amazing calm of a brilliant turquoise lagoon. The colour was so iridescent it seemed unreal. We anchored off the small town of Taravero and were the only boat there, a scene of almost extra-terrestrial unreality it was so tranquil and the colours so vivid. We did not go ashore until the next morning when we found Chinese Fred running the supermarket, ever the business men, and we hired bikes from him to explore. Of course the atolls are flat, in contrast to the mountainous Marquesas so it was easy cycling even though the bikes were a little rickety. It was Malcolm's birthday the next day 4th September and what an idyllic spot for one... an excuse to celebrate if we needed one ...so first we visited the pearl farm and again it is the Chinese who dominate the industry. There were so many bags of black pearls in the pearl farmers home but most were misshapen but the sheer volume was rather extraordinary. We had a birthday supper on board with champagne cocktails and a birthday cake... impressive on board Baringo in the middle of the Pacific.

Fakarava was the next atoll we sailed to and is the second largest in the group, luckily with a wide northern pass so easier to enter. We had to leave Kauehi at 03.45 on 5th September to get the falling tide to leave through the pass but our exit was rather rougher than our entrance and our speed rose to 10knots, but we were launched into the ocean swell without any damage. Malcolm caught another large dorado on this journey so we had another delicious sashimi lunch. We arrived at Fakarava in the afternoon and this pass was easy although we had timed it with the tide which is obligatory for a safe transit, once through we then followed the buoyed path to the anchorage off the main town Rotoava. This atoll is popular with sailors with good reason as the south pass at the other end the lagoon is a diving mecca through which you can do drift dives and snorkels but sadly we did not have the time to do that. However the lagoon itself is pure pleasure, so calm it is like sleeping on land and the colours never cease to amaze. The atoll is the home of Fakarava Yacht Services run by a French couple and their two small children and provides all a yacht could desire, laundry, coffee, good inter-net and bicycles. There were the usual beautiful deserted beaches, French cafes, restaurants and supermarkets and all enhanced by the wonderful relaxed and friendly Polynesians. The weather for the second and third days of our sojourn in Fakarava was rather rough with wind and rain so John and I stayed on board to catch up with running repairs but Malcolm and Glynis are made of sterner stuff so braved the wind and rain on their bicycles. Our stay here was only three days so on 19th September we went out through the northern pass to Anse Amyot where we could anchor outside the atoll reef so no need to go into the lagoon. There is a restaurant there owned by Gaston and his Polynesian wife Valentine who were very hospi-table. Gaston earns his living by fishing and we were there when he brought his catch in for the transport vessel to take it to Tahiti. It was a very busy morning with the sharks circling the catch which was in a separate pool and the two dogs running around barking to scare them away which was all very entertaining. Gaston also showed us his photograph album and visitor's book and in it much to our surprise was a photo of Pippa Blake the wife of the tragically murdered sailor Peter Blake who Glynis and Malcolm knew from New Zealand. Glynis bought four lobsters from Gaston's catch and Valentine cooked them for us and we ate them for lunch, a real treat, then departed for Rangiroa the largest Tuamotu. The route to Rangiroa was initially in the lee of Apataki atoll which gave calmer seas but stronger currents in the relatively narrow passage, so we had to watch the navigation carefully to avoid being swept onto the reef. It is not a place to just plot the heading and let Poppy do the rest. Before all the modern technology and GPS the Tuamotus were known as the dangerous archipelago because of their poor visibility even with radar and the strong currents between them. In fact, later when were in the hard standing in Raiatea we met several yachts who had had reef encounters but we were aware of the dangers so were as usual very cautious and luckily avoided any damage.

We arrived early for the Tiputa pass into Rangiroa so we dollied outside for a couple of hours waiting for the tide to turn and at the appointed hour entered even though the water looked a little frothy, this was our early days of pass navigation. Once in our speed dropped to 1.0 knot in a supposedly rising tide! John put the engine revs up more than ever before and we slowly inched into the lagoon all holding our breath and very pleased we had ordered the turbo charged engine, but it was a scary moment. We learnt from the local dive boats that because of the excess ingress of sea water into the lagoon the inflow with the rising tide is always delayed. Once in the calm of the lagoon we anchored near the pass and relaxed. Malcolm and Glynis did the shore reconnaissance and found the lovely Relais

Josephine overlooking the pass and promptly booked dinner there for the following evening. The first evening we contented ourselves with "Snack Lili" for supper. Snack is the name for the all the local restaurants. Rangiroa has more tourists because it is a bigger atoll and has some larger hotels and an airstrip but it was not too crowded. We did the usual cycling around and bought some pearls, difficult to leave Polynesia without them and then had a wonderful meal at Relais Josephine preceded by a cocktail of vin de corail overlooking the pass with its erratically moving water full of sharks. The vin de corail as its name suggests is wine made from vines grown on the coral and is being researched by the University of Dijon with some success judging by the bottle we had. The next day we had amazing snorkelling near the pass. We attached the dinghy to one of the navigation markers and saw so many fish, one group in such a large bunch I thought they were a lump of coral first, truly amazing. We could not resist another cocktail on the Relais Josephine terrace overlooking the pass with the added attraction of watching the huge cruise ship "Paul Gauguin" leaving through it.

The water looked much calmer than when we had entered. We had another wonderful snorkel on our last day, then Glynis cycled at top speed to find more pearls a quick lunch at Snack Lili, coffee and the internet on the Relais Josephine terrace before departure then back on board to leave. The lack of rolling in the lagoons make them very hard to leave and the motionless nights aboard are a real rest after the ceaseless movement of the Pacific rollers, but we had to go to keep on schedule so on 16th September we motored through the pass with the water with us this time, sadly leaving the Tuamotus but heading for Bora Bora one of the Society island and as long as we arrived safely we were sure that more treats were in store.

# CHAPTER TWENTY TWO

# Bora Bora

## *September 2014*

The journey overnight to Bora Bora was varied although the sea was quite confused with sharp waves from different directions which made for an uncomfortable ride in the first 24 hours. By the dawn of the second day the wind died and we motored the last few hours into Bora Bora through the pass. The Society islands are a mixture of the Marquesas and the Tuamotus because they have an outer coral reef but an island has remained inside the lagoon... the best of both worlds but it does mean that the passes are easier to negotiate as there is less water in the lagoon, the space being filled by land. We picked up a mooring outside the Bora Bora yacht club which is very pleasant with reasonable facilities and good internet and an excellent restaurant where we could dine overlooking the lagoon and Baringo. Malcolm and Glynis hired a car to look around the island which is quite small and the most touristy of the Society islands but with the usual white sandy beaches and an unusual and very photogenic rock formation, a volcano with the top blown off in the centre. We were planning to come back to Bora Bora after meeting our next Hong Kong crew in Tahiti so we could afford to get on with some boat tasks. John replaced the engine fan in the stern of the boat which keeps the engine cool, it makes a noise when the engine is started but unless we listen specifically for it we don't know if it has stopped working, just one of the many things to remember and as Steve Dashew says constant vigilance is required. The shower pump for the forward shower had also not been working but it had not been too much of a problem because we were swimming so much and showering with the transom shower but now thought we might find a new one here but we did not, so that still remained on the to do list. Bloody Mary's is the renowned restaurant in Bora Bora with sand covered floors and a wide choice of seafood and fish which you choose from a table before it is cooked and a few Bloody Mary signature cocktails later it appears at your own table cooked and garnished, all very delicious.

We moved to another anchorage in the lagoon in the hope of finding some good snorkelling and coral but we were not rewarded although the anchorage was pleasant. Time was running out and we were to meet Simon and Jo Davies in Papeete, Tahiti as they were joining us for a Society island cruise and Malcolm and Glynis were leaving. So on 21st September we sailed from Bora Bora to Tahiti overnight. We were able to motor sail through Raiatea another Society Island just to have look and also in the hope it might be a shorter route, then overnight motor sailing to make the course and reach our destination in time. At dawn the mountains of Moorea hove into view and at 14.00 we were in the Quai de yachts in Papeete. We orientated ourselves and became accustomed to a big city again and not a particularly nice one either, a stark contrast to the great beauty we had spent the last few weeks enjoying but maybe we could get the elusive water pump here. We had our first experience of the Roulottes which are vans parked in the park serving a variety of cuisine. We chose Chinese food but it proved to be a poor choice but still an enjoyable evening with lots of local interest.

# CHAPTER TWENTY THREE

# The Grand Reunion Papeete and Society Island Cruise 1

## *September 2014*

Tuesday 23rd September was change over day, Malcolm and Glynis moved out and Simon and Jo moved in! We celebrated our exchange with champagne and lots of chat.

We hired two cars the next day to see what we could of Tahiti. We stopped for lunch and our chatter was overheard by the restaurant owner Roger a retired Rhodesian police officer who had sailed from England to Tahiti with a friend in 1970 without all the modern gadgets that we have. He kindly invited us all to his magnificent home where we saw the newspaper cuttings of his voyage and met his Chinese wife and grandson and looked round their wonderful tropical garden; we vowed to come back next year but sadly never did. The Quai de yachts was not really a pleasant berth and that evening we were summarily asked to move by a motor boat who parked next to us. But we could not get the anchor up, we were moored stern-to with the anchor securing the bow so we had to drop the anchor chain and leave our precious Rocna on the bottom and tie a fender to the end of the chain to keep it afloat in the hope of finding a diver to rescue it the following day. One of the heads was now blocked, not sure why, we changed the mechanism but it remained stubbornly blocked and we could not find a new pump for the shower despite trekking all over town from one chandlery to another. We did find Topdive and a willing diver who arrived at 17.30 and rescued the Rocna which took one hour, there is so much debris one the bottom for it to get caught on, but we were very relieved to have it back. Then it was a sad farewell to Malcolm and Glynis, what fun we had had, a true adventure which left us with lifelong memories.

We prepared for our cruise and checked out the Quai de Yachts but did not leave until the next morning so that evening we watched some Polynesian dancing in the local park which was great fun. It was a 06.00 start on 27th September to reach Moorea in the calm and refuel en route at Marina Tahina further down the coast. This involved crossing under the aeroplane flight path for which we had to radio for permission which was granted unless a plane was landing. With everything comfortably executed we were off to Moorea and were anchored in Cook's bay before lunch. The lagoon of Moorea is much narrower than that of Tahiti and really only navigable along the northern part of the island. There are two big bays for anchoring but getting from one to the other requires leaving the lagoon through the reef and re-entering. The 29th September was Jo's birthday so something else to celebrate which we did by hiring a car to see the island and then a birthday meal in a local restaurant, but it was a wet dinghy ride back to Baringo. We now had two clear-cut divisions on board, the engineering department Simon and John and the domestic department Jo and Julia, no surprises there. The engineering department tackled the blocked heads and with skill and determination pulled the culprit plastic bag from the piping. The domestic department dinghied ashore to the supermarket to find provisions, so a fair division of labour. We moved to another anchorage outside the Moorea yacht club to find the internet as Simon was in the process of selling his house, but it was not ideal because of the limited space so after a tense night with 33 knots of wind and the anchor alarm on we used the internet and then departed for Oponohu Bay which was rather nicer but there were more yachts there. The snorkelling was good with plenty of fish but only dead coral sadly. We found a wonderful roulotte for lunch run by a French lady married to a Japanese diver and they had brought their flat pack Japanese house with them from Japan. We dined there as well as the food was excellent and then saw more Polynesian dancing at the nearby Hilton Hotel. The engineering department swung into action again this time repairing a leak in the deck and then repairing another leak in the dinghy, it was starting to look like time for a new dinghy but the man in Turkey who had repaired it said we should keep it as long as possible as the newer dinghies are not made to this standard now. On 5th October we left Moorea at around 16.00 for the next Society island Huahine which was an overnight sail away, but the weather was reasonable and we fortu- itously missed the squalls which kept threatening us. We arrived for breakfast and anchored near Fare the main town. Huahine is much quieter than Tahiti and Moorea and we had a good lunch at the Huahine yacht club the first day then hired a car to have a look around. In fact Huahine is two islands Huahine-Nui and Huahine- Iti linked by a very short bridge. We found an interesting marae… a sacred Polynesian place of worship and then a pearl farm so a good day out. The weather was quite rainy but we managed a few snor- kelling trips but only found dead coral but always lots of colourful fish. We moved along the lagoon through the buoyed passage in the pouring rain to Avea Bay where the water is very clear and the sandy bottom easily visible and there is also a rather nice hotel just on the beach. We enjoyed more snorkelling and the culinary and cocktail offerings from the hotel before returning to Fare by Bourayne bay in the hope of seeing some coral but again we were disappointed. This was quite a deep anchorage but surrounded by beautiful scenery.

On to Raiatea the next day the 13th October motor-sailing this time and we stopped overnight in Apu bay and then off to Bora Bora the next morning and back to the Bora Bora yacht club and another excellent dinner there. Next day we hired a car to drive around the island which takes very little time so lots of stops at beaches, time for a good lunch and cocktails at the Sofitel Hurricane bar over the water. We decided to move Baringo a little further down to the Maitai Hotel moorings for a change but it did not prove as nice as the yacht club for dining. We then moved to Bloody Mary's moorings still further down and by chance met a Brazilian couple with a car who took us to a new Japanese restaurant where we had an excellent very Japanese meal. The next day was very wet and windy so we walked to nearby Matira beach and dined at Bloody Mary's after a very wet dinghy ride over! The next day it was back to Bloody Mary's at lunchtime because they kindly agreed to print some documents for Simon to process the house sale which was not really proving easy from such a distance but Simon's perseverance was rewarded with success. We moved again to Toopua island and then on to the east side of the island through a very tricky buoyed passage with reefs close on each side not made any easier by doing it in a squall, but the anchorage at the end was lovely, shallow crystal clear water with the anchor and chain clearly visible. Finally the weather improved and the sunshine returned and we found a group of manta rays while snorkelling off the beach a rather ghostly sight like underwater birds.

On Tuesday 21st October Simon unusually began to feel unwell, aching and headache which we diagnosed first as possible sun stroke but as it got worse we realised he must have Dengue fever which is endemic in Polynesia. He had probably been bitten in the garden of Bloody Mary's so Baringo briefly turned into a hospital ship with Simon resting in the saloon taking regular Panadol and having his brow mopped by Jo. We briefly returned once again to the Bora Bora yacht Club before leaving for Raiatea on 22ndOctober in an unpleasantly strong head wind so the journey took us rather longer than usual. We were pleased to get into the Raiatea lagoon at last and anchored in Hurepiti bay at dusk but annoyingly hit the bottom luckily without causing any major damage. We moved to another anchorage the next day with Simon still not well so we were sure he had caught Dengue but he rested while we snorkelled in the miraculous coral garden which you can actually walk around but floating is also an option and here we finally saw beautiful living colourful coral. The Raiatea lagoon has two islands Raiatea, the larger one and Tahaa the smaller, so we then went to see Tahaa and anchored there but we were beginning to feel Simon needed some blood tests to see if it was safe enough for him to fly on to New Zealand so we moved again and moored alongside at Uturoa the capital, indeed the second largest town in the Society Islands, where there was a hospital. The doctors were there and blood was taken and we got the results the next day and although proving that he did indeed have Dengue he could fly safely to New Zealand. After some shopping we moved around to the Carenage where we were leaving the boat for the southern hemisphere summer(our winter) and spent the night in the entry basin, not the greatest place for a last night for Simon and Jo but they had a very early start the next morning so getting in by dinghy with the luggage could have been difficult especially had the outboard not been co-operative. It was another sad farewell on 27th

October and we then went to anchor off to prepare for Baringo's haul out and our own departure. The wind and rain did not help getting the sails down, we had to pick the chance when it came but we managed and were ready for the lift out on 3rd November so back into the basin this time stern first and we touched the bottom. The travel hoist here was small so we had to take the back stay off and the wind generator down but the guys were very helpful and all was done with a cheerful smile so Baringo was placed safely on the ground. The Carenage leaves a little to be desired in terms of cleanliness and facilities and with Simon having just been bitten and infected with Dengue we decided we should stay in a hotel while finishing off the work on the boat. We then discovered the amazing Raiatea Lodge, a luxurious hotel in such a beautiful building and such wonderful food. The two French owners were kindness itself and our bed was strewn with flowers when we arrived. That is one of the loveliest things about Polynesia, flowers are everywhere. We left a few days later and returned to our land life.

# CHAPTER TWENTY FOUR

# Year Two in the Pacific Ocean Society Island Cruise 2

## *June – October 2015*

After family Christmas and New Year celebrations in Chamonix and five months teaching medical students in Hong Kong by 18thJune 2015 we were ready to return to Baringo. It was a long flight to Papeete via Los Angeles and a night arrival so necessitating an overnight stop in Papeete before we could fly on to Raiatea. We found a local bed and breakfast in Papeete, Hotel Ahitea run by M.Bodin and his wife who met us at the airport and showed us to our flower strewn bed, a truly Polynesian welcome. One of our bags had not arrived but we hoped this would not be a great problem but the more serious problem was that John had left his "Surface" computer on the aeroplane and his passport in the taxi. These events did not make for a good night's sleep but there was nothing we could do at midnight so early the next morning we sought the help of M.Bodin and he quickly found the passport in the taxi and we collected the green bag from the airport but no sign of the surface computer which must have been stolen. We took the 16.00 flight to Raiatea on 19th June and we had extravagantly booked the wonderful Raiatea Lodge again so we were met efficiently and whisked back to another flower filled bedroom and an amazing supper on the hotel terrace.

We had decided to spend this year in the Pacific as it had been such a fantastic experience last year and more importantly we wanted Vanessa and Henry to have a taste of it as well. There were a lot of different places to visit and even repeat visits were going to be fun. We considered trying to return to the Marquesas but this proved too difficult, sailing back eastwards into the strong prevailing trade wind. It can be done but it means waiting for windows of opportunity when the wind changes and we thought we might not have the time for that so we arranged for Henry and Vanessa with Antony to fly later to Papeete and we would meet there.

It was now Saturday so we did not think we could get into the Carenage to see Baringo but luckily the gate was open and we went on board to find the bilge full of water, rain water we thought which had overflowed from the blocked companionway door drain. After pumping all afternoon we cleared it and then returned to the luxury of the hotel for a swim and dinner. The hotel had bikes so we could get to and from the Carenage easily but the work did not start in earnest until Monday when the yard was in full swing. Regine the sailmaker came for our sails which were in need of repair and we thought we would report the theft of John's surface computer to the Gendarmerie but they refused to treat it as a theft only a loss so a wasted journey. We spent the day on the boat and shopping for necessities in town but life was made so pleasant knowing we would return each evening to the hotel for a swim and another delicious supper. We were working our way through the hotel menu but the standard never dropped. Although the staff at the Carenage were a delight with a great sense of humour, it was pretty dirty and washing facilities were a cold shower and very basic toilet so we felt after working for five months in Hong Kong we could afford a touch of luxury.

After four days at work we took a break and drove around the island to see it from land rather than sea which was an interesting change. We drove all the way round and found a waterfall with a pool to swim in, had a picnic lunch and found another hotel but confirmed we had chosen the best one which anyway was much closer to the Carenage. When we had left Baringo last year we had moused all the halyards and sheets as well as removing all the sails so there were several days of work to get her back into sailing mode but the more often we did it the quicker we became. The sails were all repaired quickly and returned by Regine and we were ready for launching on 30th June, but despite promises it would happen it did not until we finally went in at 13.00 the next day. The Carenage is very crowded so other boats always have to be moved for any boat to get to the basin and be lifted in, this obviously takes a bit if time but Baringo was gracefully lowered in and the backstay was quickly reconstructed, the wind generator was still dismantled from the lift out, we would get that up later. The motor failed to start when we tried to leave the basin, a repeat of the experience when we had arrived in Marmaris but Nicolas found a loose wire in the solenoid and off we went this time to a mooring which was much easier than anchoring because the water is quite deep just off the Carenage

We still had fresh water in the bilge and John finally traced it to a leak in the hot water tank which would need attention but nevertheless we were happy to be afloat again having our cocktails in the cockpit looking out over the sea. I have not worked out why this is something so special but I only know that it is. We always needed to wake early to hoist the sails as the wind usually picked up later in the day and because of the strength of the tide in a light wind the boat lay to the tide and would therefore be at right angles to the wind which was not what we needed for easy hoisting and furling. When we did get the right conditions we made a mess of it this time getting the furling lines the wrong way round, forgetting the battens, and getting a halyard wrap which required John going up the mast to unwrap! Because we had taken so long over the small jenny it was now impossible to hoist the big jenny before the wind came up and so we decided to write step by step instructions for ourselves for next time and be more efficient. Next on the agenda was the leaking water tank so we asked Dominique the manager of the Carenage for help. Nicolas came to our rescue but the tank had to be removed to be repaired on land. To add insult to injury John had broken his teeth eating a pineapple so there were trips to town to the dentist and he now needed a new bridge so it would be a few days yet before we could leave. The 4th July was very stormy and we were joined by several yachts taking shelter on this side of the island, no outdoor jobs were possible so John decided to remove and dismantle the non-functioning shower pump and found a small piece of plastic had stuck in the mechanism and once removed the pump worked perfectly which was good although we had wasted money buying another one, but now we had a spare. The next few days of bad weather prevented us from doing several of the jobs but when it was calm enough Nicolas returned and replaced the repaired water tank. We had to wait for John's dental bridge to arrive from Tahiti which took a few days and the weather continued in the same stormy fashion so leaving in that was not an attractive prospect anyway.

By 10th august the weather brightened although we still did not have the big jenny in place we decided to motor to Uturoa the capital of Raiatea and moor alongside and no sooner had we tied up than a Canadian electronic engineer came by offering his services. As our electric winch switch and also the wind generator were not working properly we immediately engaged him and he started investigations there and then. He returned the next morning and finished off and both problems were solved. We were now regular customers at the local café in Uturoa, La Cubana, after many visits there last year because it was the only place in town where we could get internet for the price of a cup of coffee. While we were there that day sipping coffee slowly enough to allow time for e- mails and other internet tasks, we saw a band advertised as playing that evening so we returned later for some music and dancing. We were only two couples dancing watched by local ladies in their marvellous flower head-dresses and the Polynesian music was rhythmical and fun.

By 12th July it was time to go and explore after nearly three weeks of repairs and maintenance so we sailed past the Carenage and the Raiatea Lodge down the western side to Pt. Tipanui in the south west corner of Raiatea where we found a yellow government buoy to tie up to. We had heard that they were being put in several bays which was of course very welcome and there was no charge. Ashore we found the oldest protestant church in Raiatea surprisingly built on an ancient marae so obviously some previous conflict of interest. Our next move was to Ha'amene bay in Taha'a the smaller island within the Raiatea lagoon. The bay is a very deep inlet on the eastern side of the island and although this is the weather side, but because the bay is long and slightly curved it provides excellent shelter and again we found the yellow government buoys. Our faithful Avon rover 8 dinghy was continually springing leaks which kept John busy with repairs but we were rather sadly coming around to the idea of buying a new one for the following year. This bay had an excellent restaurant the "Taha'a Maitai" owned and run by a Frenchman who was an excellent chef and very obliging, and had internet! There was also a good supermarket; it was always interesting to find how well the essentials of living were provided in Polynesia despite its remoteness and life certainly seemed comfortable and enjoyable here and unsurprisingly a refuge for many ex-patriot French in search of a particular life style. We hired motorbikes and drove round Taha'a in search of Jo Dassin's beach recommended by Lonely Planets and we visited Patio the main town. Jo Dassin's beach was well hidden and a walk beyond the end of the road but was deserted and beautiful as described. There was lots of opportunity for hiking around this large bay and we did as much as we could in between the rain storms which were more frequent than we had expected, in fact the weather that year was poor and we started to worry about the children's visit in case they should not see the islands at their best. On one of the fine days we hiked over the hills from Ha'amene bay to the town of Patio through the tropical forest which gave us a wonderful view of the bay and Baringo bobbing gently on the mooring. We had been told the wine in the supermarket there was a good buy but in fact it was disappointing on our visit. It was by then too far and too late to trek back, night time jungle walks are not a good idea, so we had no choice but to hitch a lift as there were no buses. No sooner were our thumbs out but a lady stopped and took us back to Ha'amene Bay even though this was not her destination, very typical of Polynesian kindness and one of the many reasons why Polynesia is such a brilliant place. Yves and Jacqueline on "Imagine" came into the bay and we had some very pleasant evenings together and we were all to meet again further along the road and indeed it was Yves who recommended the agent who finally sold Baringo.

We stayed in the bay for eight days, we were not in a rush this year as we had no long passages and the lack of time pressure was very enjoyable and as always there is never great enthusiasm for leaving the calm of the lagoon for the rough and tumble of the ocean. We moved round to Hurepiti bay where we had hit the bottom last year but managed to avoid that this time and we could still walk back to our favourite watering hole "The Tah'a Maitai" and get the internet. We needed more provisions by then so decided to sail to Uturoa but it was Saturday, charter boat change over day so it was far too crowded so we continued to Fa'aroa Bay on the east coast of Raiatea another very deep and sheltered bay and with the welcome yellow government moorings. We went up the river which flowed into the bay in the dinghy, all leaks repaired for the moment, and it took us through thick tropical forest until we met farmer Andre who showed us his farm pointing out the different fruit and vegetable plants and presenting us with a huge bunch of bananas. We were well and truly in easy cruising mode now, swimming, reading, sleeping and watching DVDs in the evening but tempting as it was we could not spend the whole season inside this lagoon so we goaded ourselves into action and focused on preparing for some ocean sailing to see more Tuamotus. We provisioned and refuelled in Uturoa which is often tricky to get into and out of as it is on the northern tip of Raiatea and so is not protected from the prevailing easterly wind. We were either blown on or off the pontoon each of which creates different challenges and certainly honed John's helming skills. This time was no exception as we had to move up and down the quay to get fuel and then move again for another boat. Luckily Yves was there to help and we tied up securely for the night finally.

On 28th July, Vanessa's birthday, the morning was calm for an easy getaway and we sprung off just before a catamaran arrived behind us, their width did not help the springing off procedure so much better if they were not there. We were heading for Tikehau about 180nm away to the north east but once out through the pass dark clouds gathered and there was a slightly nauseous oily sea so we pulled into Huahine to wait there for better conditions. We tried to phone the birthday girl but no luck, the iridium phone seemed less reliable in the Pacific, maybe because there are fewer satellites. We set off again the next day but the weather had hardly improved, it was Henry's birthday the 29th July and we did manage to connect to speak to him and It was then out into a grey cloudy day. It was not easy to make the NE course to Tikehau and John was not at his best after so long in the flat lagoon, the mal de mer arrived but we pressed on and after three days we were waiting outside the pass into the Tikehau lagoon at midnight. The rest of the night was spent dollying up and down waiting for dawn when we could then anchor in the Admiralty recommended spot just outside the entry to the pass, it would have been too dangerous to approach that close in the dark. From there we could watch the water in the pass and by now we had discovered understood the magic Admiralty calculation tables and after two hours we entered very smoothly at high water slack. It was interesting to observe the water become smooth quite suddenly just at the correct moment we had calculated. We were through at 13.30 and motored along the marked channel, always so reassuring in the reef strewn lagoons, and anchored again in a beautiful peaceful spot. We felt very thankful to the French for their excellent navigation marks everywhere, all well maintained and accurately positioned, it would be a different story without them for us and all the other yachties.

It is really hard to describe the wonder that is the Tuamotus, remote but not harsh, tranquil and natural but with all the creature comforts of life, plenty of food: lagoons full of fish, fruit and vege-tables growing and other requirements like wine, yeast and flour for baguettes delivered regularly by the good ship Aranui...all rather amazing.

Tikehau was no exception to paradise, and we really enjoyed

exploring the atoll and meeting the unusual people who had decided to make their life there with the delightful Polynesians. We saw how baguettes are baked and ordered our daily supply of these and croissants, found another wonderful beach and found internet at the local Hotel Hotu owned and run by an Estonian. We cycled around the Motu with its calm lagoon side contrasting to the rough and wild ocean side and returned to our by now favourite bar in the Hotel Hotu and even managed to get some documents scanned and sent with the help of the owner. The lagoons are full of uncharted reefs so we rarely strayed outside the buoyed channels once inside so in order to see the rest of the Tikehau lagoon we took a tourist boat; Tikehau as we learnt is a honeymoon destination and we shared the trip with three very elegant Italian couples all in chic beachwear! We were taken to the Isle D'Eden a paradise created by a Taiwanese religious leader then to L'Isle des Oiseaux full of Noddy terns and white Gigi birds all unafraid of humans, then a lunch of poisson cru on the sable rose, a feature of the Tuamotus and is what its name suggests, then the sharks came and ate the left overs. Finally, we saw two huge manta rays on our return trip, a very memorable day out. It was certainly hard to drag ourselves away from Tikehau as we had easily fallen into the lifestyle here, ordering then later collecting baguettes daily, walking and swimming then ending yet another perfect day with a cold Hinano beer for cocktails at Hotel Hotu.

On 7th August we made the break and headed for Ahe atoll about 126nm to the east, we made our choices for geographical reasons and from recommendations from the pilot books and Lonely Planets. It was a rough ride there, the weather so far this year had been far from clement this year, we had 30 knots of wind but because we were between atolls the sea was relatively calm. It was another dark arrival at 03.30 outside the Ahe pass so we tried heaving-to to rest but with our "slutter" or solent rig this does not work all that well so it was dollying again until daylight with the bright red light of the pass in view giving us some comfort. The certainty of knowing that dawn will come is a great solace in these situations and it never failed us, so with the daylight we went for the pass at 08.00 with the ingoing tide and peace reigned once again inside the lagoon. The generator stopped unexpectedly while we had been dollying outside so that needed to be tackled. We could of course charge the batteries with the main engine but this was expensive on fuel and noisy so John settled down to diagnose and treat the problem; it was the impeller, so easy to change and we had learnt the need to carry plenty of these from our days in the convoy when impeller hunts had been the rage, so we quickly had a working generator. Now in impeller mode John wanted to change the engine impeller but it was impossible so he had no choice but to wait. The poor weather limited our excursions but in fact Ahe had recently been hit by a typhoon so the village was a little sad and the surroundings rather scruffy apart from a wonderful solar panel farm. Ahe lagoon is enormous, but it was not buoyed so we were too nervous to explore it in Baringo who still had to take us several thousand miles, and there were no boat trips in Ahe. So here we spent most of the time on board as the wind was so strong getting the dinghy afloat from the deck was tricky so after five days of constant strong wind we departed for Fakarava atoll on 11th August. The pass transit went smoothly, this time we had a catamaran just ahead of us so had the luxury of seeing how it fared in the pass and could then go through with confidence after it. It proved to be a more pleasant overnight sail passing Apataki and Taou atolls and we sighted Fakarava at dawn so slowed a little to reach the north pass at the appointed time but our entry which was supposed to be at slack water did not go as planned because the inflow was continuing and rushed us in at 9.5knots. We knew where we were after our visit last year and were happy to anchor and reacquaint ourselves with the Fakarava Yacht Services family who we were very happy to find still in residence. We enjoyed Fakarava to the full fearing it might be the last visit so we concentrated hard on soaking up the atmosphere of tranquil beauty and the friendliness of the people and also tasting the local food and of course drinking Hinano beer which is to be found everywhere thanks to the supply ship Aranui. On 18th August we went to the south pass which we had missed last year and really wanted to experience, and luckily there was a well-marked channel southwards across the lagoon and a great anchorage off the beach at the southern end. It was a sunny day and the colours were at their best, white sands and brilliant turquoise water untouched and totally unspoilt. There were several yachts near the south pass as the diving and snorkelling is so popular but this did not spoil the scene. The local beach restaurant was Lisa's where we dined with a French diver and a few cats and dogs and a small brown piglet, all very entertaining company. We really wanted to try a drift snorkel in the pass so got the local tide information from the French diver but the weather was so poor and our dinghy and outboard slightly less than robust so in the bad conditions we decided not to risk it. We contented ourselves with the local snorkelling which was lovely and quite safe and there was living coral there. We met a much more adventurous French couple from whose boat we had seen nappies hanging out to dry and when we met in our dinghies found that they had a toddler and a babe in arms and had been to Antarctica in their boat! We decided not to leave by the south pass in the rough weather, it is much narrower and therefore rougher than the north pass and we had heard a lot of banging from one boat braving it through so it was north again early on the 23rd August to leave by the north pass. This was less convenient for our next destination but wider and therefore much safer. We needed to wait at anchor off Rotoava for the right time but having worked out the time perfectly when it came we could not get the anchor up, it was stuck round a coral bommie! We manoeuvred here and there and it finally came up but not without being within an ace of Baringo crashing into a coral reef making our already racing hearts go even faster as we were worried we would miss the time for the pass. We did make it out and we set sail for Tahiti to meet Vanessa and Antony. We were now sailing on a south west heading but it was a rough passage as the wind had been so strong for the last few days so a big sea had whipped up making it hard work on all fronts. On the second night out Poppy went briefly on strike just after we had finished supper, luckily we were both in the cockpit but were too slow to realise her absence and did not hear the warning buzzer as the wind and waves were too noisy and in a second we had crashed jibed which gave us a fright. No damage was done and of course we had the preventer on but the episode made John think about our preventer system and he later changed it for a better and safer one. We righted the problem and carried on to see the loom of Tahiti and the Mount Venus light at dawn on 25th August. We had decided to try Marina Taina after our experiences at the main Quai de yachts last year but in the end this turned out to be a bad decision as once alongside we found ourselves stern to right at the end of a pontoon, either being blown too far off or on at risk of colliding into the next door motor boat as we could not secure the lines adequately to keep us stable. We could see our plank from Baringo's stern to the pontoon was going to make loading Vanessa and Antony's luggage precarious but there were no other places available in the marina. We prepared the boat for their arrival and on 30th August we drove to the airport at dawn to find them already there. We loaded the baggage onto the boat using the dinghy, the plank was clearly inadequate but Antony and Vanessa braved the walk.

That afternoon we drove to Venus Point where Captain Cook tried to observe the transit of Venus across the sun in 1769. This measurement had the aim of making improved astronomical measurements of the solar system which could improve nautical navigation which was dear to Captain Cook's heart. Later in the afternoon we swam off PK23.5 beach but after where we had been it was disappointing, certainly Tahiti is not the nicest Society island so we decided to leave the next day for more perfect pastures and were away by midday and straight into a force 7 breeze. Under the flight path, through the pass and with three reefs in the main and a furled jenny we were in Moorea only 17nm away in no time and anchored in Opunoha bay where we swam and then had the Hendrick's gin Antony had brought for cocktails. We knew our way around now as we had done this trip the previous year with Simon and Jo so we booked dinner at the Hilton Hotel overlooking the sharks and returned the next night for a sumptuous buffet and Polynesian dancing. Antony and Vanessa inevitably only had a short holiday here so it was really just a taster of each place so on 3rd September we did the overnight sail to Huahine and arrived in the morning to find a free mooring buoy off Fare Avea beach was next on the cruise, with such lovely clear water it could not be missed and it was sunny so we had the best of the colours and great snorkelling. On 6th September we sailed to Raiatea and found the coral garden empty so plenty of space to anchor and the coral garden did not disappoint. We were then off to Bora Bora to meet Henry and had a good sail there and tied up once again to a Bora Bora yacht club buoy at 17.30 and had yet another delicious dinner at the restaurant.

Henry arrived on 8th September and we went to meet him at the airport on the ferry, the only way to get there but a pretty ride, meanwhile Vanessa and Antony hired a jeep to explore Bora Bora. Once all back on board it was a move to a Bloody Mary's mooring and a Bloody Mary's dinner that evening. We thought we would anchor off Matera point to try and see the manta rays but they were not there and by then our mooring buoy had been taken. The wind picked up so we stayed the night off Matera Point but because of the bad weather we could not get ashore to the Japanese restaurant we had found last year. Vanessa and Antony had booked a hotel on the eastern side of Bora Bora where most of the overwater hotels are but they had managed to find a more local establishment as the prices are exorbitant. We motored through the narrow, marked channel, at least we knew what to expect this time and found the hotel and it proved a very good choice with Vlad a friendly Russian proprietor and a few small but well- appointed cottages near the beach to sleep in and a nice terrace overlooking the sea with a restaurant. We could not get very close to off load Vanessa and Antony and their bags in fact Baringo briefly touched the sandy bottom trying so we retreated and returned to our former anchorage. We had all the anchoring co-ordinates from last year, and John did a sterling dinghy ride in 30knots of wind taking Antony and Vanessa and their bags to the hotel. Despite the rough conditions and the parlous state of the dinghy and outboard he did come back. The hotel lent us kayaks so we could get back and forth easily under our own power rather than that of the unreliable outboard so we had the best of both worlds, enjoying the hotel facilities from our anchorage. We showed off the manta rays to them all, they always seem to be there, and then it was goodbye to Antony and Vanessa who left on 12th September. Henry was still with us so we did more snorkelling there in another spectacular coral garden, then we went to Motu Topua for more of the same. We hired a car the next day so Henry could see the island from the land as well, so it was beautiful beaches, exotic cocktails and supper in the Maitai hotel under the stars. We then left Baringo on the Bora Bora club moorings and because Henry's visit was so short we flew with him to Papeete and had a night with him chez M.Bodin and a farewell supper. Henry departed very early the next morning and we returned to Bora Bora. Luckily the weather had been quite good while the family were with us but that changed rather quickly and it was back to rain, wind and cloud again but we nevertheless returned to the eastern side of the island to have a few days there hoping to use Vlad's internet which we successfully did.

Rather than using the dinghy for the whole journey to Vlad's hotel we tried to walk there along the beach near to Baringo where we left the dinghy. After a few minutes walk we met a lady who warned us against leaving the dinghy there out of sight so we turned back and we went over to Vlad's Hotel in the dinghy. We visited the rays again always fascinating and eerie to follow but that day John started to feel unwell. We then sailed to Raiatea as John was still unwell and fortunately we had an easy sail with full main and jenny for the first time this season! We anchored in Hurepiti bay in bright sunlight so easy to see now where we had run aground anchoring at dusk the previous year. John was still feeling unwell and we presumed he had Dengue Fever like Simon, he had probably been bitten going into the undergrowth for a call of nature while we had been walking along the beach trying to reach Vlad's hotel. We retired back to Fa'aroa bay for John to recover which was the perfect place to rest, an idyllic spot, so we stayed there for four days and by then John was feeling better so we left to refuel in Uturoa and then on to Ha'amane Bay. It continued windy and stormy and John had developed the typical dengue rash but was at least feeling better in himself. We were battered over the next few days by wind and rain so had some pretty rough dinghy rides ashore for provisions and the internet, but most of the time it was impossible to get ashore. The wind was so strong that we had waves in the bay with white horses and one afternoon the dinghy overturned with the outboard on.

The starboard side had deflated, another leak, making it was unstable. The outboard was dunked as well so needed an immediate wash in fresh water but it required a new spark plug to make it work. We were due to leave Raiatea on12th October so needed to get to the Carenage to prepare Baringo for the hardstanding but the weather did not make this easy. By 5th October we felt we had to brave the journey and it was very windy with waves and white horses even in the lagoon. We could not pick up a mooring buoy at the Carenage because of the strong wind so anchored off and made it in with the dinghy when the wind allowed to organise our lift out, there was no chance to get the sails down that day. We made a 05.45 start on 6th October and managed to get both foresails down and stowed and we were lifted out on 7th October and got the main down on the hard. There are so many jobs to do before leaving the boat and with so much rain it was difficult getting things stowed dry but we managed somehow and flew off on 12th October for our land and air travel to Rapanui (Easter Island) Peru and Bolivia before heading home.

# CHAPTER TWENTY FIVE

# The Western Pacific

*May – December 2016*

Our time on land had been more than usually eventful because Antony and Vanessa got married on 15th March 2016 at Fulham Palace in London. Luckily we finished our work in Hong Kong earlier this year after only two months and sadly it was to be our last teaching contract but at least we were in time for the great wedding. It was a wonderfully happy occasion with excellent speeches. Antony's family came over from Australia as did some of his friends and the venue was perfect and although it was cold there was no rain. Once the excitement was over we were able to return to Baringo a little earlier than normal which was useful as we had a long passage across the western pacific to Australia.

We arrived back on Baringo on 8th May 2016 by the same route as last year and had the usual warm Polynesian welcome of flowers and music. We succumbed to the delights of the Raiatea Lodge for a third time but it would be the last and we did not stay for so long this time. We found Baringo still in the Carenage and this time it was oil and water in the bilge! We had ordered a new mainsail from UK sales in Hong Kong where Barry who knows everything there is to know about mainsails organised the new sail as they had all the original measurements, this was our third and probably last order. Regine had agreed to take delivery of it and it had arrived safely. Our other new purchase was a dinghy which had arrived from China via Hong Kong thanks to Myles Winter. It had arrived just before we left at the end of last year but we had barely had time to unpack it then so we had that to look forward to. Regine arrived with the new mainsail, so stiff and awkward to move around but when we had a closer look the cars attaching the sail to the mast were not there so we had to rush to her loft and remove the old ones and drill holes in the new sail to attach them. It is a wonderful Harken system of ball bearings inside the cars which make for very smooth hoisting and more importantly quick dumping. The water in the bilge annoyingly was the hot water tank leaking again, so it had to come out for a second time and be repaired. It was located behind the water maker which had to be partially dismantled for the removal and this did not improve its performance but there was no choice. The 11th May was our last night in Raiatea lodge (they were full not surprisingly for the following weeks) but we did not want to stay on board in the Carenage. We had found the Sunset Motel which we had tried to stay in two years before but they had been full hence our stays in the Raiatea Lodge but this time there was plenty of room as it was early in the season. We had a large bungalow in the spacious grounds which ran along the seaside. It had a kitchen, sitting room, bathroom and bedroom and a large verandah so very spacious with internet, ever the necessity, in a nearby bungalow. It rather reminded us of the Gambia where we had worked for three months, and lived on a similar large compound in a similar large bungalow in a tropical setting. We needed a car now as the Sunset Motel was further from the marina but this came in useful for shopping and other searches and avoided taxi fares. It was comfortable enough but not quite the luxury of Raiatea Lodge.

Work on the boat continued where possible as it rained intermittently and so we had to alternate indoor and outdoor jobs depending on the weather. On 15th may we were unlucky enough to be robbed. We had gone from our bungalow to the internet bungalow and I had left my rucksack behind and only taken my iPad and on our return only about 20 mins later the mosquito net was torn and the anti-theft window had been easily unscrewed. The rucksack was gone and our money with it, my French wallet with euros in it, my diary and a few other minor items. For an unpleasant minute I thought the passports had gone as well, I had hidden them so safely I could not find them immediately but they were there. We called the police who came very quickly and shone a search light on the crime scene which revealed another hand bag of mine which must have looked of interest to a thief but had been abandoned on the ground as there was nothing in it and the gendarmes also found the robbery weapon, a large screwdriver. We had to tell Madame the next morning and she was very upset and apologetic. We then had to make a formal report to the Gendarmerie for possible recovery of stolen goods and our own insurance claim. We felt pretty low and very foolish not taking the rucksack to the internet bungalow. We thought it was one of the local people staying in a nearby bungalow who had seen us leave and seized the opportunity. We were not staying in the main tourist area of the Motel as it was not properly open for the season but in one of several bungalows occupied by locals. We never saw any of the stolen goods again of course we did not expect the money but they might have thrown other useless things away. A few days later while looking for something else in the grass around the bungalow I found my Nokia mobile phone which had been lying in the rain but miraculously still functioned. Work continued on the boat, the water tank was removed once again, John had to reconstruct the Gibson lift on the new dinghy and we now needed a new outboard after the dousing of the old one last year had caused complete failure. We found a four stroke Suzuki in Uturoa that was not very powerful but light enough for us to lift into and out of the dinghy without a mechanical hoist. In fact the lack of power was never a problem. the rubber of the new dinghy rather like the dacron of the mainsail was very stiff and getting the floor boards to fit was rather a marathon but it did get easier over time. We sought help from a you-tube video but this only showed two Chinese men mantling the dinghy ridiculously quickly and easily, so not much help to us!

We were ready to move back on board on 20th May and Madame was so kind and gave us an even more reduced price for the bunga-low in addition to the free baguettes she had delivered every morn-ing. An even greater favour was that she had got some New Zealand dollars for us as we had only just discovered this was the currency of our first stop Nuie and we had none and not being natives of Raiatea we could not get any ourselves from the local bank. Madame was a real saint and when we finally cleared our room and met for the last time she came with a huge bag of wonderful pamplemousse. We were in the basin by 16.00 that day and stayed overnight as it was quite late by the time the boys had put the backstay up and they also kindly put the wind generator up as well. It was then time for a beer with Simon the chief and the rest of the yard workers, a regular occurrence on Friday evenings we discovered. It was Simon was really who held the yard together, a very hard worker, nothing was ever too much trouble and he was under the water checking keels in the basin one minute then at the top of a mast the next. On Satur-day 21st May we were back on a mooring outside the Carenage and it was time to struggle with the new dinghy which was much larger than the Avon and therefore more difficult to manoeuvre and with the extra weight of the aluminium floor boards which were not light. Now the Gibson Lift was a necessity not just a luxury. We found the floor boards finally slotted into place flat when the dinghy was in the water and it was lovely to drive around and much better for transporting heavy loads and jerry cans of diesel. During our routine rigging check John had discovered that there was a fracture in one of the shrouds which would have to be replaced before such a long journey. The rigging expert came over from Papeete and arranged replacements from there and he would return at a later date to replace the broken sections but we had to go back into the dreaded basin for him to do that.

We worked often in the rain making, mending and hoisting the sails when the weather permitted. We also had quite a social time with "Ganesh" French friends of "Oukiok" whom we had met on the convoy and Kendal an American single hander and Peter and Vicki on Carango who had suffered a major gear failure on the ARC and had been delayed in Raiatea while their boat was being repaired. We all enjoyed swapping our sailing stories over drinks and meals. The mooring we were on belonged to Chantier Naval the smarter yard next to the Carenage and they were quite expensive so after seven nights at £10 per night we retreated to Ha'amene Boy to continue the preparations and wait for the new shrouds to arrive from Papeete. We used the new mainsail on the way up and it looked beautifully white and pristine, we thought we would be safe enough inside the lagoon with the broken rigging and we were. The yellow mooring buoys were still there but this year they were no longer cost free but at least less than the Chantier Naval buoys. We serviced the winches, provisioned, mended a stanchion and for a change of scene we went to Tapamu bay opposite the coral garden with a magnificent view of Bora Bora which has such an iconic silhouette. It was time for the new rigging to arrive so we returned to the Carenage and on 1st June we went into the basin for Fred the rigger who did not arrive until the following day but we could stay in the basin overnight rather than having to move out then in again. During an evening of passage planning we had realised that we did not have a chart to get us to Nuie which we had decided to go to rather than the Cook Islands after discussions with a very nice Austrian couple sailing that way with their baby on a catamaran. The Cook Islands had gained the reputation of overcharging visiting yachts and having difficult bureaucracy so Nuie which we had never heard of before seemed a better option. We ordered the necessary charts from Hong Kong and they duly arrived promptly by air. We were thankful for the usual Hong Kong efficiency, as we could not really have left without them and we collected them from the airport before our departure. We had to spend one afternoon back at The Riaitea Lodge as news from the UK on EU referendum was looking bad so we felt we needed to send our remain votes in which took an afternoon of printing and scanning documents with the help of Laurent the owner who was most obliging and anyway we were all on the same side. As we sadly found out later it was to no avail.

Fred eventually arrived armed with metal coils and rather precariously climbed up the mast rather precariously supported after half the rigging taken been taken off and he replaced the damaged sections. It was another night in the basin but nearly all, it is never all, the work was completed and on 4th June we did the shake down sail to Bora Bora and returned to the Bora Bora yacht club moorings. Strangely we had a northerly wind but we thought this was due to a system we had seen to the south, we were watching the weather closely to assess the best time to leave for Nuie about 1000nm to the west. The wind was really strong over the next three days so no imminent departure yet. We needed to refuel as well which entailed driving with six 20litre jerry cans and two 5 litre ones about 1.5 nm across the lagoon to the nearest fuel station and then returning with them full and loading them onto the boat. We stowed them in the aft heads shower room low down and secure and we never had any problems with this system. John had rigged a new preventer as planned, much safer with the ropes coming from the bow to another rope attached to the end of the boom. This meant the preventer could be easily undone and changed from port to starboard by unclipping and reattaching the preventer ropes to the rope on the boom overhead in the cockpit. The bow end of the preventer was secured to the stern winch via a block mid ships and another on the stern cleat. It worked really well and can be recommended although we never tested it under stress as we never had any more inadvertent jibes but it certainly made our planned jibes safer and easier. We were more vigilant about Poppy going on strike. Rain squall followed rain squall and we just had to wait for better weather to leave and it could not be a Friday because leaving for a long passage on Fridays is unlucky so we never did. On Monday 13th we went to the Gendarmerie to check out and to find eggs but there was not one on the island we were told! The new dinghy was so big we could no longer store it in the stern port lazarette so we had to wait for it to dry in the sun which we now had and then stow it on the lower bunk in the bunk room, not ideal but we got used to it being there. At 15.15 that day after the all clear from Emmanuel our weather forecaster we left Bora Bora and sailed west.

The wind was fine but the swell was very uncomfortable so it took us both a few days to get used to it and feel more energetic. The wind was directing us too far south so on day two we jibed and then the wind became more SE and we jibed again, John's new system worked very easily and we had main and jenny with varying degrees of reefing depending on wind strength. We had radio "skeds" with the pacific Magellan radio net and with Carango a 55foot Amelle who was on the same route but a little further ahead and faster. The "skeds" reduce the feeling of loneliness on a long ocean passage and are very comforting and also informative. We rolled along and the further we got the calmer the sea became, relatively that is, and when the wind became more southerly we could make a better course. We changed time by one hour on day five as dawn was really late, we had a nasty squall then the wind disappeared and we motor sailed but at least we were on course with the motor and we had a wonderful full moon. On day 7 we had a SW wind so were sailing up wind for a change, one of those windows for yachts going east, but it only lasted for just over 24 hours and it was back to the usual downwind style until it changed again as we approached Nuie. We could not see any land as we approached because Nuie is a very flat coral island. In fact it is the largest uplifted coral island in the world but it has not been lifted very high so we did not see the island until we were about 8nm away, a very smooth black pancake floating on the sea. We radioed Commodore Keith of the Nuie yacht Club to ask how he recommended entering the moorings, which were about half way along the west coast. Should we go north or south of the island? The Commodore advised south so we rounded the southern tip and sailed north up the east coast. With the shelter from the land we dumped the main and went in on jib alone very calmly. We rarely make a night entry but had been assured by Carango that it was easy to drive in and pick up a mooring. We took him at his word and entered as carefully as we could but still managed to run over an FAD (fish aggregating device) about which we had been warned but at night it was impossible to see it. Luckily we passed over it swiftly and the rope cutters on the propeller shaft did their work so we only saw it fly by and it did not snag. The port was illuminated brightly making any leading marks hard to distinguish but we knew the location of the moorings from Carango and we cautiously motored in until we saw the other moored yachts and easily picked up a buoy helpfully painted with illuminous paint. We celebrated with a nice cold Hinano and then slept.

# Nuie June 2016

Nuie is a coral island so anchoring is impossible but the Nuie yacht Club support several mooring buoys off the east coast for visiting yachts otherwise there could be none. If the wind changes to westerly it is a mass exodus as the moorings become untenable but luckily such winds are rare, the trade winds from the SE dominate almost all of the time. Commodore Keith had instructed us to come ashore early to meet the officials to check in so we needed to mantle the new dinghy to get there so no lie in this morning. Landing here was quite something as there was no facility in the commercial port for dinghies and no beaches because of the coral. We went alongside the concrete harbour wall to find a huge hook hanging from an electric hoist on shore. We then had to grab the swinging hook before it caused a head injury, attach it to the Gibson lift, climb onto very slippery steps with the bags and documents and quickly turn on the electric hoist at the top of the steps to lift the dinghy up before the hook came off. In a swell lifting the dinghy up and down a few feet with each wave this was not very easy! Using the electric hoist we could manoeuvre the dinghy onto a dinghy dolly and move it to a dinghy parking space and then most importantly remember to lower the hook down the wall for the next dinghy. After that we were ready for the officials whom we met 1.5 hours later but we had a chance to look around the immediate vicinity. We checked in and then found the famous Nuie yacht club a small hut with internet and some books but no café but this was more than made up for by the marvellous local cafes and restaurants in Alofi the capital where we found ourselves. The restaurants were excellent and when bureaucracy was over we had the most tasty lunch in a shore side café. It tasted so good but perhaps this was in comparison with the on-board cuisine for the last week.

We heard the disastrous news of the referendum on 24th June while in Niue, which was very depressing even though we were thousands of miles away so tried to cheer ourselves up by hiring a car and driving round the small island exploring the numerous coral tracks which are paths leading over and through the coral to the sea. There are occasional small sandy strips so swimming is possible off rocks in some places. The eastern side of the island was in poor shape after a typhoon hit a few years before when many Nuie people moved to New Zealand and never returned so there were many abandoned dwellings and a bleak atmosphere. We saw amazing coral formations and a coral forest on our way round, needless to say nowhere was crowded. On the southern tip of the island there is the only tourist hotel The Matavas resort which is visited mainly by New Zealand tourists. We drove to the university campus passing the very elegant New Zealand ambassadors house, then the golf course and had cocktails in a cliff top bar watching the supply ship from New Zealand start its return journey, this would be a good time to provision! We finished off with an excellent Japanese meal and then back to Baringo after lowering the dinghy with the hook down the wall but the swell was much less now and we were used to the system. Sunday was a quiet day for non-churchgoers and even swimming was forbidden so we planned our next leg to Samoa and checked the weather for the passage which was to the north east. We checked out on Monday 26th June packed the dinghy away and by afternoon were going along the leading line towards the open ocean once more.

Samoa was 400 nm away so it was only two nights out at sea and it was the usual squally bumpy passage we had learnt to expect and as we were quite close hauled the waves were extra bumpy but at 13.30 on 29th June we sighted Upoli Island, the main but not the largest Samoan island.

# Samoa July 2016

Rather than enter the marina in the capital Apia we earmarked Faga-loa Bay along the north coast which we could make before dark which looked straightforward for anchoring for the night. How wrong we were, it was full of reefs and the GPS had us in 1.0 m depth when the depth metre read 50M, we could see the reef but the chart was at least 0.5nm out so we made a hasty retreat and dollied until dawn outside Apia. We had missed the 30th June because of the date line and had therefore arrived on Friday 1st July but we went into Apia harbour and waited for clearance which took some time as we were the last in the queue after the commercial vessels. It took persistent calls to finally enter the marina where half the pontoons had been blown away by a typhoon a few years earlier but there was enough space for us and quarantine and customs arrived promptly and cleared us in.

"Junior" the self-styled marina manager came to see us straight-away and took us to immigration and offered us excursions and other treats so we were a little suspicious but he was honest and indeed took us on an excellent trip round this beautiful island a few days later. We walked into Apia to get the measure of the place and liked what we saw and found a good supermarket, much needed, as provisioning in Nuie had been limited and extremely expensive so we needed fresh fruit and vegetables and bread which always run out the earliest. There was a lively but noisy bar The Edge at the marina so we sampled drink and food there. On Sunday we went to church, we had always intended to go in The Marquesas and the Tuamotus but had never made it so here we were very close and no dinghy ride to get there. It was a wonderful experience seeing all the ladies in their finery and hearing the choir singing beautifully but the downside was a long self-congratulatory sermon by a visiting medical missionary but it was worth it. We had read about the renowned Aggie Grey's hotel in Apia in the cruising guide but it was no longer, it had been taken over by the Sheraton with total loss of historical character and it was not open yet. Junior's tour was on the 4th July a clear sunny day and he took us to Robert Louis Stevenson's home Vailima now a museum but preserved as the home he had lived in, then to a Bahai temple in a beautiful tranquil setting with large gardens surrounding it. Samoa is very mountainous so has many waterfalls one of which we visited and swam in the pool at the bottom. Then a delicious lunch at Seabreeze Hotel, the fish is so deliciously fresh here, then Junior took us to look over Faga-loa bay where the geography of the reefs was easy to see from a height.

We were trying to get to Tokelau one of the rarely visited islands but our negotiations with the Tokelau affairs office in Apia came to nothing so we never made it there so decided to sail directly to Wallis next. We also explored the possibility of sailing to the other Samoan island Savaii but there were no local charts and anchoring did not look that easy so we hired a car and took the ferry over and toured that island, so empty but just enough facilities to make it comfortable for visitors. We spent one night there in a Fale, a sleeping hut on the beach which was magical. There is plenty of interest to see, blow-holes where the guide got dangerously close to the powerful blow of the sea through the larva holes to throw coconuts in to be shot high into the air, a church still standing surrounded by an old larva flow and beautiful waterfalls and verdant mountainous scenery. We wished we had stayed longer but after returning to Upoli we used the car to return to Vailima as we wanted to walk up the hill to see RLS's grave with his apocryphal epitaph. We still had a few more days for errands and maintenance jobs and luckily about five minutes walk from the marina there was a small beach with very good snorkelling which we frequented most afternoons for relaxation after time spent in the town. We planned to leave on Thursday 14th June rather reluctantly as Samoa was such an easy sunny place but in fact we did not leave because we could not get off the pontoon safely with the strong wind and a large neighbour restricting our space and no help available. So we waited until 05.00 the next morning when the wind was light and we got off the pontoon smoothly but it was Friday so we felt obliged to overnight at anchor in the harbour and leave on Saturday.

It was Saturday 16th July so we could now leave, we motored along the north coast of Upoli then Savaii past the Apolima Strait between the two which we had crossed in the ferry, then westward to Wallis. The passage was about 450 nm everything was going well as we motored passed Stevenson's Hotel where we had stayed on Savaii when suddenly the screech of the engine overheating alarm went off. I immediately switched the engine off and on investigation John found the fan belt had broken. We were sure we had a spare but it was rather well hidden in a black plastic bag and folded up very small so John had an unpleasant few moments searching in the spares compartment unable to find it, meanwhile we were drifting closer to the coast! Of course he found it and quickly replaced the broken one and we were on our way again. The wind did not establish until we were quite far out of the lee of Savaii the next morning and then we had a nice SSE breeze so were on a reach. That afternoon while I was off watch the oven fell off its gimballing support on the left side and was tilting alarmingly as a result. I woke to make tea to find this, John had been in the cockpit and not noticed or heard the collapse. No tea today and cold baked beans for supper, luckily cocktails were uninterrupted. We could boil the electric kettle when the generator was on but that was all. The next day the 18th July Wallis was in sight and we went to the Honikulu Pass which is renowned to be quite tricky as it is long and narrow and to our great surprise another yacht appeared so we were able to compare the times we had both calculated to be optimum for entry through the pass and we agreed. It was Wallis time and we were an hour different from Samoan time so we had to wait a little longer for the low water slack and when the water in the pass looked smooth "Seanote" went through and we followed and motored up the buoyed channel to anchor off Mata Utu the capital.

# Wallis July 2016

Wallis also known as Uvea, Futuna and Alofi are the Hoorn islands and are grouped together administratively as a French overseas territory. Wallis is the most attractive for sailors because it has a lagoon whereas Futuna does not and the anchorage there is not sheltered. The people are Polynesian but there are quite a lot of French people living there teachers, police and military, considered by some to be a hard ship posting but it is hard to imagine why, but there were others in search of the lifestyle. Checking in was easy and Mata Utu though small is not very compact and with the total lack of public transport we did a lot of walking. On our first foray we were delighted to find "La Cave de Wallis" a very well stocked wine shop and a Carrefour selling baguettes, the French certainly know how to make their mark in distant parts. Our first priority was to try and get the oven operational so we went to the garage to see if they could do any welding or lend us a soldering iron, but no and after a few visits to other possibilities we drew a blank. However we did arrange car hire but only for the weekend as during the week all the cars are booked by French workers arriving to service the island facilities. While at anchor we managed to put the oven on some support so we could now cook at least but we still needed to find a solution for the next voyage. "Seanote" was still anchored next to us and when they came over for a drink they told us that when we had met at the pass they had almost run out of fuel as they had not been able to buy any with US$ in the northern islands of Fiji, so it must have been very tense for them going through the pass. This was maybe why they had gone first so we could have helped if needed.

We had managed with a struggle to get a local 4G SIM card for the internet which was very sketchy indeed here not surprisingly. We did the necessary provisioning and did a lot of walking which is no bad thing after passage making and sampled a local meal but Mata Utu was not the best anchorage offering no shelter and we were facing directly into the wind. So we moved to Gahi further down the east coast on 21st July which was slightly more sheltered. Seanote was already there as well as another yacht both travelling eastwards.

It was a pleasant bay and we hitch hiked easily into and out of Matu Utu until we picked up the car at the weekend. We drove round the island over the weekend the most notable aspect of which were the amazing churches at least one in every village, each a completely different style and some with marvellous interior decoration. We found a crater lake and in which American war weapons had been sunk after the war but we only saw beautiful white birds soaring over it. We then went to see the Hihifo airport, empty of course as there are not that many flights but it certainly fills up when there is one. We ended the day by joining a church service in the cathedral on the front at Matu Utu listening to the marvellous Polynesian singing, then back to meet the Gahi yachties for supper at the local restaurant. There are no signposts in Wallis not even to the airport but there are no tourists so presumably no need. Sunday was another day of travel and shopping, we found Carrefour, Super U and Intermarche, all very familiar from Chamonix then we drove around the island and hiked to a lake. We had to take the car back on Monday but we had decided to stay in Wallis for the local festival later in the week commemorating the day Wallis and Futuna officially became a French overseas territory. So we hitch hiked in and out of town and did the usual jobs on the boat while waiting. John had miraculously found a spare gimbal in the sanctuary box of random items and we got the oven secured again.

We had booked a tour at the local cultural Centre for the next day as we were now staying to see the festival and some of it was a repeat of what we had found on our own but we were taken to a ruined old Tongan meeting house and possibly palace dating from the Tongan empire which had ruled Wallis in the 10 century. There was not that much left but it was interesting and our guide was keen to impart what knowledge she had. Polynesian history is steeped in mystery as nothing was ever written down and the oral history was lost after the Europeans arrived. So your imagination can run riot trying to construct what actually happened, they were certainly great navigators who over many years spread from China to Easter Island and New Zealand.

We had to go early to customs and immigration as they would all be closed over the festival and we were hoping to leave immediately afterwards. The festivities were over Vanessa's and Henry's birthdays and we saw lots of dancing in front of the king's palace and the accompanying music was very lively, indeed the whole spectacle was very entertaining as was watching the locals all enjoying it as well. We hitched a ride back and hoped to be away the next day. We packed the dinghy away to make an early start but the weather was not good and we missed the time for the pass. We had a rendezvous in Vanuatu with Bob and Sandie Llewellin who were going to sail with us to New Caledonia so there was some time pressure. We checked with Emmanuel for the weather and he advised staying for another three days because of storms en route which we would inevitably encounter. So we followed his advice and were boat bound until 2nd August as we did not want to unpack the dinghy, but there are so many little jobs to do we were not idle and we had Foyle's War on DVD to watch in the evenings which was very entertaining. The weather was squally so we could not do very much swimming around the boat either so we actually managed some reading in the cockpit, we often see other yacht crews doing this but we have hardly ever had the time. The appointed day arrived, the 2nd August and we finally left Gahi Bay. The other yachts were going eastwards and had departed a day earlier to take advantage of the westerly wind. The morning was calm and we watched the Honikulu pass carefully before traversing it and had 2knots pushing us through with just a few eddies. The reefs so close on either side with their breaking waves made it a tense experience. In fact every time we went through a pass tension was high as if we had lost control of the boat we would have been on the reefs in seconds.

We were out in the Pacific again heading south west to Fiji about 245nm as the crow flies but it was not a direct route to Savusavu our destination on Vanua Levu the second largest island in Fiji. The start was a pleasant reach but by early the next day the winds were back to normal and the swell increased so we continued with two reefs in the main sail and a reefed jenny. After two days of quite unpleasant swell we entered the passage between Taveuni island on our port side and Vanua Levu on starboard, with land on both sides the swell decreased and life became sweet again. We jibed round the point going north east to Savusavu and arrived at dawn in calm conditions on 5th August.

# Fiji August 2016

The Copra Shed marina which is situated up a creek was very welcoming and help arrived immediately to help us onto a mooring, despite the early hour. All the usual bureaucratic officials came to the boat to inspect us before we could move to a berth. This time the problem was shore power and finding the right electrical connections to bring electricity to Baringo, but we succeeded finally after much plug changing. It was the start of the Rio Olympics so we could watch some of it on the television here, when it worked. We only had one contact in Fiji from a school friend of John's who had worked here and the contact Geoff just happened to be the owner of the Copra Shed Marina and an experienced sailor, such a coincidentally great stroke of fortune. He took us out around the local area and showed us where John's friend's house was, in fact next to his own! It was pouring with rain so it was a short trip but Geoff showed us the damage to the hotels that had happened during the recent typhoon only a few months earlier. Geoff also gave us a detailed route through the reefs, of which there are so many, to get us over to Vudu point Marina on the east side of Viti Levu. We had studied the charts for a long time thinking about a safe route across and decided to avoid all reefs and take a very long route out at sea but Geoff's route saved us a lot of time and was so easy and very enjoyable as the passages between the reefs were very wide and well-marked.

The marina had most facilities including a very good restaurant and of course our first purchase was a new fan belt. It rained very heavily the first three days and this exposed a leak in the big saloon windows so all the head lining had to come off which makes such a mess to live in but it had to be repaired, not for the first time, but this gave us the time and excuse to watch more Olympic sports hoping for better weather. On Tuesday 11th August we hired a car for the island tour over the mountains to Labasa a sugar cane town on the northern side and it was like a trip to India, wonderful Indian food, colourful saris, Indian shops and of course Indian people. They were running the sugar cane factory on which the town depended. We had an excellent meal and then drove back along the coast and found an Eco Lodge where we had tea with the owners and saw two yachts at anchor in the bay we were overlooking rather wishing we had allowed more time in Fiji as there were some marvellous bays and anchorages. Initially we had not felt it would be an easy place, so had not planned to spend much time there but It proved to be much nicer than we had anticipated. We had been worried about the reported racial tensions between Fijians and Indians which might have created a sinister atmosphere but we neither saw or felt anything of this. In addition we were there when Fiji won the rugby sevens Olympics and so there was great celebration and excitement. We used the car to get the gas cylinders filled which we succeeded in doing here, we carried four cylinders during the trip as filling them was often not possible due to connectivity problems. We also bought four new pillows, the humidity that builds up while the boat is on the hard does nothing for pillow preservation or the preservation of any other fabric on the boat as any Hong Kong boat owner will know.

On 11th August we left the marina said goodbye to Geoff and initially anchored just down the coast off the Cousteau resort in order to make a very early start for the journey across to Vudu Point Marina on the west coast of the main island Viti Levu. We left next morning at 04.30 it was still dark but the start of the passage was initially across the Koro Sea so a clear reef free sail, the reef navigation did not start until later after it was daylight. We followed Geoff's route carefully, some of the passages between the reefs were beaconed but not all but it was a fine day so we could see the reefs easily. The wind was strong up to 40 knots as we crossed the final open water to Viti Levu, through a pass and then we were inside the surrounding reef with all the calm and tranquillity that brings. This inside passage was much wider than it had appeared on the charts and we anchored as instructed by Geoff off Voli point and had a very pleasant night. We continued on around the north coast of Viti Levu in the inside passage the next day. Some of the beacons were missing, and those in place were not as well maintained as the Polynesian navigation marks but the passage was wide and the reefs clearly visible. This was not at all as we had imagined and a very pleasant surprise, and once again we wished we had allowed more time in Fiji. We should have arrived in Vudu Point marina that day but were tempted by another night out at anchor so we spent that night in Saweli Bay and on 14th August we finally tied up at Vudu Point Marina It is an unusual style of marina with all the yachts tied bow to on the inside of a circular basin lined with a concrete wall with appropriate attachments for mooring warps and platforms to get ashore with varying degrees of difficulty depending on the height of the tide. The facilities were very satisfactory but we awoke the next morning to find the next door boat was in the process of eliminating a rat from their vessel, something we had dreaded on our circumnavigation but had not yet happened to us, we had put rat poison down each time we had left Baringo but this reminded us of the ever present possibility of rats. We needed to leave as soon as possible to meet Bob and Sandie in Vanuatu but Emmanuel's forecast was not auspicious so we had to wait a few more days. We found the First Landings resort within walking distance and enjoyed an Indian meal there, Fijian Indian cuisine is first class direct from India. We took the opportunity to visit Lautoka by taxi, a very pleasant town with wide streets and an esplanade. By the 18th August the weather was far from ideal so we delayed another day but we had discovered that paperwork was needed for Bob and Sandie to enter Vanuatu on a one-way ticket. They were going to leave from Australia after their sailing trip so this delay gave us time to organise that while we had access to modern technology in the marina office. We finally extricated ourselves the next day at 16.00, anchored in a nearby bay and prepared for the journey. We met one of the more interesting circumnavigators while in Vudu Point a very plucky Japanese couple in a 38foot X boat, not the typical round the world boat, they had sailed from Japan and were going to New Zealand, they were small in stature which fitted their yacht.

On Saturday 20th August we were underway through the Malolo pass on a westerly heading to Port Vila, Vanuatu. Initially there was little wind but it had picked up by evening. Poppy turned herself off again and we jibed but John's new preventer mechanism worked very well and it was much easier to manage rectifying the jibe. The wind died down again and became more easterly and as we can't sail dead down wind we had to go off course, it became the worst of conditions sloppy sailing with light wind from behind and a beam swell and it certainly did not help John's seasickness. The light wind was later replaced with a series of squalls so a very wakeful night going on main alone with three reefs. The wind shifted to a more favourable ESE the next day but the swell was unpleasant presumably left over from the previous few days of bad weather while we were waiting in the marina. Bob and Sandie had already arrived in Port Vila and were taking some land trips; timing for visitors is often a problem because of weather but as sailors they understood and did not waste their time there. We arrived at 23.00 on 23rd August and decided to go into the Quarantine mooring bay even though it was dark but it was hard work finding an anchoring spot as the depth was very variable either too shallow or too deep and little in between but after two attempts we were settled and the next morning we were escorted into Yachting World moorings. We prepared the forward cabin for Bob and Sandie then we all met for lunch and we were certainly very pleased to see them.

# Vanuatu September 2016

Bob and Sandie moved on board and that evening we celebrated their wedding anniversary at "The Chill" a restaurant overlooking the water recommended by Carango and had an excellent meal, all the dishes we ordered arrived but in a confused order but this did not alter our enjoyment. The next day we did the usual formalities and provisioning and internet, Port Vila is slightly scruffy but the ladies in their frilly party dresses improved the scene. Bob and Sandie had done an island tour but we decided against so we left promptly after 48 hours and headed for Erromango an island to the south en route to Tanna to see a volcano at first hand, health and safety would not have allowed this in many other places! It was a great help having another person on watch for the night out and we anchored off Erromango the next morning. We had the bay to ourselves and swam and enjoyed the beauty and tranquillity of this mountainous island. A canoe arrived bringing paw paw, pamplemousse and bananas and its owner David announced he was the Commodore of the Erromango yacht club and would take us for a tour of the island. We went as agreed and found a beautiful scene with green trees and a slow flowing river with grazing cattle, scenery reminiscent of a Constable painting. We wandered around with David and visited the yacht club which had accommodation and was very clean and neat. We signed the visitor's book and noticed that Carango had preceded us.

We departed for Tanna the next day eagerly anticipating visiting the active volcano there which we thought would be well worth seeing. It was a day sail past other islands which provided shelter from the wind but it certainly picked up in the gaps. We anchored in Resolution Bay, Tanna Island at 16.00 and had it to ourselves. We could see the belching smoke of the volcano as well as lots of smaller steaming vents on the hillsides. Our first visitor the next morning was a guy in his canoe asking us to charge his mobile phone! Technology has obviously arrived in even this faraway island. In fact we found a solar panel powered telephone charging centre when we finally got on shore, which was quite sophisticated and well used. Of course we were here to see the volcano so we organised this straight away with a trip that afternoon, the optimum time for a visit is dusk because the red glowing larva is more dramatic. We met the guide at 15.00 and were driven to the volcano where much to our surprise there was a visitor's centre and lots of tourists, unbeknown to us there was a hotel nearby. We watched some dancing and then had to wait for the chief to decide if the trip to the volcano was safe that day. Luckily the chief gave his assurance and we drove to the base of the volcano and then hiked up to the rim. It was certainly fire and brimstone with a vibrating growl as the crater spewed molten larva and rocks into the air. Each time is seemed to get more fierce and the land shook frighteningly and we thought this is the big one and prepared to run but thankfully it never was. Pieces of magma some quite large were thrown into the air around the rim so hats were advised. It was a mesmerising sight the full force of nature just a few yards away, quite unforgettable. The light was fading so we were herded back to the vans and then the four of us, still stunned by the experience, took our car back to Resolution Bay. Overnight the wind changed with the result that we woke to find Baringo was covered with volcanic ash, this was a first, and it was quite difficult to clean off even with the help of a little light rain. We left later and no sooner were we motoring off the coast of Tanna than John thought he saw an oversized dolphin but it was a broaching whale no further than 100m to starboard so we slowed to let it pass across the bow in safety.

We were now heading to Ouvea one of the Loyalty islands off the west coast of New Caledonia and after a rough overnight sail in the usual 25-30 knots with sea to match we sighted Ouvea on 30th August at 09.00 and sailed to enter through Passe Coetlogon into the Ouvea lagoon but we had to wait for a cargo ship to leave first. The water was a magnificent iridescent turquoise and we were the only vessel there, we had had so many deserted anchorages while in the Pacific that our memories of the crowded Mediterranean made us wonder if we could ever go there again, we had been truly spoilt. The first day there the wind blew 30 knots all day so a shore party did not happen and it was even too rough for a swim. There was a long sandy beach beckoning but this would have to wait. The next day Bob could wait no longer to show off his swimming gear which perfectly matched the colour of the water and he braved the wind and the relative cold and swam, but it was not until the day after that conditions allowed Bob, Sandie and John to go ashore to investigate by which time a New Zealand yacht had joined us in the bay. There was little to find ashore as the main town was much further away up the coast and it remained so windy manoeuvring the dinghy was hard work so we were glad to have some crew with us to help. We prepared to set off the next morning to New Caledonia aiming for the Passe Thio but it would depend on the course we could sail but we wanted to enter the lagoon as far north as possible so we had the maximum sailing inside rather than outside the lagoon on our route round the Southern tip of New Caledonia.

# New Caledonia September 2016

The high mountains of New Caledonia soon came into view, red jagged and irregular and almost certainly why Captain Cook named the island as he did as this would also have been his first view. We achieved our aim and entered through Passe Thio at 14.00 and headed south inside the lagoon and anchored in Toupeti Bay another scenic empty anchorage. The lagoon of New Caledonia is the largest in the world and provides perfect conditions for water-sports and so many beautiful anchorages, in fact a lifetime of sailing could be spent here! The next day we continued on southwards in the lagoon to the next anchorage. New Caledonia is a very long thin island and we were aiming for the southern tip, to round it then sail north again on the western side of the island to Noumea the capital. We anchored again alone in a recommended bay for the second night and we swam in the late afternoon, it was warmer now and on the following morning we did not need an early start so we explored the river which entered the bay in the dinghy, always good fun. Then we left to get through the Canal de Havannah at the southern tip of New Caledonia with the flooding tide. When we arrived the channel was full of eddies, frothing as if a thousand living creatures were battling underneath and the tide was still ebbing! We decided to motor through rather than wait as the Admiralty had described rough water here and it might get even worse, so it was a bumpy ride through but the motor helped us and it was extraordinary to watch the behaviour of the water. We managed only 3.0 knots over the ground of speed through the channel then at 15.00 three hours after we had predicted the tide changed and we went a little faster into Baie de Prony one of the many splendid anchorages in New Caledonia. There was lots of choice of anchoring spots in this large impressive bay and we had a peaceful night, not a ripple to disturb our sleep. We wanted to get to Noumea to check in the next morning which dawned sunny and calm so we left just after 07.00 as there was another channel Canal Woodin to get through ideally with the water with us which we managed, there was nothing like the disturbed water of Canal de Havannah. It was a lovely sail, wonderful scenery with the backdrop of the high New Caledonian mountains. We arrived at Port Moselle Marina at mid-day, tied up and then checked in at the various offices in town. Finally the biosecurity inspector arrived on board and took the remains of our fruit and vegetables from the boat but luckily there was very little left and the local market was about five minutes from the marina with stalls piled high with all varieties of fruit and vegetables. We enjoyed getting acquainted with Noumea a very French city with all the good things that brings, we had some excellent meals and met up again with Yves from "Imagine" in Noumea

Originally Bob was going to sail with us to Australia but we did not want to leave New Caledonia so soon and because we had got slightly behind schedule with the weather delays Bob and Sandie decided to stay and fly to Australia together later on. We now had the delightful prospect of exploring this wonderful lagoon with them. While wandering around the chandleries we spotted a glistening new oven identical to our own and we bought it there and then but it had to be fitted just before we left so we could avoid the import tax. We organised all this easily but had to wait until later to see it in place. Bob and Sandie had a useful contact in Noumea, Herve, who managed super yachts but he kindly agreed to look after our non-super yacht while we were away in Australia later for Antony and Vanessa's wedding celebration there.

We sorted out all the travel arrangements and on 8th September we intended to go to the fabled Isle des Pins about 70 nm to the south east but the wind was so strong from that direction it proved impossible so we retreated to the beautiful Ilot Maitre and picked up a mooring to wait out the wind. The next day was no better so we gave up the idea of Isle des Pins and headed north instead still with 35 knots but at least from behind. We found an earlier anchorage than originally planned so we could get shelter from the strong wind and as we rounded the point into the bay the wind speed hit 50 knots, presumably some land effect so it was a speedy arrival into the bay. The anchorage although beautiful did not offer much shelter from the wind so we could neither swim nor go ashore that day. The scenery around us was very wild and woolly like the country's name sake. The wind is usually lighter in the morning so we snatched the chance of a swim before going north again to Isle Ducros. The cruising guide recommended Baie de Moustiques but fearing what the name implied we tried another bay but we ran aground briefly so returned to Baie de Moustiques hoping the wind was strong enough to stop any insects reaching the boat. It was a windy night so early next morning before the wind picked up we moved to what we hoped was a more sheltered side of the bay and re-anchored. It was a quieter day anyway and we went ashore and found wild horses and admired the savage scenery around us which was very beautiful. The frustrating restrictions of the wind were disappointing as this limited our shore explorations and swimming off the boat but it was quite restful in some ways with siestas and evenings watching DVDs and early nights. On 12th September we started the return to Noumea stopping at another anchorage on the way down in which there was a new town being constructed and it did not look very attractive so we then returned to Ilot Maitre which is a lovely small tropical island with a small resort and a coral reef in good condition within easy swimming reach. There were lots of kite surfers speeding along the lee shore, plenty of wind but no waves so ideal conditions for them. We returned to Port Moselle on 14th September as Bob and Sandie were leaving the next day.

After Bob and Sandie had gone we hired a car to see the national park Riviere Bleu but not before we had a look at Yate where we had anchored after entry into the lagoon. Riviere Bleu is the home of the national flightless bird of New Caledonia the cagou which is a beautiful delicate grey bird and very shy but which thanks to our guide we did see. It was now that we had another try for Isle des Pins as the wind was still SE on the nose but not nearly as strong as before. On 17th September we left at 11.15 so got a foul tide in Canal Woodin only making 2-3 knots over the ground but we were anchoring off Isle Ouen on the western side of the canal which was not far and once in the anchorage the effect of the tide disappeared and we had a wonderful moonlit night. Really there is a lifetime's sailing in the New Caledonian lagoon, so many perfect anchorages, so empty and flat water despite the wind. We reached Isle des Pins at 15.30 the next day after a motorsail into the wind. Here the bay was quite crowded but it is an exceptionally beautiful place so we had to share it. We hired bikes the first day to Vao admiring yet another church and more beautiful beaches with turquoise water but when we returned the bikes I realised I had lost the camera. We retraced our steps and went to the hotel where we had had coffee but no sign of it, what a blow, not the camera of course but the photos but nobody had seen it. We dejectedly returned to Baringo and just as we finished lunch a dinghy came towards us with a rather nice Frenchman holding our camera aloft. He had found it, looked at the photos and seen the name of the boat and asked another sailor to bring him and the camera out to us in his dinghy. I think he must have been a policeman because of his detective work finding the owners of the camera and he only asked for a kiss as thanks, not too much of a problem!

The Piscine naturelle here is an amazing natural swimming pool surrounded by coral reefs with clear water washed by the tides and indeed it almost empties at low tide. The best way to get there is by pirogue, a local canoe with a small sail, which goes across a lagoon with curious limestone rocky outcrops on the way, then it is walking through jungle and across a riverbed to the piscine. Of course it is popular but its natural beauty is not spoiled as there are no facilities to ruin the picture. The next day we hired a car to tour the island and felt a great need to return to the Piscine, it is so unusual and natural as its name suggests and the water is warm because it is shallow and the colours so wonderful. We could have easily stayed longer here, it is indeed a magical island, unspoilt even though it is popular with tourists and yachties. However, the next day we motorsailed back and made it to Baie de Prony just before the Canal de Woodin to anchor and try for a better tide in the morning. This we got and we were soon in our berth at Port Moselle to be greeted by "Ganesh" whom we met later in the marina bar to catch up. On Saturday 24th September we flew out to Brisbane, then to Sydney to see Malcom and Glynis and finally to Melbourne to join Vanessa and Antony for their Australian wedding celebrations.

# CHAPTER TWENTY SIX

# New Caledonia to Australia

## *November 2016*

We arrived back in Port Moselle on 8th November to prepare the final passage of the season to Bundaberg, the closest port in Australia to New Caledonia so a popular route. We had joined the Down Under Rally, a yearly event to help cruisers cross from New Caledonia to Bundaberg in company and with it a few discounts and gifts as well as information. We were too late for the rally itself but that did not seem to matter to the organisers. The money we paid them was outweighed by the discount we received in the Bundaberg marina where we were putting Baringo in the hard for the summer (our winter).

We had to get the new oven fitted now just before we left New Caledonia to avoid the tax, luckily the old oven was still cooking and gimballing but probably not for much longer. The fitter arrived but some fittings were not correct so he left the oven on the saloon floor, so no hot dinner that evening, but he returned the next day and fitted it with new pipes and took the old oven away. How smart and shiny the galley looked now! So gleaming I felt I could hardly cook. We started the check -out procedure and had a marvellous supper at "Le Marmite et Tire Bouchon" which had been recommended by Yves and more than lived up to his recommendation. It was last minute errands for the next two days, always the same worry about running out of food on a long passage, although the calculated length is easy to provide for who knows if we could be becalmed and engineless and out at sea for longer than anticipated so inevitably we always overprovisioned. It was here we heard of the next political catastrophe Trump was elected President of the United States, oh dear.

The 13th November was the day we left for Isle Signal on the way to Dunbea pass, the exit from the New Caledonia lagoon. We used the time here to clean the hull to improve our speed on the crossing. We had been going progressively slower over the last few weeks despite occasional cleaning attempts so it needed some serious work. John took the gas cylinder so could go deeper under the hull and clean the propeller and shaft, we worked hard to clear the growth along the hull which was really thick after the stay in Port Moselle but we also managed some time for snorkelling. We met the couple moored near us while viewing the coral and they were going in the same direction so we arranged a radio sked. with them for the crossing. We checked our SSB radios that evening and everything worked, the weather looked favourable and so next morning we checked with Emmanuel if it was clear to go, and it was. We woke to find Platinum IV had already gone but we spoke to Vanessa and Henry first and by 10.50 the wind was quieter and we motored in a light wind in a calm sea, we were still inside the lagoon, and left through Dunbea Pass. The first two days were sunny and we had a full moon, always very welcome, the trade winds were as normal with quite a rough sea but we were making good progress. The weather was often sunny but as always occasional squalls passing by not always hitting us thankfully, so we made good speeds and the wind became more southerly on day five so we could move a little further north nearer the correct course. As we approached the Australian coast we were over flown by a coast guard aeroplane to whom we were supposed to reply on VHF, as we learnt later, but as our VHF was turned down we did not hear their call, so we had not replied. We were not accustomed to the Australian surveillance! We had been warned about the sudden storms that may hit as we neared the Australian coast and which were impossible to see coming. We got one as described at 19.20 on 20th November and the boat rounded furiously to the wind and Poppy could not cope, we dumped the main very quickly, the beauty of single line reefing, and then continued on the furled little jenny alone. We later discovered that the sudden force on the little jenny during a jibe had torn the terminal fitting off the slider! It remained rough for the rest of that night as we approached the coast which we could not see as this part of Queensland is very flat, quite unlike the majestic mountains of New Caledonia which can be seen from afar. As we approached the day after the storm we jibed as we had somehow slipped too far south and came up to the cardinal mark on rocks off Fraser Island which marks the entry to Hervey Bay at 02.30 on 21st November. We had hoped to get some relief from the swell on entering Hervey Bay but it was not to be. Later on the same morning at 10.29 we sighted a small insignificant hump on the horizon and this was Australia, a rather understated sighting for such a huge landmass, no wonder the early navigators kept missing it. We sailed slowly across Hervey Bay not wanting to arrive too early so we could delay the inspections until the following day. We knew all our fresh food would be confiscated as biosecurity is very strict in Australia and a twenty four hour delay would give us a chance to eat some more. We found the cardinal mark to the long runway of lights into the Burnett River where the marina was, followed the path in and anchored in the river opposite the marina berths. Platinum IV had arrived and we would meet them the next day. This was the end of the Pacific sailing and what would turn out to be the highlight of our circumnavigation, but there was more to come to complete in the following year.

Bundaberg Marina was first class, clean, well maintained and efficient with friendly staff and lots of help to berth alongside. Once berthed the following morning we had to wait for the authorities and we were thoroughly checked for termites but had the chance to eat the last of the fruit and salad for lunch before what remained was confiscated, including pumpkin seeds which had come from Australia. The inspector was a very large Torres Strait Islander and managed to break part of the wooden toe rail by pulling on the stanchion to get on. We had a delightful and unexpected welcome from the OCC (Ocean Cruising Club) representative who happened to be there and then another welcome drink from Platinum IV, so a very sociable arrival. We needed to arrange a haul out date and prepare Baringo for that, do some shopping and organise communications with an Australian SIM card, but it was all quite easy in the local village Burnett Heads. The marina had excellent facilities, spotless showers, a well -stocked chandlery and a restaurant and was walking distance from Burnett Heads.

We were lifted out on 29th November and we had booked into the cabins at the Burnett Heads caravan park rather than stay on board on the hard. They were just perfect with the colourful rainbow lorikeets who seemed quite tame flying around feeding in the bushes just outside the front door and occasional wild kangaroos on the grass in front such a joy to see. We could hire a car from the marina so spent a day having a look around the area, mile after mile of sugar cane and very flat with only one unspectacular mound which is presumably what we saw from the sea but we did find what were purported to be meteor craters to add to the excitement. It was quiet and the roads were in good condition and Bundaberg is a typical Queensland town with old fashioned public houses and wooden buildings and of course the rum factory.

We left on 2nd December for Europe and hopefully our first complete skiing season for a few years as we were no longer working in Hong Kong.

**Crew at start of Pacific crossing**

**Malcolm's catch**

**Downwind sailing in the Pacific**

**Approaching Marquesas at sunset**

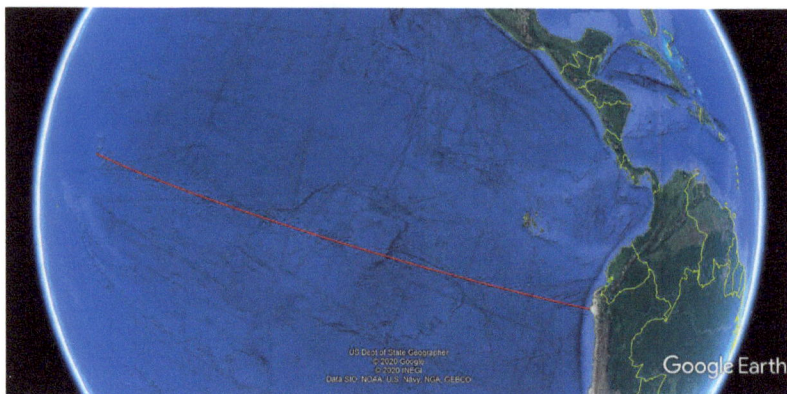

**Pacific route**

**Gauguin's grave Hiva Oa**

**Baie de Vierges, Fatu Hiva**

**Ua Pou Marquesas**

**Tikki**

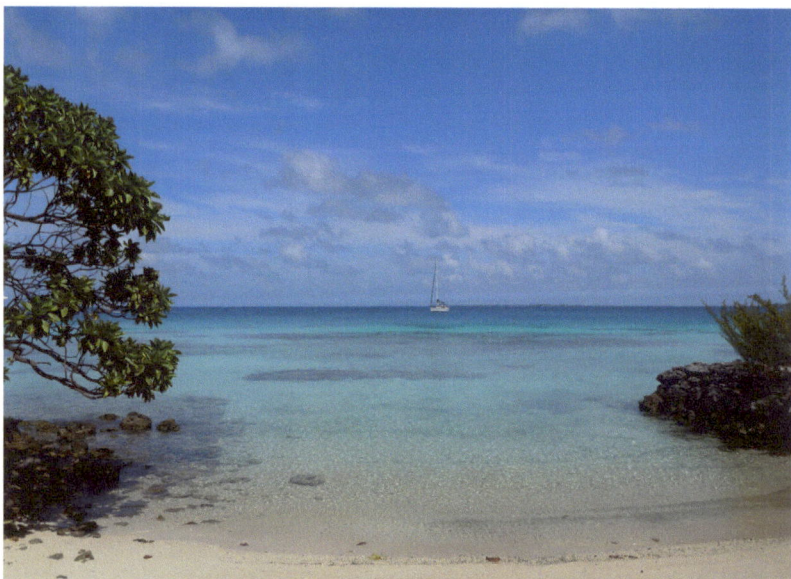

**Anchorage in Fakarawa island Tuomotus**

**Avea bay Huahine island**

**Outside the reef of Bora Bora**

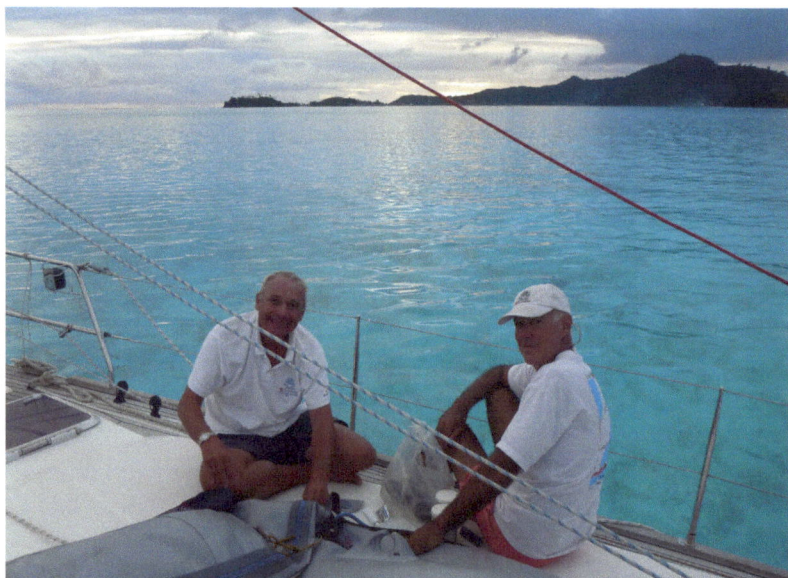

**Engineering department at work in Bora Bora**

**Gift of bananas**

**Bird**

**Local ladies lunching Tikehau**

**Pacific sunset**

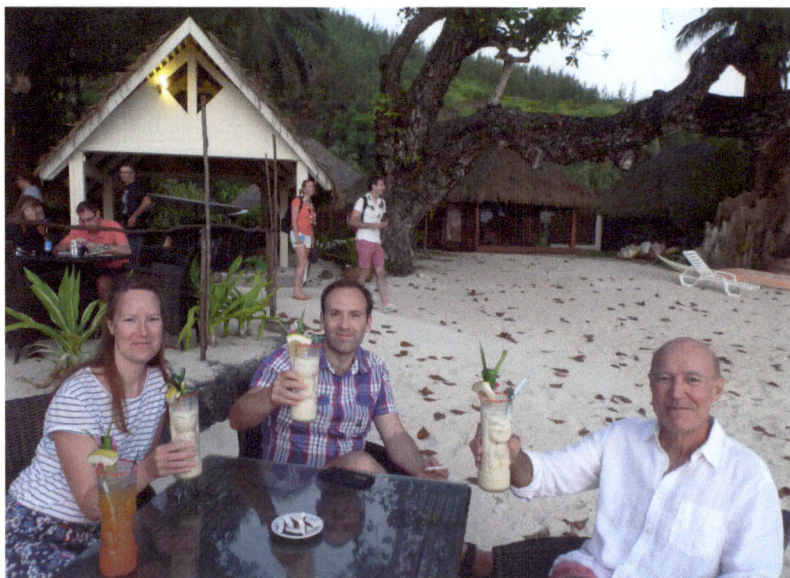

**Cocktails in Avea Hauhine with Vanessa and Antony**

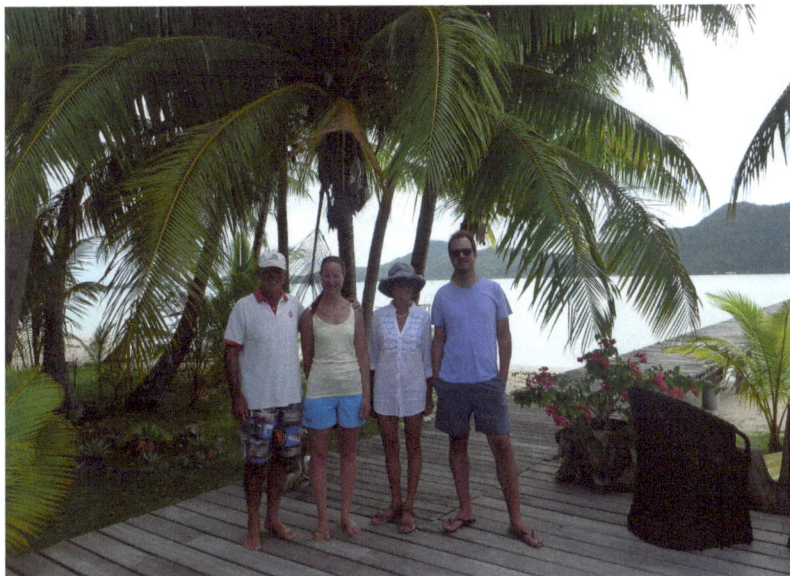

**Family at Russian hotel Bora Bora**

**Turquoise water in Bora Bora**

**Raiatea carenage**

**Mooring at Niue**

**Gibson lift in action**

**Coral chasm in Niue**

**Shore line of Niue, impossible to anchor**

**Cathedral Apia Harbour Samoa**

Church in solidified lava

RLS grave

**Wallis island Matu Utu**

Cave de Wallis

**Church interior Wallis Island**

**Wallis celebration of French connection**

**Savusavu Fiji**

**Coprashed marina Fifi**

**Sugar cane lorries queuing into factory Fiji**

**Tanna volcano Vanuatu**

New Caledonia East Coast

New Caledonia West Coast

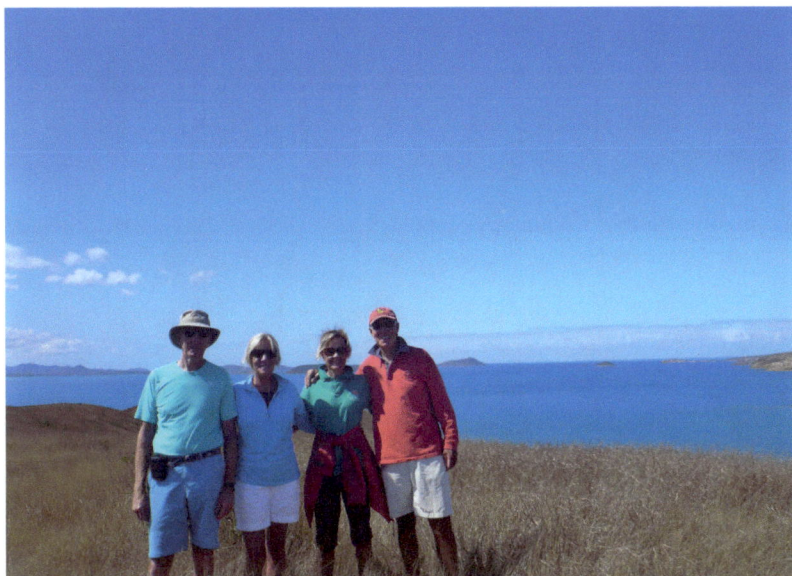

**With Llewellins, West Coast New Caledonia**

**Ile des pins**

**End of the Pacific Passage, Bundaberg Australia**

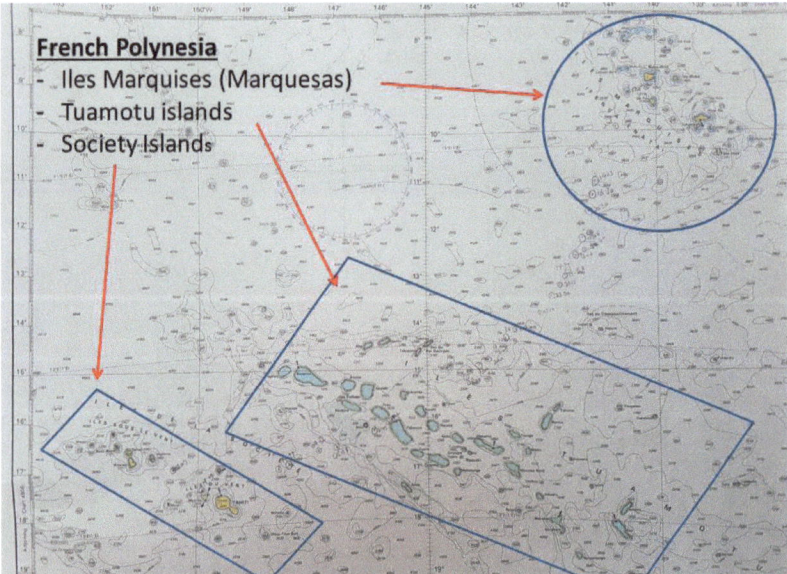

**Map of Polynesia**

CIRCUMNAVIGATION

# PART FOUR

# CHAPTER TWENTY SEVEN

# Bundaberg and Hervey Bay, Queensland Australia

## *May 2017*

On May 8th 2017 we returned to Baringo. We decided to stay on board on the hard this time, hoping the time would be short as the work needed on Baringo had already started, a mark of the Australian efficiency here. A storm came over maybe part of the typhoon near New Caledonia and it was also quite cold. We did the usual pre water entry checks and provisioned at the IGA supermarket in Burnett Heads, we needed ice to keep the fridge cool while on the hard as we could not run it on the electricity without being in the water. Luckily IGA ran transport back to the marina so bringing back heavy things to the boat was easy, really a wonderful service. After three days we were lowered back into the water at high tide and helped back onto the pontoon without incident.

There had been a few storms as expected over the summer in Bundaberg and during one of them two of our mousing lines had broken and we found the advice in the electronics bible to rethread them using bicycle chain but actually it was too thick so we made our own tool, a shackle pin with a hole in it to which we could tie the loose end of the mousing line, heavy enough to fall but slim enough to enter the hole in the mast! The sails were being repaired, almost a yearly task as the winds are so strong in the oceans and the sails are up day and night. The main is always the hardest work to get on with the cars and the split pins to be individually attached and then the sail cover, the lazy jacks and reefing lines. On 13th May we received a call from Vanessa to tell us she was pregnant, wonderful news but the pregnancy was making her feel very ill so we returned to look after her on 15th May leaving Baringo in the water half ready for sailing.

We stayed for two months until Vanessa felt better and then it was Henry and Claudia's wedding in Chamonix on July 29th also Henry's birthday. It was a very happy occasion; a weekend of celebration and parties and Vanessa was well enough to fulfil her bridesmaid's duties although looking a little larger now!

On 6th august we returned to Baringo again and decided we could not go further north and make it to Indonesia and Malaysia this year and we could not leave Baringo any further north along the Queensland coast because the typhoon risk was too high and the insurance company would not permit this anyway. So, we did some local sailing around Hervey Bay which lies between Fraser island and the Queensland coast and is a favourite breeding ground for the migrating Humpback whales. We had a ghastly journey back by air from Geneva with serious delays and all the knock-on effects including a twenty four hour stay in Dubai which was less than inspiring. We were both very tired and had picked up the inevitable colds on the way after so much waiting in airports and queuing for hours. We gradually recovered and continued preparing Baringo for the Hervey Bay excursion, we were quite looking forward to some easy calm sailing without any overnights! We had also been in discussions with an agent to sell the boat in Australia but the tax implications were too tricky, tax needed to be paid before the boat could be marketed and if the boat did not sell and we left Australia the tax was not refunded. After the grim journey we had just had from France to Bundaberg we decided we should get Baringo a little closer to sell her and also we could complete the circumnavigation. So we booked Baringo into the hard standing for a second year for the summer (our winter), luckily there is no shortage of space here for boats the land is flat and empty for miles around.

In the process of rethreading the mousing lines John discovered the rigging was torn again, not in the same place -the starboard intermediate this time- but it would have to be repaired of course but luckily we were not in a great hurry as the rigger had to come from Brisbane.

We heard the sad news on 10th August that Antony's father had died and so we flew to Melbourne for Ian's memorial service on 17th August. Vanessa was not able to go because of her pregnancy. After that we were meeting Diane and family from Hong Kong on the sunshine coast, we had planned to take the boat there but with the disruptions this year time had run out so it was more land travel, but very enjoyable and interesting to see that part of the coast. We returned on 21st August and Colin the rigger arrived on 25th August and renewed the broken bits. As usual there seemed to be the usual myriads of small jobs to be done before we could finally leave and also the weather forecast was not that good so there always seemed a reason for procrastination but we did need to get Baringo out of the marina soon! The outboard motor was giving problems, I think we had left the fuel in the tank rather than draining it out and with the summer heat it had become sticky and blocked the outlet pipe to the engine, apparently a design fault and quite common so we found out later. Finally, on 27th August we were at anchor outside the marina for the night, to hoist the dinghy on board and get away early on 28th August which we did and we sailed into Hervey Bay heading due east toward Rooney Point the northern tip of Fraser Island.

## Hervey Bay, Queensland Australia, September 2017

We had a good sail over to the east as the wind that day was more from the SE so close reach in 22knots resulting in a very pleasant crossing. We had discovered our port winch had jammed which was surprising as we felt we had given them all tender loving care over the years carefully following the Lewmar instructions and admiring their amazing construction and engineering which enabled them to take such force at times but using such tiny springs and other minute metal parts to do it. We had two port winches so hoped we could manage with one on an inland water. Baringo was pleased to be free again and we had a peaceful first night off Fraser island. It is the largest sand island in the world and the beach on the Hervey bay side seemed infinite and we could anchor anywhere along its length going south towards the passage around the southern tip to the open sea. We saw whales every day and could hear them singing to each other at night through the hull, they came very close to the boat but we never felt threatened as I think these whales are used to coming here every year to breed and so know all about man made vessels. We tried to tackle the jammed winch the next morning but on dismantling it we found the mechanism was totally stuck rather than broken and despite oil and vinegar applications nothing moved. We had to forget it for the moment and maybe order a new one for next year. We stayed put for the next day going ashore in the dinghy when the wind allowed, the outboard was still not working quite as it should and there was a strong wind despite being on the sheltered side of Fraser island, but exploring the infinite sand was amazing, sand as far as the eye could see and very empty although we did have the company of two motor boats and another yacht but with so much space they were scarcely noticeable. On 31st August the wind had picked up even more and being so close to the northern tip of Fraser island we experienced a swell of about 1.0 M presumably coming round the northern tip of the island, all the other vessels had moved out of the discomfort zone so we followed and went further south following the long sandy beach and anchored off a lagoon which we could explore the following day. Catamarans and small draught vessels could enter the lagoon but it was certainly not for us. We met one of the other yachts while walking and they advised us to carry sticks in case a dingo approached us, a useful piece of local knowledge which we followed. We did see a dingo on a later forest walk but it did not show much interest in us, maybe it saw our dingo sticks!

Further down Fraser Island we had to cross the Sandy Strait which is quite shallow but of course well marked, it is safety conscious Australia, and we sailed down to Booker island and anchored off there to wait overnight for a high tide the next day to get around Boonlye point which we could only do at high tide and even then our depth went to 0.8M below the keel. We woke early for the tide but did not see any of the other anchored yachts looking as if they were moving so we waited, checked the tide tables and despite seeming to be the only ones to move we weighed the anchor and left but just as we did another yacht went ahead and we followed it through the shallow passage which was very reassuring. We continued all the way to Tin Can Inlet in a strong northerly wind as there was not enough space in the recommended shelter of Gary's anchorage. On the way down we passed the Wide Bay Bar which leads out into the ocean and is the route to take going to Brisbane but it requires careful timing as it is shallow and the full force of the ocean enters and exits with the tide so conditions can become rather dangerous. We were not heading out there thankfully.

We arrived as far south as we could go and anchored in the Great Sandy Strait marine park with many house boats, yachts and fishing vessels. Although the water was flat the wind blew as Fraser island is not that high and the winds always seemed strong whatever direction they came from. The northerlies start late in the season around now so yachts that have ventured north along the Queensland coast in the winter can now return if they have not gone too far. On a calm morning on 6th September we ventured ashore to explore Snapper Creek which flows into Tin Can Inlet and found a yacht club and a restaurant where we returned the following morning for a full Australian breakfast and then strolled round the seaside park which was very neat and tidy with lots of information about the local birds. Even here which is not a place of chic style or affluence everything was well maintained and clean. This is something we found everywhere in Australia and made travelling there very pleasant.

On 8th September it was time to head north again and as a southerly wind arrived so we used it to sail north and this time found a space in Garry's Anchorage. We passed the Wide Bay Bar and as it was calm several yachts were doing the passage through that day. Garry's anchorage is popular during the strong winds as it is very sheltered from all directions but it was calm today so Garry's was quite empty. It is a good place from which to walk in the Fraser Island forest it was here we saw our first Dingo who followed us back to the dinghy. We planned to leave the next morning to get the tide through the shallow channel but we mistimed it and just anchored on the side of the channel and waited for the next day. We considered a dark transit because it looked well marked and easy during the day but contemplating it at night we decided against. How the dark changes the appearance of things, everything always looks more menacing. We got through the next morning, so easy in daylight and we headed towards the local Urangan marina as we needed more provisions and ...the internet! Our needs fulfilled we left the after two nights but into a strong north westerly wind which was not ideal for getting back into Bundaberg. We tried to stay in the marina for longer but there was no space so it was out into the sea again and we had a good sail despite the adverse wind direction and anchored in the Mary River estuary. We stayed all the next day in the estuary waiting out the strong northerly wind with about five other boats who were all much further up the river where we could not go because of our draft. Of course they looked as if they were much more sheltered so we let out more anchor chain to secure our position and waited for the southerly wind forecast for the next day. It arrived with gusto and suddenly we were on a lee shore with more than enough anchor chain out to get uncomfortably close so it was a speedy departure to avoid actually making contact with the shore. It was quite rough outside the confines of the river estuary but as the wind was behind us from the south it was not too uncomfortable, in fact better than expected, so we sailed on to Woody Island and anchored there overnight. The southerly wind was blowing the next morning so we headed north towards the Burnett River. During the day the wind gradually veered SE the E then NE but we managed to sail all the way to the wonderful "runway" lights which guide yachts from quite far out into the Burnett River and we were anchored in the river by 16.30.

On 10th September we returned to the Marina and started the

process of packing up Baringo for another summer (our winter) on the hard. We had not thought we would spend so much time in Bundaberg but we grew to like it, the Marina was really excellent and all the staff so helpful and pleasant and everything was so convenient. We went to the excellent huts in the Burnett Heads camp site for our last night rather than face the rigours of staying on Baringo on the hard and then left on 20th September.

# CHAPTER TWENTY EIGHT

# The Queensland Coast
# Bundaberg to Cairns

*April – September 2018*

The 9th April 2018 saw us back on board Baringo and there she was on the hard as we had left her. There is always some anxiety on the final approach to get our first glimpse but here at least we felt we could rely on the marina to tell us of any major disasters if they had happened. The flight had been trouble free this time so we felt more like tackling the task of getting afloat quickly. It had been a very stormy summer and two boats in the marina hardstanding had been blown over, fortunately neither were next to us but in one case the foresails which had not been stowed had unfurled and caused the boat to fall and the other was a catamaran which had just been lifted up by the wind and deposited onto another vessel. We felt all the work getting the sails down each season had been worth it! Also during the time we were away the Lady Musgrave a small passenger boat taking tourists to the nearby Lady Musgrave island had crashed into the marina pontoons and not only damaged the outer pontoons but also the boats alongside them. Apparently a new captain had been driving that day and had not been told how to operate the second engine so when the first one failed he lost control. So it had been quite an eventful season for the marina and we felt relieved to have escaped damage. The perennial problem, or one of them, on arriving back after a long absence is finding things because stowage had usually been done in a hurry and we hid anything that might be tempting such as torches, the knife, spanners, binoculars and radio equipment to mention a few so it often took some time and patience to unearth them all from their secret places.

On 12th April Baringo was lowered into the water and we were back in the marina to finish the departure preparations. There was always help on hand here as getting into the berth was tricky because of the tide and the wind, Baringo is high sided and so has significant windage and no bow thruster. We had a new water tank this year after continuous leaks despite two repairs in Raiatea and also a new big jenny which had arrived from Hong Kong. We had reluctantly decided against the extra expenditure of a tape drive sail and opted for the cheaper Dacron as it was to be our final year sailing. The tape drive sail had been excellent and lasted a long time given its usage and maintained its shape and most importantly was aesthetically pleasing, so now our foresails did not match but as they were rarely flown together perhaps this was not such a problem. It was a pity we could not manage with the old one for the final year but it would not have been worth the risk as it was this sail that got the least rest. The Queensland clock was not to our liking as it was light very early in the morning and dark by 17.00 so not suitable for us as late risers, it seemed to be dark very soon after we had started our afternoon! The next few days were spent putting the halyards back, the mousing had held up this time, getting the sails and covers back on and erecting the wind generator which was now much easier after the Canadian electrician in Raiatea had organised the wiring more efficiently. We had to change to Australian gas cylinders now because we could not fill our own and they were looking decidedly rusty, as if they might puncture any time so beautiful new shiny white new cylinders arrived and miraculously the chandlery made the connections work so we would have hot meals for the rest of the journey.

We travelled to Brisbane on 18th April to collect the new water tank and take the life raft to be serviced which was well overdue as we had been unable to get this done anywhere in Polynesia, it was not a French brand! We stayed with our friends Robin and Jane Bradbear, medical friends from early houseman days, and their wonderful brown spotted dalmatian dog Bronte. It made our time there fun and gave us a chance to look around Brisbane. We actually bought a new four-man life raft rather than service the eight man one we had bought for the Philippines races when we did have eight crew. The expert at the servicing centre said that if we were two people in an eight man raft it was likely to roll over and over and would be very dangerous as well as being unpleasant. He managed to sell the eight man one later which defrayed some of the cost of the new one. The philosophy for sailing really has to be avoiding serious regrets about expenditure when in awkward and perhaps dangerous situations out in the ocean when it would be too late to wish you had spent those extra few dollars.

We were back in the marina by the 18th April and arranged for the water tank to be fitted and were pleased to find the new life raft fitted into our locker easily as although it was a smaller raft the container was different and we had had some doubts but they were pleasantly and quickly dispelled. The marina here had started life as a fishing port and this industry was still going alongside the marina and there was a fish bar and a fish shop next to the marina office where we could buy either cooked fish or fish to cook, all of course so very fresh and very delicious, so we made full use of both facilities while we were there. Every Friday evening there was a cruisers party in the marina with free beer and wine and some sausages and bread so for us the former was more interesting! This time we went along and met several sailors doing the same route as us, as well as the local boats cruising the Queensland coast in both directions and it turned out to be a fruitful evening as some of the sailors we met proved a great help further down the line when they were ahead of us. We had a new problem this year and that was to mend the holding tank pump because we planned to cruise the Whitsunday island on our way north and a holding tank was required to cruise there. We had not used it for the last few years so had not bothered to repair it. There were always plenty of other repairs to do but this time there was no escape but after John dismantled it, cleaned it and checked the electrical connections it worked! We mended the jammed winch with the new parts but in the meantime we had discovered a can -do engineer Trevor in the more industrial part of the marina and had taken the old winch to him as well as the stuck wheel for the step hoisting mechanism and he fixed both in a trice. Clearly it was a matter of the right tools as we had struggled for hours with both items without any sign of success and had broken a clamp in the process! We had lost Emmanuel our weather forecaster this year nobody we asked could trace him but at least we knew up the Queensland coast the forecasting would be available on VHF and accurate.

The 1st May, John's birthday and departure day but the wind was so strong by the time we had done the last minute errands and paid our debts we delayed until the following day to try and leave earlier when the wind is usually lighter. We spent the night of the 2nd May anchored in the Burnett River to rig John's new preventer system and then we were as ready as possible for the open sea. We had planned to sail overnight the first night out but the trade winds were strong 25-30 knots and the sea rough and when we heard over the radio another sailing vessel being advised to stop at Roundhill Creek and as we were feeling less and less like an overnight sail we wondered if we could follow suit. We contacted the VMR (volunteer marine reserve) to discuss our options. The VMR stations are all the way up the coast and it is rather like the air traffic control system, you check in from one to the other as you move up the coast. Apparently they are not meant to give advice but luckily for us they broke this rule occasionally and that evening we received precise instructions from them about where to anchor with our draught in Roundhill Bay. We could not get into the more sheltered creek and although it was still quite rolly in the bay it was a big improvement on being out at sea. Many of the anchorages up the Queensland coast are river estuaries and shallow so it was a continuing problem trying to find enough shelter as we were unable to get very far into the rivers. Catamarans are much better suited to sailing along this coast and we saw plenty of them anchored in sheltered water while we sat outside in the wind and the swell!

The next morning we tested our safety alarms and I set off my personal EPIRB accidentally so again the VMR to the rescue, they had heard the signal but put two and two together that it was us and unlikely to be an emergency in the bay. We called them on the VHF and they cancelled the call but it was a real test which was reassuring although inadvertent. We tried for another overnight sail but the sea was very rough and because we had a choice as we were near the coast we stopped again in Pancake Creek which everyone said was very beautiful and indeed we had planned to spend some time there originally but with the preparations taking a long time we now did not have enough time for that but we did get a flavour of it as we arrived by lunchtime. We had the excellent Alan Lucas pilot book which described all the anchorages of the Queensland Coast in great detail and with his own depth measurements so it was easy to choose the best ones for us all the way up. The next one we chose was Hummocky Island a very pretty small island with a rounded hilltop. We passed Gladstone a large industrial aluminium port on the way up and heard the VMR hard at work keeping track of the day boats going out to the reef to ensure they all returned safely and keeping a watchful radio eye on everyone, such an excellent service. Hummocky was a good anchorage, a small bay but we were the only vessel and the wind was calm.

Our next stop was Great Keppel Island a popular stop along the coast so several yachts at anchor in the bay including some we had met in Bundaberg, but how the wind blew here! Luckily we went ashore the first day and walked along the beach but the next day we were boat bound with 30 knots of wind and 40 knot gusts but the waves were reasonably flat. We had meant to go to the marina that day but delayed for twenty four hours as the wind was forecast to be less by then. We were flying to Hong Kong as we had sold our flat and needed to sign documents in person. John was then going to Beijing to work and we were leaving Baringo in the marina while we were away. The wind was less the next day but it was pouring with rain as we motored over to Rosslyn Bay Marina where luckily help was on hand to get alongside and the next day 8th May we flew out of Rockhampton the beef capital of Australia.

I returned on 15th May after the successful sale of the flat and John arrived on 21st May and we left the marina on 22rd may. I wrote some of the book while I had the time and provisioned in the local town Yeppoon which was an easy bus ride away. The marina was very pleasant with good facilities something we would find most of the way up the coast in the marinas we stopped in. We left the marina and anchored off Keppel North island just opposite and slightly north of the previous island to finalise Baringo for another passage. We were meeting Jane Houng from Hong Kong in Airlie Beach in the Whitsunday islands so had another deadline to meet so could only hope the weather permitted our timely arrival. The trade winds really blow very strongly along this coast and at this time of the year are at their strongest and although the sea was relatively flat inside the barrier reef Baringo could take quite a hammering when out in these winds so we tried to avoid the really strong days where possible. We left at 06.00 on 23rd May heading for Pearl island and had a good sail with jenny alone and with a few planned jibes we arrived at Pearl Bay early so decided to continue to Island Head Creek to get a few extra miles in, but this proved a bad decision. Island Head Creek was very shallow, without navigation marks and with lots of sandbanks so the anchorages were either too deep, too shallow or too close to a sandbank. After a near miss with one of the sandbanks we retreated and tried to hurry back to Pearl Island against the wind and tide and anchored there just before dark.

It was a long run to the next anchorage off South Percy Island, the only possible trade wind anchorage on this stretch of the coast so not much choice. We had a lot of wind shifts that day with rain as well so we worked accommodating it all and we arrived before dark and chose Alan Lucas's recommended spot to shelter from the strong winds we knew were coming over the next few days. It was a difficult anchorage as the bottom was stony, after all we were in Rocky Ledge Bay! The tide was about 4 meters so we needed enough chain to allow for that and used the anchor Buddy this time as with the strong tide we would swing and we wanted to avoid getting the chain around the keel. We had heard this rather alarming story from an Australian in Taha'a about how it had happened to him, not something we could have thought possible but we were now aware of it in the prevailing wind and tide conditions here. Overnight the wind blew fiercely and both snubbers had come off overnight as well as the extra rope we had put on the chain to take the strain off the windlass. Because the boat was sitting to the strong tide and not the wind the snubbers became loose and non-functioning and then had undone. By morning as well as the loose now non-functional snubbers all the chain had come out and we just caught it before the string in the anchor locker took the strain and would have immediately broken with the loss of chain and anchor. With all the chain that had come out the buddy was stuck on the bottom now fouling the chain and holding the boat down. We motored forward to take the strain off and the Buddy freed and we retied the snubbers and then remembered the anchor chain hook which Roger Eastham the boat yard manager in Hong Kong had added while he was looking after Baringo. We had very rarely used it preferring the snubbers but in this situation it worked perfectly taking the strain when the snubbers did not. How thankful we were that we had it and the new system of the snubbers and the hook worked excellently. The wind blew and blew and it as here that we experienced "bullets" for the first time, really strong sudden gusts of wind of at least 60 knots hitting the boat making her swing furiously on the anchor chain such that during one such bullet the snubber snapped! We then had to raise the anchor chain to replace the broken snubber in between the horrible bullets. In addition, to add to the already unpleasant enough experience as Baringo swung with the wind and tide the chain moved across the rocky bottom making a sickening grinding noise and a vibration we could feel below in the saloon. The whole boat seemed to shudder in a way we could feel in our bones, it really was the worst anchorage we had ever had easily beating the excessively rolling one we had had in Thailand. We considered leaving for West Bay on North Percy island but it looked unprotected and small and we did not want to have a wasted journey and have to return. We sat out the next day dreading the afternoon bullets and the grinding chain but there was no escape. Three nights was quite enough and as the wind calmed some what we made our escape on 27th May waiting for the high tide to help get the anchor up more easily. After all the swinging and grinding we felt sure it must be stuck around something but to our delight it came straight up and we were free and sailing towards Curlew island for the next night. This was a lovely anchorage and we wished we had been here for the last three nights rather than South Percy as it had a sandy bottom, a welcome absence of grinding and was very calm. We had looked at the chart for this bay and thought it might be too small and difficult to get into as the entry was around a sand bar but once there it was all very easy with plenty of room although we were on our own. What a relief to be away from South Percy, forever etched on our memories as the anchorage from hell.

We left for Scafell island the next morning and sailed as usual with jenny alone downwind and we could soon see the high mountain peak of Scafell in the distance. The route is scattered with many islands, not all of them are suitable for anchoring but Scafell had been recommended and indeed there was a very sheltered bay, the only risk being concealed coral heads only visible at low tide. It is always rather alarming to see them emerge in a place where we might have anchored! We are now routinely using the snubbers with the hook to anchor as the tide was strong and the boat almost always lay to the tide rather than the wind even at the strength it was. We could now enjoy our usual evening routine of cocktails, supper and a DVD again. Scafell is just south of the Whitsunday Islands so we should be there in time to meet Jane. We moved the next day and made it to Shaw Island, jib alone again was enough and easy to manage and there was now lots of choice for anchoring as there are many islands in the Whitsunday Group. We knew we had arrived as we saw the first charter boat in the Shaw island anchorage, it is a very popular charter area as the islands are beautiful and therefore a popular cruising ground. We wanted to get the tide to make the final journey to Airlie Beach which meant leaving at 00.30 on 30th May and we had a magical night sail with the full moon, wind behind and tide with us adding 2.5 knots to our speed. All the navigation marks were where they were purported to be and at 05.30 we anchored in Funnel Bay on the mainland just south east of the Port of Airlie Marina. After a short sleep we moved into the marina only to discover there were no showers and no laundry! Jane was coming by train from Cairns and we were all to meet at Proserpine later that day. We had to get the bus to Proserpine to meet Jane's train and happily we all met at Proserpine railway station later that afternoon.

## The Whitsunday Island Cruise No. 1

Disaster had struck on the way to Port of Airlie marina in the form of a blocked heads! Of course just as guests were arriving and even though John tried his best to unblock it there was no sign of any movement. We did not want to delay Jane's cruise so we made do with one heads and a pot de chambre and set off on 1st June for Nara Inlet. The Alan Lucas book gave us some detail of the Whitsundays enough for us to get around and our first stop was Refuge Bay in Nara inlet on the southern end of Hook island. We did an evening dinghy excursion and enjoyed the peace and emptiness of the surroundings. Jane being a lady of letters was delighted to play Banagram with us in the evening often accompanied with a whisky and dark chocolate. Our anchorages had to be chosen in the light of the prevailing wind which for now was the SE so our next stop was Butterfly Bay on the west coast of Hook Island. We found a mooring buoy there and swam and snorkelled, all very relaxing. Whitehaven Bay was said to have a beautiful beach but once we rounded the northern tip of Hook Island to try and get there it became a battle to continue so we turned back and anchored in a very calm Stonehaven Bay on Whitsunday Island. The next day we motored the short distance round to Sawmill Bay and tried to walk up the Whitsunday peak but had left it too late to reach the top but we swam and snorkelled as usual but there was very little living coral. One of the hazards of swimming in this area of Queensland are the jelly fish which are invisible being very small and transparent, but nevertheless deadly within seconds. Certainly a very serious threat but apparently they are not around at this time of the year, only in the summer, so we took the risk and lived to tell the tale. On 5th June Jane's cruise was over and it was back to Airlie beach across the channel between the North and South Molle islands avoiding the strategically placed mid Molle reef. The passage had the welcoming name of Unsafe Passage but we were pleased to find port and starboard markers present to guide us through and we were soon tied up on our marina berth. We had earlier discovered a lagoon swimming pool a short walk from the marina, very cold and full of sun seeking backpackers from all over the world but at least a safe swim! We went there for a final swim before our farewell dinner in the local Italian restaurant. It was an 04.00 start the next morning for Jane's bus to Proserpine station for the train to Cairns, so it was a sad au revoir but we had introduced Jane to the pleasures of boating and Banagram.

We went back to sleep before starting on unblocking the heads. Malcolm and Glynis were arriving a few days later so the need was urgent. Our boat neighbours were very helpful bringing pumps and manpower but to no avail. We went to Abel point marina and hunted for help from anywhere we could think of and finally John prevailed upon Andy to come, he took pity on us as it is far from any worker's favourite job. His first try was unsuccessful but he came the following day with a special pump and the blockage was removed. The following day it was the fridge which needed attention (not the freezer which Edgar had fixed in Panama) and it seemed it had run out of gas so it was refilled. Although no leak was detected there probably was one but we could only hope it might last us out if it was a slow one or at least keep the beers cold on the next cruise. We provisioned and tried to refuel running aground in the attempt which was not even successful as the machine would not accept a foreign credit card so we left anyway as we were only going across to Hamilton island to meet Malcolm and Glynis. We stopped on the way over at Happy Bay where there used to be a resort but it had been destroyed in a typhoon and was deserted apart from the caretaker. We then motored the short distance to Hamilton Island Marina to greet Malcolm and Glynis.

## Whitsunday Cruise No. 2

Hamilton island is the main resort island of the Whitsundays with large hotels, buses, shops and restaurants and of course people in abundance. Malcolm and Glynis arrived by air direct from Sydney and as soon as they arrived we refuelled and left for Bay 20 for the night. Malcolm and Glynis knew the area well and had brought a more detailed cruising guide to the islands so we could plan a route better informed. We explored the mangrove lined creek in Bay 20 going to its entry point in the dinghy, beautiful scenery and lots of birds. The wind was now NW so we were able to go to different anchorages to those we had visited with Jane and later that day we moved to Chance Bay. From there we could walk to Whitehaven beach which is truly magnificent, acres of the finest white sand and clear water for swimming. We then moved further north along the east coast of Whitsunday island to Tongue Bay and picked up a buoy. The tides are quite significant and we saw some people stranded on the shore with their dinghies which they could not carry across the rough coral in the low tide. Our evening entertainment was again Banagram reminiscent of our Pacific anchorage evenings on board, great entertainment and there always seemed time for just one more game. We had no chateau Clos to improve our vocabulary but I think we finished the whisky.

The next morning we walked to a view point overlooking the magnificent Whitehaven sands before sailing to the smaller Border island to the north west. There we walked up a goat track to the top for more wonderful views over the sea and islands. It is certainly a perfect cruising area with plenty of anchorages and only short passages to get around. We were very lucky to get the sustained NW wind because in the normal prevailing SE trades these anchorages would be impossible. We then went to Marcona inlet on the south of Hook island and then Sawmill Bay for the last night. The strong wind had returned and we had quite a rough trip back to Hamilton Island Marina motor sailing into 30 knots of wind but the tide was with us and we made it in time for Malcom and Glynis to get their flight back on 17th June so it was au revoir again. We stayed in the marina until the wind had settled a little and took the opportunity to take the bus round the island but it was not the highlight of the Whitsundays. The wind allowed our departure on 20th June and we motored across to Port of Airlie Marina before leaving to go north again.

# Airlie Beach to Cairns, June – July 2018

We left Airlie beach on 22nd June and went through the Gloucester passage and anchored the first night in Edgecombe Bay just south of Passage Islet and had a quiet night. We were just doing day hops up the coast to Cairns where we would leave the boat and go back to France and UK for some of the summer. The next stop was Cape Upstart a huge mass of rock jutting dramatically out into the sea. We passed several commercial vessels outside Bowen and as John had a suspicion that our AIS (artificial identification system) was not working we asked one of the vessels to verify if they could see us but sadly they could not although we could receive their signal. Something we would need to investigate at Townsville further up the coast. We had the usual jib alone, sailing downwind all the way to Cape Upstart and it loomed from some distance away just a huge lump of land jutting out into the sea. We rounded the cape and sailed down the west side assuming we would find good shelter behind such a monstrous hunk of land but no, it was still pretty windy and choppy that side and as usual too shallow for us to get very close in. We sailed up and down looking for calmer patches of water but it all looked much the same so we chose a spot but there was a lot of wind and slapping of waves most of the night. When we left the next morning we were very surprised to find the wind shadow much further out so we had to motor for the first hour or so until we found the SE wind again, very contrary. The next recommended stop was Bowling Green Bay formed by a very flat peninsula a sharp contrast to Cape Upstart. We jibed round the flat peninsula and went into the depths of Bowling Green Bay but shelter was not to be found. The waves were also quite rolly so we decided to turn back out of the bay and go to Magnetic island off Townsville which would mean dark sailing but not overnight. We contacted the Townsville Coastguard and they would wait to receive our call when we had arrived. I had a list from Yeppoon of all the VMR stations up the coast with their radio call frequencies and phone numbers which was very useful. We were logged onto the system so felt someone would notice if we failed to arrive and check in. It was a good sail although not much moonlight but good visibility and we rounded cape Cleveland and were anchored in Horsehoe Bay by 21.00. The preferred SE corner of the bay was full of yachts so we anchored off but it was a significant improvement on Bowling Green Bay. We stayed on the boat all the next day tidying up, cleaning, checking the oil and doing other small jobs which do not get done with visitors on board. On 27th June we motored over to Breakwater Marina in Townsville to get the AIS repaired and the Raytheon display unit replaced as the screen was going black on the inside. We had been in touch with them by e-mail so they were prepared for our arrival and came over very quickly. Peter came for the AIS and found the wire at the stern from the dedicated AIS GPS was completely corroded, just powder! He replaced the wire and the antenna and it worked again. Of course there is a lot of salt water near the stern so corrosion was inescapable there. The Raytheon multi-display unit was also replaced with a much smarter newer version.

I had worked in Townsville for a few months in 1978 and wanted to have a look round so In the afternoon we took the marina car and went up the local viewpoint Castle Hill for the view over the town and then drove down Ross River Road where my surgery had been but there was no sign of it now. The whole town had grown enormously since my last visit and was quite unrecognisable. We left the marina the next day and returned to Horsehoe Bay to the same anchoring spot. We were still continuing to manage the left over administration from the sale of the Hong Kong flat so it meant e-mails, printing and posting letters and documents, none of this land work is easy while on board but we did manage to finish the necessary at the local post office on Magnetic Island. There were some lovely coastal walks from Horseshoe Bay to other less populated bays and we had found a stand up paddle boards for hire so intended to try that for the first time the next morning. However the generator stopped while we were just topping up the batteries before leaving so stand up paddling was replaced by generator stripping to find the cause of the sudden stop. After changing the seawater filter and the impeller it still did not work but John diagnosed the problem as a corroded water flow sensor and once this was removed it worked perfectly. The sensor would need replacing and the day was gone! The next day we walked to an old second world war fort which had been built on a hill to look out for any Japanese boats approaching but this had never happened but the fort was interesting to walk around and the added attraction is wild koalas along the route. Monday 2nd July was a public holiday so we could make no progress with the generator so we finally got out on a paddle board, our first time and we really enjoyed it, nice warm water so no nasty shocks falling in. We completed the day of rest with a long walk to the end of the beach but the memory of our lovely day was marred later when I realised I had left the camera in the public toilets.

We motored over to Breakwater Marina again the next day this time for the generator to be repaired, sadly just out of warranty now so quite a costly repair with a new water flow sensor and new heat exchanger and labour charges which are not cheap in Australia but at least the work is well done here. Before we could spend any more money we left Townsville on Friday 6th July and headed north again for Cairns.

The first stop was Juno Bay on the west side of Fantome Island and the following day we wanted to get into the Hitchinbrook Narrows a natural inside channel which was said to be quite dramatic with high mountains on either side. The scenery this far north was much changed from Bundaberg. The entry was near the town of Lucinda and was complicated by several shifting sandbanks but we thought if we timed it for high tide we could get in. We checked in with the Townsville VMR to log our plans but we were warned not to enter because the sandbanks made the entry too shallow for us and were always shifting so any charts would be totally inaccurate, so feeling lucky to have checked we continued north on the outside of the Narrows admiring the high mountains rising from the sea but only on one side. There was little wind today but a left-over swell so the boom swung noisily. It is always difficult to tie down, we tried so many ways but never found the ideal solution; really our boom was too long for the boat and this may have been the problem. We spent the next night south of Gould Island at the northern end of the Hitchinbrook Narrows and as the forecast was for very strong wind we decided to sit that out there in the shelter. We received a call from the VMR volunteer checking we had arrived safely …such a service. We stayed for the next day and John continued his job of trying to stop the water maker leaks. We could still make water but the leak was very persistent perhaps because of all the dismantling needed to replace the water tank so many times, anyway it kept him busy while waiting out the gale. On 9th July we sailed to Mourilyan harbour in the mouth of the Moresby River. It is an old sugar port and the entrance is quite narrow with high rock walls on either side, easily missed unless you know where it is but all that is taken care of now with chart plotters and GPS, traditional navigation skills are becoming a dying art. It was a difficult place to anchor because there were lots of piles, vessels and empty buoys but after one false try we found a place a little too close to two other vessels but luckily it stayed calm and we had an eventless night there as we had swung with the tide in unison with the other vessels. The next day we found a SW wind outside and wondered about putting the main up but soon the SE returned so we were glad we had not bothered and continued on as usual with jenny alone with two reefs but still making good speed. At this time of the year there is little let up of the trade winds along this coast we found and we were glad we had invested in the new jenny as this was the only sail we used on this downwind passage up the Queensland Coast. Fitzroy island lies just south east of the cape we needed to round in order to reach Cairns and we considered stopping there but it was crowded and with a resort so we opted for Mission Bay just around the cape and anchored in 30 knots of wind. The holding was good and the night was fairly peaceful. At 07.00 the next morning we started out for the Blue Water marina near Cairns, we needed the high tide to get in as it was far up a mangrove creek but we made it without running aground and were greeted by Rick the manager who helped us tie up in the wonderfully calm water, the rolling had finally stopped. We had hoped to meet Andrew and Jila Peacock in Singapore on 24th October as they were going to sail up the Malacca Straits with us but when we examined this plan in detail it was apparent we could not make it so we made a later rendezvous to give us more time. It was a long way up the rest of the Queensland coast and through Indonesia even with minimal stops. The watermaker man arrived and fixed the leak and then we biocided it as we would be away for a few weeks. This stops any growth in the system and protects the Clarke pump from damage.

We hired a car as much to get to the airport reliably as anything else but also used it to see Cairns and the botanical gardens and the esplanade where we surprisingly saw a sign in the middle of the urban area warning of crocodiles on the town beach. They are very numerous here now because killing them is prohibited and this has allowed their numbers to increase rapidly. The tide was right out exposing a huge area of mud flat which was not really that attractive and we never found a true city centre. On the last day we drove to the interior to Kurunda for a jungle walk, then to the Barren river gorge then onto the Atherton tablelands, a wide open space, then to Yungaburra to try and see duckbill platypus but we were not lucky. Once back on board for the evening we packed up ready for departure. We did not take any sails down with Baringo staying in the water so leaving was not so complicated this time. On 16th July we flew back to a European summer.

# CHAPTER TWENTY NINE

# Cairns to Thursday Island

## *September – October 2018*

I arrived back in Bluewater Marina on 19th September and found Baringo in good order and a letter in the cockpit from someone interested in buying her. Rick the marina manager clarified that he had met the interested party and told them we were going to sell soon so we kept in touch with them but in the end they did not buy her. I cleaned the inside of the boat did some provisioning and contemplated the next passage further north where the Barrier reef becomes much closer to the mainland and so the channel becomes much narrower. There were two navigable channels one old one and a new one called Lad's Passage which was shorter but had nowhere to stop and we felt might be busier with commercial traffic. John arrived on 21st September after his time working in Beijing so we could now discuss this choice but it was a difficult decision so we did not make it immediately. There was some time pressure as we had another date to meet Andrew and Jila in Singapore where our circumnavigation would be complete but we still had a lot of water to go. We wanted to get the rigging checked professionally and the hull cleaned and checked after so long sitting in the marina and both revealed nothing amiss. We needed a lot of provisions as we did not think we could get much in Thursday island and we did not plan to stop very much in Indonesia. It is one thing shopping but another stowing the food and then remembering where it is as by now I seemed to have more than one stowage list! We were delayed by one day because a cruise ship came into the fuel dock and blocked it for the day but luckily we found out before we had untied our warps and moved.

Departure day was then 27th September and within a few minutes of motoring up the mangrove channel we had run aground with little time left of the rising tide! John revved backwards and forwards, I tried to hang off the boom and after a few anxious moments which always seem longer than they are we were through the mud and moving again. Once more into the swell and with jib alone in the SE wind we sailed north, pleasantly for a few hours intending to do one overnight to get some miles under our belt. It all roughened up as the night started with a vessel on collision course and we could not manoeuvre easily in the strong wind but after a chat on the radio it changed course. We were very glad to have our AIS again as at least the big vessels could see us early and with this the old rule sail before steam has been revived. There were several islands and reefs to avoid but with the dawn the wind settled and we had a nice reach around Cape Flattery before going downwind again to reach Cape Melville by afternoon and anchor in the bay behind the cape. We motored up and down looking for a sheltered spot but there was none as usual. There were campers on the beach here actually a lovely place deserted and unspoilt. In the absence of Emmanuel, Malcolm had agreed to keep an eye on the weather for us which was such a help so we had news of strong SE winds for the next five days. We pressed on as the Great Barrier Reef was so close now the sea was never rough even though the wind was strong so we felt braver to take it on. We crossed Princess Charlotte Bay the next morning then through the Flinders group of islands and finally decided to take the inner older navigation passage rather than the newer Lad's passage because we could stop if needed and it proved to be good decision as we did need to stop to sit out the gale. It was nice sailing during the morning but in the afternoon an errant NE wind picked up and we were heading straight into 30 knots of it. We only had the reefed small jenny, too windy to get the main up but we did not move too far sideways and we were glad to reach Morris Island where we could anchor which we did in 40 knots of wind. It is a very pretty low -lying, sandy Robinson Crusoe island so gave no protection from the wind. The next morning did not look inviting for a departure so we stayed next to Morris island for another day which was a good chance for us and Baringo to rest from the stress of such strong winds on us all. The wind was lighter next morning and we left early at 05.45 to make the most of the lighter breeze and we arrived at Portland Roads really the last outpost of the far north of Queensland. We anchored easily with a few fishing boats and a dive boat. We could see there were about five houses visible on the shore and not very much activity. It would have been interesting to go ashore but it was far too windy and the dinghy was packed away in the bunk room so not easily accessible. We made the mistake of leaving the following morning in our effort to keep up with schedule, and had a horrible day in 50 knots of wind in a very narrow part of the inside passage with several large vessels coming up and down also constrained in their movements by their draught so it was not always possible for either of us to move. We really regretted leaving the comfort of Portland Roads but there was no way back. Baringo was under considerable strain even with a small handkerchief of sail, especially Poppy who does not really like downwind helming in such strong conditions. Luckily the sea was relatively flat being inside the reef. We avoided any collisions with the passing commercial vessels, as we talked on the radio and they could alter course enough to make room for us all and one casually wondered why we were out there in such conditions! We had to press on to Cape Grenville and were very happy to round the cape through the outlying islands and anchor in the bay behind even though we still had 40 knots on the sheltered side but at least we were not sailing anymore and could get out of the wind ourselves below deck. We stayed one more day here until Malcolm said the forecast was for light winds for the next five days.

We left this bay on 4th October at 04.45 and headed towards the Albany Passage at the very north of the Australian mainland. It is quite narrow and so we needed to time our passage with the tide to get through easily. We sailed northwards in the lighter SE breeze and the tide turned to a favourable one at mid-afternoon so this would take us through the passage. We decided to furl the jib before entering the passage in case of flooky winds and it was just as well because during the rough passage the shackle on the foot of the sail had come off and it would not furl and the lazy sheet had jammed in the process of trying before we realised the problem. Fortunately, we had time and space to sort it out and replace the shackle before we entered the narrow passage. There were some strange rips at the entrance but the passage itself was rather beautiful and wonderfully calm with attractive very pale pink rocks each side gently glowing in the setting sun. Just the other side of the passage is Shallow Bay where Joshua Slocum anchored in his journey up this coast so we followed suit and had a peaceful night in there and compared to many other anchorages up the coast it did not seem too shallow. Tomorrow Friday 5th October was the final leg to Horn island in the Torres Straits which separate Australia from

Papua New Guinea. Horn Island is opposite Thursday Island and it is a more sheltered anchorage and we could easily take the ferry over to Thursday Island to do the administration and check out so although we could have anchored off Thursday island we took the Horn island option. We rose early again at 05.20 and motored around the navigation marks and Scott Rock to find the anchorage off Horn island. It was quite crowded with fishing vessels and empty buoys but we found a spot on the second try. We launched the dinghy from the foredeck and went ashore to take the ferry over to Thursday Island, about a 15minute ride, to check out and see if we could find any provisions. The check -out produced a problem as it seemed our Australian cruising permit was out of date even though we had thought we had renewed it in Bundaberg but we did not remember receiving a document after the renewal so we had no paper to present. Luckily it was on the computer so we escaped without penalty and the check-out was very simple and we were even allowed to stay until Monday to get ready for the next passage. We found a surprisingly well stocked but not surprisingly expensive supermarket and bought a little more fresh fruit and vegetables. The next day we had to fill the jerry cans with diesel and carry them from the petrol station to the dinghy which was about 500 meters and no trolleys to be seen. A kind Torres island gentleman helped me with mine as it was a bit of a struggle and he was much larger and stronger than I was. The Torres Straits islanders are generally large and different from the Aborigines. The tide and wind are both very strong up here and on one occasion during the afternoon we seemed to be swinging wildly out of tune with the other vessels which made a collision possible and John realised it was because the sprayhood was acting like a small sail and once we took it down we swung like everyone else. Sunday dawned very calmly and we took the opportunity to change the jib sheets around so that the knots were in different place, we felt they had had so much strain during the journey up the coast that before we left we should move the point of strain. No sooner had we finished than the wind picked up; we had become accustomed to these very short wind free intervals and took the chances quickly when they came. There was one other yacht at anchor and we heard their tale of a broken gear box when they were at anchor on one of the islands near Albany Passage and had been towed into Horn island to wait for a new one. One had eventually arrived but after struggling to get it into position which was extremely hard work it was the wrong one and did not fit and they were now waiting for another one. So there was not much they did not know about either Thursday island or Horn island after their prolonged stay up there. They were hoping to return to Brisbane in the spring northerlies when they had sailed up, so a rather sorry story. The night before we left we had a phone call from Russ whom we had met in Bundaberg and who had just completed the same route that we were planning and had now arrived in Malaysia. He had several very good tips about the forthcoming route. He advised downloading i-sailor for navigation as the navionics charts we were using were quite inaccurate in Indonesia and also told us about a marina in northern Lombok which was a really good stopping spot, both bits of information which proved invaluable on this leg. We left Australia on Monday 8th October to cross the Arafura sea to Indonesia.

# CHAPTER THIRTY

# Thursday Island – Singapore

## *October – November 2018*

We left Australia on Monday 8th October to cross the Arafura sea to Indonesia and we woke that morning to a huge tide running in the passage between Thursday island and Horn island but only a light wind. We were waiting for the fridge to be checked again as we thought it had run out of gas knowing there was probably a small leak. Jack finally arrived but said all was in working order and no gas was required so we raised the anchor at 11.30 by which time we had wind and tide against us. We had to take a circuitous route out going back the way we had entered the passage round Madge Reef then turning to pass south of Thursday Island and into the Normanby Passage where we then had the tide with us and were pushed along at 11.00 knots over the ground. By 14.00 we were through the final navigation gates leaving the Torres Strait Islands fading into the distance behind and the gleaming turquoise Arafura Sea ahead.

The first night was quiet and no traffic, we were sailing nearly dead downwind with jib alone jibing intermittently to make the westerly course to Saumlaki on Yamdena Island one of the Tanimbar group in Maluku province, the easternmost of the Indonesian islands. We hoped we could check into Indonesia here and get the short stay visa and cruising permit. We had decided our passage through would be short and therefore had not got the long stay visa which can only be obtained outside the country. The next few days saw us jibing to make the course in quite calm conditions with clear skies and beautiful sunsets and dawns which we savoured appreciatively knowing this was our last long passage and we would not experience the solitude of the open sea for much longer. The fishing boats which had been so pleasantly absent in the pacific now started to appear along with the occasional fisherman's marker flag placed in what seemed like far too deep water but they were there and unlit. The days slipped by with ease, light wind, calm sea and sunny weather such a change from the battle we had had up the Queensland coast. The watch system went uninterrupted and a large pod of dolphins came by. It was really perfect conditions and we did not worry we were only making 4-5knots, we did not want to destroy the tranquillity by motoring. We also wanted to time our passage for a dawn arrival on a working day so the offices would be open and we felt it was nicer out at sea rather than in Saumlaki port. By day five the wind had almost gone but rather than motor and arrive on Sunday we just dollied with the little jib tied down going along in roughly the right direction at 2.5 knots, there was very little swell so we had a wonderfully relaxing day with no vessels and the sea to ourselves. At 03.15 on Sunday there was still no wind and we had no excuse to wait any longer in this magic seascape so we motored towards Saumlaki hoping to make a dawn arrival. The sea was glassy and at 07.00 we sighted land and rounded up into the bay to anchor in the port. We were trying to compare the accuracy of the depth readings between navionics and i-sailor but despite using two systems we still ran aground although this was because the recommended anchorage way points that we were aiming for were totally wrong. We revved the motor and moved off deeper water without any damage and anchored in 16.9 meters depth further out. We had a visit from a local boat who said they would help us with formalities the next morning. We refuelled the boat from the jerry cans as we needed to refill these while in Saumlaki, we had been warned of the absence of wind during the Indonesia passage so we needed to keep plenty of diesel on board. We had a range of 1000nm with all jerry cans and the fuel tank full.

On Monday 15th October we launched the dinghy and drove over to the ferry pier where we to meet our visitors from yesterday whom we hoped would reveal the complexities of Saumlaki and Indonesian bureaucracy. The water was filthy and the pier and ferries in a poor state of repair, such a contrast to the spotlessly clean and well-maintained environment of Australia where no damage or scratch was left unattended, here repair and maintenance were a distant dream. We had arrived early so sheltered under the pier for some shade as even this time of the morning the heat was strong. We could not see any landing pontoon or steps so just waited for the people with local knowledge to arrive which they did and told us to climb over steep piles of random blocks of stone to get ashore. We left the jerry cans in a shop and then on to the Quarantine office where we waited for four hours with no air-conditioner and not even a fan. The immigration officers finally arrived with their computer and we got 30day visas which put a time limit on our trip but rather surprisingly no money changed hands. Hige who became our link man and was extremely helpful arrived at the office and came with us back to the boat with the officers for the inspection which was uncomplicated and then back to the office again driving through dense rubbish in the water to which the locals seemed oblivious. Hige took us to get Indonesian SIM cards which took at least another hour and finally we all went for lunch and a much-needed cold beer. The town was very scruffy and dirty, everything partly broken and damaged and never repaired. Hige took us for a short excursion around the larger town in a friend's car and showed us a long wide boulevard of smart government buildings, what a contrast! We tried to fill the jerry cans but it was not allowed so Hige said he would do it the following morning as he had contacts, always the magic way. We had to return to the SIM card shop to connect to the telephone network and that took another hour and then some shopping which really needed Hige's help as one sterling pound is nearly 18,000 Indonesian rupia so far too many noughts to calculate quickly, even small items were in the thousands. It had been a tiring and hot day and on our return journey to Baringo we saw a French catamaran had arrived so we went to say hello to find that one of their propellers had broken. They were hoping to get it repaired here so we promised to introduce them to the can-do man of Saumlaki... Hige...

The next day we had to return to the office to check out. We had hoped that once checked in to Indonesia we would not have to check in and out of every port we stopped in but we did, so it was another morning in the office oven but I excused myself and went shopping with Hige again. The Frenchman from the catamaran was there trying to get a long stay visa for Indonesia but this is impossible once you have entered the country, they have to be obtained from an embassy outside so there was lots of discussion and Hige was very helpful and also he could help with their broken propeller. We finally had our clearance and thought it was all over but no Hige said we had to go to the Harbour master's office, our hearts sank dreading another long wait but here the process was quicker and the office cooler. Hige had only been able to get 35litres of diesel rather than the 50 litres we had wanted but certainly better than nothing. Loading these now heavy jerry cans down the steep slope of slippery jumbled rocks was tricky but for Hige everything was possible. We dropped Hige onto the French catamaran on our way back and then prepared to depart, hoisting the jerry cans and then the dinghy onto the foredeck which the Gibson lift made so easy. We tied it down on the foredeck then stowed the provisions and by 13.00 we were on our way.

We had to weave a passage through the Indonesian islands, a long thin archipelago lying east to west with our final destination being Singapore. We had not planned any stops but knew we would have to have a break somewhere en route but would just see how things evolved. We had Stephen Davies's pilot book with lots of information and advice about the passage. There was no wind initially so we motor sailed with main and little jenny. John had put in the way points for the journey threading between islands to make the shortest route, passing south of Pulau Babar then north of Pulau Sermata then on to Pulau Kisar. On the evening of 17th October all the instruments stopped working... Poppy was steering wildly, our SOG (speed over the ground) was reading 1.8 knots... what to do... switch everything off and on again always the first move to try... and order was restored! There were always land lights on the islands we passed, Indonesia is a very heavily populated country and this did nothing to disprove it. The new problem on this passage was that the engine coolant was not siphoning back into the reservoir and we actually never worked out why but simply siphoned the coolant from the engine back into the reservoir. While motor sailing we slept in the forward cabin as the engine noise aft was not very restful but all continued smoothly and we passed south of Pulau Wetar. Malcolm was giving us weather forecasts but none of any wind so we were using oil and diesel in quantity and the tank was now only half full. Refuelling from the jerry cans is always a very messy job despite our best efforts with lots of rags to hand but diesel inevitably gets onto the teak and into the cockpit on the soles of our feet so it is not a task we relish at any time least of all at sea although of course it is only needed in windless calm conditions. Pulau Wetar is a large island so we were south of it for about 12 hours and finally picked up some wind there but soon black clouds gathered with lots of lightening so we added motor to the wind to try and get away although it is always difficult to predict the direction these systems will take but this time we did escape and enjoyed the remains of the wind the system had delivered.

By next morning we were along the north coast of Pulau Alor and decided to refuel and then calculated that we would have enough fuel to motor to Lombok where we now planned to stop in the marina recommended by Russ. That evening we got a strong south west breeze so not very good for our westerly course so we motored into it but when it reached force 7 we had to go off course to sail with it but it became more favourable later so our course improved. Just before dark John noticed that the jib sheet was at a funny angle and we realised it was caught round the mast spinlocks and could easily have pulled them all off with the forces generated when we winched it in and we would have been very lucky to have seen the problem in the dark. Steve Dashew's "constant vigilance" is the watch word at sea! We had also left a hatch open under the dinghy while sleeping in the forward cabin and now with the rougher sea the mattress was soaked with seawater! The next day was a mixture of motoring and sailing with the wind up and down and from all directions and not really as forecast but maybe this was the land effect, we were now north of Pulau Flores. We were always trying to calculate the miles we had from the remaining diesel when we passed places where we could possibly buy some but it had not been simple in Saumlaki and without Hige's help in a strange port a stop was not very appealing so we continued making a guestimate that we should make it to Lombok.

Over the next few days we had some nice sailing with the wind from the SE but it was mixed with motor sailing as it never lasted more than a few hours. After many calculations we were now confident that we had enough diesel. To reach Lombok but now we needed to do the correct speed to make a daytime arrival. We had really strong wind 35-40 knots for two nights on 22nd and 23rd October which seemed to come from nowhere and was not a storm, the sky was completely clear. We decided it must be a land breeze from the very high land masses of the volcanic Indonesian islands but it was so much stronger than any land breeze we had experienced before. It was hard on Baringo and on us so we decided we should try and anchor to avoid a third night of such wind and luckily we had some anchorages from Claire of Apsara as well as those in the cruising guide and miraculously one of Claire's was just right for us, en route and a late afternoon arrival. The wind was calm during the day but we did not want another bad night if it could be avoided so we found Potoppupu Bay on the north west of Pulau Sembawa and anchored. It took two tries as the first time we were in 17m depths but when we swung it changed to 1.1 m so that would not do. Jim Howard the American cruiser said you never really master the art of anchoring you can only strive to improve and I think that is very true even after the hundreds of times we have anchored it is always a guess as to where Baringo might end up.

We were pleased to be stationary and avoid another windy night and we both slept very well. There was an inner bay through a narrow channel which might have been more protected but there was no information on either Navionics or I sailor about depths or hazards so we stayed outside. We were now close to Lombok and the overnight stop had given us good time for a daylight arrival. We left at 04.00 on 24th October to ensure this and as soon as we were out of the bay we had 35 knots of wind, so much for windless Indonesia! We reefed down and made good speed towards Lombok but just as I had gone into the saloon for a short rest John saw a sea snake coming over the coaming on the starboard side into the cockpit. Once he realised he was not hallucinating he shouted to me to shut the companionway hatch, disaster if the snake got below, and I gave him the wooden oar which we kept handy in case of boarders and he did the dirty deed and killed the snake which had hidden in the coils of the halyards in the cockpit. It probably thought they were fellow snakes. We really had no choice as sea snakes are amongst the most deadly of snakes and we had recently read of the death of young English man who had found one in the nets of a commercial fishing boat he was working on and in trying to get it out had been bitten and died. We can only presume the snake had climbed up the anchor chain the previous night. We recovered from the shock, it all seemed so unreal but now Lombok was looming into view, a very high dramatic volcanic peak. The wind changed to westerly so it was straight into it to get to the marina so that took our minds off the snake and wondering if there was another one lurking somewhere. There are many mobile phone masts on the Indonesian islands as part of the tsunami and earthquake warning system so we were often able to connect with our local SIM cards so we could now call the marina and get some entry instructions. Interestingly Navionics had the marina way point in the next-door bay but i-sailor was correct so it was lucky we were aware of the inaccuracies of the charts here and of course we looked where we were going as well. We decided to pick up a mooring although there was a small pontoon. This is always difficult in a strong wind but after four tries we were attached.

In the morning we saw another yacht arrive and go alongside the pontoon and it was "Intrigue" a well know Hong Kong boat so over the next few days we had many long chats over a few beers. The marina was perfect, all services available, fuel, water, bar, restaurant and all offered with smiles and grace. We were so pleased we had found out about it as originally we had planned a more northerly route to Singapore missing Lombok. It was a wonderful stop and we needed fuel anyway. The diesel arrived the same day and we loaded the jerry cans that afternoon, an excellent service. We still needed more so we refilled them again after putting their contents into our own fuel tank, and then brought the refilled jerry cans back to be stowed on board. This was very hard and messy work in the extreme heat. Intrigue had the detailed Indonesian cruising guide so we took a few anchorages for the rest of the journey from that which was very useful and planned the passage. On 27th October we took a taxi to provision in Mataran the capital of Lombok and about an hour's drive away and we were very surprised to see how the village just behind the marina had been devastated by a recent earthquake. We had heard about the one in Sulawesi a few months before but nothing about Lombok and when we had heard an earthquake mentioned by the marina staff we had assumed it was a much earlier one. Many of the houses were just piles of rubble and there were a few tents for people to shelter in, surprisingly the road was quite intact but although our driver had lost his house he seemed quite pragmatic about it, part of life in Indonesia maybe. We drove over the green hills and saw lots of monkeys and had some good views and the provisioning was reasonable but often in Asia the supermarkets look very well stocked and exciting but on closer inspection there is little that we wanted to buy. We had left Baringo alongside the pontoon to be cleaned and after stowing the food we stayed there as the wind increased as usual in the afternoon and we had a good evening with Intrigue in the restaurant. Much as we would like to have stayed here we had to leave on 28th October and we were out into 30 knots of wind once we left the shelter of the bay. The sea was too rough to hoist the main, we should have done it in the bay as we were close hauled in a westerly breeze but it gradually moved south then south east and so we were downwind once more. We sailed past the Bali volcano at sunset and we approached Pulau Kangean leaving it to starboard. We had a quiet night but the sea was very confused so not really comfortable sailing with the irregular rolling of the boat. There were significantly more vessels now both commercial and fishing, we were passing north of Pulau Madura and Java. The fishing vessels all shone bright green lights at night which was new since we were last in Asian waters, but this meant they were clearly visible and all behaved sensibly and kept out of our way so much less troublesome than before, and they often gave a bright white flash to tell us they had seen us. The next way point was Pulau Bawean in the middle of the Java sea between Borneo and Java so we were well on the way now. We were approaching the gap between the southern coast of Borneo and Pulau Belitung and Stephen Davies recommended two possible "gates" to go through safely and avoid the ever present reefs. We therefore kept closer to Kalimantan passing through the easternmost gate. We had wind from all directions and of varying strengths so the sail plan was in constant change and there was quite a lot of motor sailing in between blows but it was certainly not the windless millpond we had been led to expect, at least not that year. There were now lots of fishing vessels at night and we were entertained with a lightening display on the night of the 1st November but luckily no wind and not much rain with it. We were heading towards Pulau Seratu north east of Pulau Belitung and we arrived to anchor there at dawn on 2nd November. It was useful to have a day stationary to refuel the tanks and use the internet to organise our marina berths in Ngongsa Point and Singapore. This was one of the anchorages we had found in Intrigue's book and the information we had from that was completely accurate but in agreement with Navionics not i-sailor this time. We had a very good night's sleep and were off again next morning with a light NE breeze so we motored into it and we only had a very short spell of sailing during the afternoon. Black clouds and lightning started in the early evening but no strong wind or rain as we headed NW up the shipping lane so lots of commercial vessels now passing us. The next day we had a few squalls with rain and short lived bursts of strong wind and as we crossed the longitude of Hong Kong today we wondered of this would count as completion of our circumnavigation if we did not make it all the way to Singapore. On 5th November we crossed the equator at 00.15 and toasted King Neptune with a Hahn beer with party hats on. He had looked after us pretty well and we wanted his surveillance for the rest of the journey. Later that day we dodged a huge squall just passing the edge of it with only 20 knots of wind but it definitely looked worth avoiding. The sea assumed a rather peculiar oleaginous quality after these squalls which seemed supernatural and a little unnerving, as if some strange creature might emerge from it. We were planning to anchor off Pulau Mesanak where we had a difficult choice of a southern bay or a northern one which depended on the wind direction and I am glad to say we got it right going for the southern bay and a north west wind blew. The entrance was marked by rudimentary sticks but clearly visible preventing us going onto the shallows each side. We had another day and night here so used the time to prepare the forward cabin for Jane who was coming to Ngongsa Point and then sailing across to Singapore with us to complete our circumnavigation. It was a very pleasant bay all to ourselves and a small village ashore so quiet we thought it must be the residence of sleeping fishermen. We left at 06.00 to our next anchorage off the town of Tanjung Pinang on the east coast of Pulau Bintan. We chose this urban anchorage to get protection from the north west wind, although we knew it would not be scenic. There was a marked channel to get into the bay but not all the markers were present, a lot of plastic bags had taken their place. Once in the estuary proper there were parked and moving craft everywhere, it was very busy because the city straddled the river estuary and there was no bridge. We anchored in the best place we could find following the pilot book's instructions and were next to a barge. It was a contrast to the previous night in every way, but change is what we thrive on. There was the usual forest of mobile masts but no 4G so no internet which is what we had hoped we might get in exchange for the noise and dirt of a city but we were not lucky here. We had no temptation to go ashore so we tried to work out optimal timing with respect to the tides to go up the Selat Riau to Nongsa Point the next day. We read that the tides can be up to 5 knots so we were expecting the worst, we had to cover 36 nm and arrive in daylight. We put all the lights we had on Baringo alight that night and we slept with the foghorn and the oar within easy reach in case of intruders. Our fears were unfounded and we passed an uneventful night and miraculously left without getting a plastic bag around the propeller, there were so many of them.

We sailed north for the first two hours amongst commercial vessels, it was now very industrial on the shoreline as well and ferries were speeding by at 30 knots in all directions but we seemed to have the current with us and at 12.00 on 7th November John sighted Singapore. We rounded the north-eastern tip of Pulau Batam and then we had a very slight current against us but we had missed the dreaded 5 knots against which would have seriously slowed Baringo up. We followed our way point into the channel to get into the Nongsa Point Marina; there are two channels in parallel here so very critical to get the correct one and not all that obvious by eye but with the waypoint and a chart plotter, not to mention the skipper's navigation skills, we made the right choice and arrived in the marina basin and not the ferry port. We were helped into the berth, given a very friendly welcome and checked in at the office.

There is a wonderful swimming pool and restaurant here as a hotel and golf course are all part of the marina so it was a treat to have a swim and a meal in the restaurant. We did some provisioning the next day then a siesta then a swim and then prepared the boat for Jane's arrival the next day. We had got into the habit of siestas for most of the voyage as in most of the places we had been it was simply too hot to work in comfort during the middle of the day and even when it wasn't the habit did not die. Nongsa Point was very hot and humid so no reason to change anything yet.

Jane must have taken a liking to sailing as here she was again joining us for the finale and she came with a lovely bottle of pink Moet to drink when and if we arrived in Singapore. We had a few days relaxing by the swimming pool, strolling round the grounds of the marina estate and golf course and dining in the restaurant which was all very pleasant. The evenings were spent with more Banagram competitions with Jane being a professional wordsmith usually winning. We checked out of Indonesia on 12th November which was the last day of our visa so we had no choice. Luckily the weather was fine and we motor sailed along the north coast of Pulau Batam which is very industrial with oily black water full of rubbish, rather a depressing sight. The end of our circumnavigation was within reach but we restrained the rising excitement, sailing can be the most unpredictable mode of transport! We chose our moment to cross the shipping channel to Singapore one of the world's busiest and then went to the Western Anchorage to be checked in. This has to be done before setting foot on Singapore soil. The process was completed while we had lunch and we arrived safely in Keppel Marina named after the same Admiral Keppel as the Keppel islands in Queensland.

Our circumnavigation was complete and the champagne flowed!

**Fraser Island, Queensland, Australia**

**Humpback whale, Hervey Bay, Queensland**

313

Aeroplane at anchor!

Percy Island anchorage looking deceptively calm.

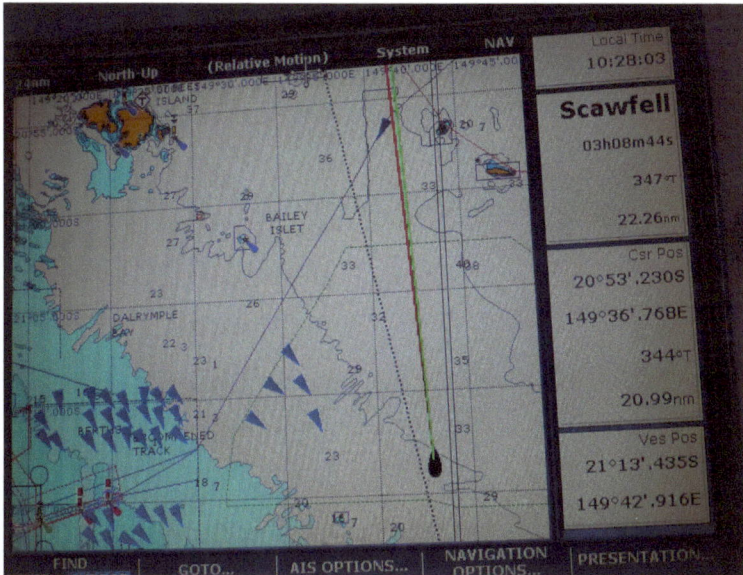

**Ships (triangles) at anchor shown on AIS waiting entry to Gladstone port**

**Islands off Queensland coast**

315

**Whitsunday islands**

**Strong trade winds blowing as usual**

**Albany passage Cape York entry into the Torres Straits**

**Horn Island, Torres straits**

**Saumlaki, Indonesia**

**Medana marina, Lombok, Indonesia**

**Bar and restaurant Medan Marina**

**Island on tow, Java Sea**

**Dawn passing Bali Mt Agung**

**Nongsa point marina**

# CHAPTER THIRTY ONE

# The Finale,
# Singapore to Langkawi

## *November 2018*

Andrew and Jila had arrived in Singapore to sail this last passage with us up the Malacca Staits to Langkawi where we planned to sell Baringo. We enjoyed a few days sightseeing in Singapore the highlight of which was the laser light show from the top of the Casino building, it felt like being in outer space so high and so many lights.

We left the bright lights on 18th November after the usual Western anchorage document exchange and we planned to repeat the first journey we had done in 2002 stopping in the same places. Our first impression was that the coast was much more built up and industrialised and this remained all the way up the coast to Langkawi, evidence indeed of the booming Malaysian economy we had read about. We anchored the first night at Pilau Pisang on the north side as there was a SW wind, a squall blew up but no lightning this time. The Water Islands were next and we had a squall during the night again which never makes for a good sleep. Then on to

Admiral's Marina, passing a now very industrialised coast through a plastic laden sea. The marina had not changed very much since our last visit in 2003 but there was a rally passing through so we had to content ourselves with a berth without electricity so we had to run the generator to have the air-conditioner. Check in at Port Dickson was much as before on our previous trip. We made a trip to Melaka by car which we had not done last time because we had been there with the children in 1984. Of course, there were many more tourists this this time but the elegant unusual pink Dutch buildings were still there. Andrew had perused the guide book during a rain storm and suggested we go to the Royal Selangor Yacht Club in Port Klang and take a train to Kuala Lumpur to see the new Islamic museum there. We had only anchored off last time so this was something new. We left Port Dixon and went up the river delta to the Royal Selangor Yacht Club passing rows of dockside cranes belonging to a huge container port. The water in the yacht club was so dirty that the water was scarcely visible underneath a thick layer of plastic and rubbish. The tide was running fast so getting alongside was not easy. However, we were rewarded the next day with the interesting train ride to Kuala Lumpur and the beautiful Islamic Museum. Not sorry to leave the Yacht Club we continued to Pulau Pangkor and this time had to navigate a new lighted path into our old anchorage in the dark but we made it safely. Once again we all wanted to do the motor bike ride we had so enjoyed last time and luckily Pulau Pangkor was still pleasantly unchanged and unsophisticated but we did find a rather beautiful new mosque built out on stilts over the sea.

The wind had not been very favourable so far so we were not sailing as much as we had expected, the NE monsoon did not seem to be well established here yet. We needed an overnight passage to arrive in Penang in daylight and this was uneventful apart from the lightning and we decided on a dawn anchorage off the NW of the island

and enjoyed a rather spectacular dawn before going around to the marina. There had been no marinas here in 2003 so we were pleased to avoid the difficult anchoring we had experienced here before and just tie alongside a pontoon although the entry into the marina had to be made through a dredged channel at high tide. But despite these problems it made our stay in Penang much easier. We hired a car and visited the Penang Funicular railway going up to the peak but it was very crowded so we then circumnavigated the island finding the temples and villages of interest with Andrew and Jila's guide book. The evening storm came with a vengeance as we were driving over the hills by now looking for a restaurant for supper. The guide book had a few recommendations of wonderful sea food meals in local villages but each one we found proved gloomy and empty, no sign of welcoming sea food eateries obvious. It was dark, raining and we were hungry but when we stopped for Andrew to top up his SIM card we found ourselves by chance under a sign for Tiger beer outside a restaurant. By now desperate we went in and had not only several cold tigers but a superb meal including a grilled whole fish, all very tasty, one of the best dinners we had but no thanks to the guide book!

Pulau Bunting was the next anchorage and this was rather curious; we were sure there would be a resort there but all we found was a deserted island with a very glossy bridge connecting it to the mainland the reason for which was not immediately obvious. We later discovered it had been built for a power station which had never happened. On 2nd December it was the final journey to Langkawi and into Rebak marina… this was our last passage on Baringo. Andrew and Jila stayed in the marina resort and then kindly organised the celebration of our safe arrival with Moet in the gazebo on the end of the breakwater at the resort overlooking the sea… quite perfect.

Baringo was sold in March 2019 to Andrew and Kylie who will I hope take her on another adventure, after all that is what she loves.

**Keppel Marina Singapore**

**Singapore Welcome**

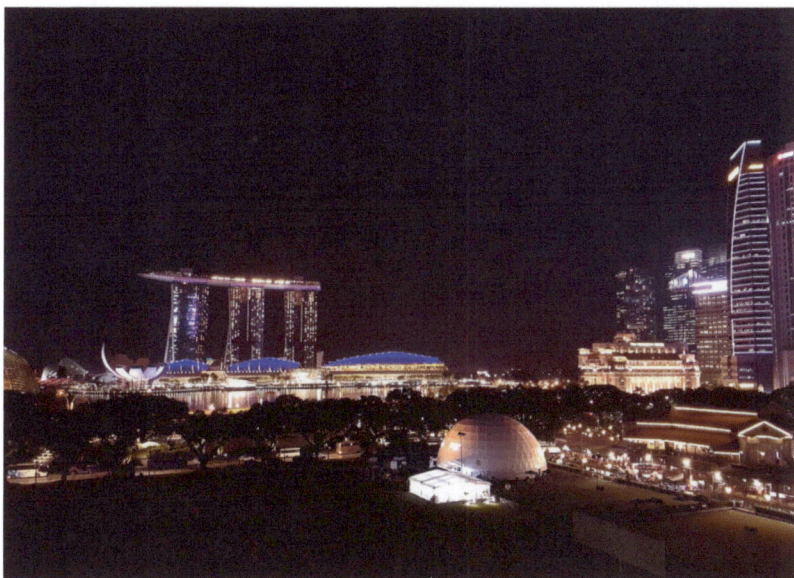

**Singapore Welcome**

# Glossary of Nautical Terms

| | |
|---|---|
| AIS | automatic identification system.<br><br>Identifies vessels on the chart plotter with information about the risk of collision. |
| Antifouling | paint for the underwater part of the hull to slow plant growth |
| Autohelm | automatic computer controlled steering device |
| Backstay | the stern standing rigging wire |
| Battens | Strengthening rods inserted into slots in the sail material |
| Bilge | space under the floor boards |
| Biocide | anti-bacterial liquid to put into the fuel tank |
| Bow | the front end of a boat |
| Bow Thruster | electric machine inserted into the hull at the bow to enable easier manoeuvrability by moving the bow independently |
| Cleat | metal fittings at bow, stern and centre of the boat to tie any ropes onto especially tying to the same device on the pontoon |

| | |
|---|---|
| Clew | the corner of the sail to which the sheet attaches |
| Companionway | the steps leading from the cockpit to the saloon below deck |
| Dinghy Dolly | lat steel trolley for moving dinghies around |
| Draft | depth of the keel from the bottom of the hull |
| Flopper Stopper | a pole put out over the side to balance a boat at rest in a swell |
| Gimbals | device to allow the stove to swing to maintain a flat surface for cooking utensils to remain in place when the boat is rolling at sea |
| Goosewing | ailing downwind with both foresails out one on each side |
| GRP | glass reinforced plastic of which the hull is constructed |
| Halyard | rope for hoisting sails to the top of the mast |
| Heads | boat toilets |
| Heave-to | a method of stopping the boat by backing the jib so that it opposes the force of the mainsail |
| Jenny | foresail |
| Jibe | a change of course causing the boom to move across the boat when sailing with the wind behind |
| Lazarette | large locker for storage usually at the stern |

| | |
|---|---|
| Lazy Sheet | the rope attached to the foresail that is not holding the sail tight |
| Mainsail Cars | small plastic attachments containing ball bearings attaching the mainsail to the mast |
| Marlin Spike | metal tool with pointed end to undo tight knots |
| Monkey fists | small bundles of knotted rope used to throw heavier longer lines |
| Mousing | replacing the halyards and sheets with thinner lines when the boat is laid up |
| On the Hard | on the ground |
| Painter | rope on the front of the dinghy to pull it along |
| Parasailor | a downwind sail with a horizontal slit to allow wind through |
| Preventer | ropes devised to slow the boom in case of unplanned jibes |
| Quadrant | metal arm attaching the autohelm to the steering mechanism |
| Reach | point of sail when the wind is at right angles to the boat (beam reach) or just forward of the beam (close reach) or just aft of the beam (broad reach) |
| Sacrificial Sheet | a rope used on the foresail to take the wear off the usual sheet when the sail is being held by the pole with the sheet running through the end of the pole |

| | |
|---|---|
| Self Tacking | a sail that moves across the boat during a tack or jibe on a slider without having to be pulled round |
| Shackle | U shaped metal link closed by a bolt to secure chain or rope to something |
| Sheets | ropes attached to the sails which can be moved to change the sail shape |
| Slider | bar on the foredeck allowing foresail to change sides when tacking |
| Slutter/solent Rig | two foresails close together on the bow |
| Snubbers | thin ropes used to take the strain off the windlass at anchor |
| Solenoid | a cylindrical coil of wire acting as a magnet when carrying current |
| Spinlocks | holding devices for sheets and reefing lines |
| SSB | single side band long wave radio for long distance messaging |
| Stanchion | metal struts around the outside of the deck to support guard rails to prevent falling overboard |
| Stern-to | Mediterranean style mooring with the stern at right angles to the pontoon |
| Tape Drive Sail | a sail made with a grid of high strength low stretch tapes covered with a skin of crosscut laminated panels |
| Toe Rail | wooden rim around the edge of the deck |

| | |
|---|---|
| Topping Lift | rope attached to the end of the boom to prevent it dropping |
| Transom | the flat surface forming the stern of a boat |
| Trysail | a small mainsail for use in a serious storm |
| Turbo | a super charger driven by a turbine powered by the engine exhaust |
| Warps | thicker ropes usually used for tying to the shore |
| White Horses | the white crests of waves indicating a Force 4 wind strength |
| Windlass | a winch for lofting and lowering the anchor, usually electronic |
| Wind Vane | arrow on the top of the mast which tells wind direction |
| Tinny | small metal boat |

www.ingramcontent.com/pod-product-compliance
Lightning Source LLC
Chambersburg PA
CBHW041959090426

42811CB00030B/1951/J